f499/00

6/00

Also by the Editors

The Titanic Disaster Hearings edited by Tom Kuntz
The Starr Report introduction by Phil Kuntz
The Starr Report: The Evidence edited by Phil Kuntz
The Starr Evidence edited by Phil Kuntz

THE
SINATRA
FILES

THE SINATRA FILES
THE SECRET FBI DOSSIER

TOM KUNTZ and PHIL KUNTZ, Editors

Three Rivers Press • New York

Published by Three Rivers Press, New York, New York. Member of the Crown Publishing Group.

Random House, Inc. New York, Toronto, London, Sydney, Auckland
www.randomhouse.com

THREE RIVERS PRESS is a registered trademark and the Three Rivers Press colophon is a trademark of Random House, Inc.

Library of Congress Cataloging-in-Publication Data

Kuntz, Tom.
  The Sinatra files: the secret FBI dossier / Tom Kuntz and Phil Kuntz.
    p.   cm.
  Includes index.
    1. Sinatra, Frank, 1915–1998—Archives.   2. United States. Federal Bureau of Investigation—Archives.   3. Singers—United States—Archives.   I. Kuntz, Phil. II. Title.

ML420.S565 K86 200   782.42166′092—dc21   99-086875
                                    [B]

ISBN 0-8129-3276-5

Printed in the United States of America on acid-free paper
DESIGNED BY JOSEPH RUTT

98765432

First Edition

To our parents, the late John J. and Madeleine M. Kuntz
—Tom Kuntz and Phil Kuntz

To my wife, Tracy
—Tom Kuntz

CONTENTS

Introduction

When he died on May 14, 1998, Frank Sinatra was one of the most chronicled celebrities of modern times—the focus of oceans of ink and miles of film and video footage at turns serious-minded, celebratory, or mean-spirited.

But one detailed record of his life, taken from a uniquely penetrating perspective, became fully public only after his death: the Federal Bureau of Investigation's extensive files on the singer and screen star. Most were compiled over the course of several decades under the watchful eyes of J. Edgar Hoover, as his agents investigated whether Sinatra was a draft-dodger, a Communist, or a front for organized criminals.

Released in December 1998 in response to requests under the Freedom of Information Act, the 1,275-page dossier is a trove of insights into Sinatra's life, his turbulent times, and, perhaps most important, the Hoover-era FBI's invasive and at times almost voyeuristic ways.

Although Hoover's FBI kept files on other celebrities, few were as voluminous, for no other subject was as enduring or controversial. For more than five decades, Sinatra was a major force in American society and popular culture, a politically active, hard-partying star who associated with powerful figures in both the underworld and at the highest levels of government through every important turn in the latter half of the twentieth century. The Sinatra FBI files offer themselves as an allegory of the American Century and its obsessions.

Extensive excerpts from them are published here for the first time. Along with a limited number of historical documents from other

sources, the files have been organized and supplemented with explanatory notes to put them in context and to highlight their revela-
tions.

Taken together, they invite a reassessment of the entertainer. Rev-
elations abound. Chapter 1 details how the rail-thin crooner with im-
peccable phrasing at first told World War II draft board officials that he
had no physical or mental disabilities, then asserted later not only that
he had a perforated eardrum, which was true, but also an irrational fear
of crowds, which was highly doubtful. With a blossoming career at
stake, could Sinatra have been feigning mental illness? Chapter 2 includes evidence suggesting an unholy alliance between press muckrak-
ers and the FBI's star-obsessed top brass, who occasionally helped
favored journalists seeking dirt on Sinatra. This new material lends
credence to Sinatra's lifelong grudge against the press.

Chapter 3 offers a disturbing glimpse into the red-baiting 1940s
and 1950s, when Sinatra was unjustifiably, in his words, "tagged [as a]
commie." Though for a time he stood by other embattled Hollywood
stars caught up in the paranoia, he became so sensitive to the charges
that, according to an intermediary, he volunteered to become an un-
dercover snitch in the FBI's hunt for subversives. Hoover turned him
down. So did the army years later, when Sinatra offered to entertain
American troops in Korea.

In some key instances, what isn't in the files is as important as
what is.

For example, although excerpts in chapter 4 and elsewhere assidu-
ously note Sinatra's interactions with notorious hoodlums, the FBI
gathered no evidence that mob pressure landed him his Oscar-winning role as the pugnacious Private Angelo Maggio in *From Here
to Eternity* in 1953. This canard is so embedded in the popular imagi-
nation that it is assumed to be the inspiration for a scene in *The Godfather* in which a severed horse's head in a movie mogul's bed ensures a
plum role for an Italian-American singer. Nor do the files support the
widely held assumption that the mob in 1942 strong-armed Tommy
Dorsey into releasing Sinatra from a contract that entitled the band-
leader to 43 percent of the singer's earnings for life.

More broadly, the files offer a striking case study of the way Hoover managed and manipulated the sensitive information at his disposal. Chapters 5, 6, and 7 detail how the FBI director, with little subtlety, made sure each successive politician who befriended the popular singer knew exactly how much derogatory information the FBI had on their friend.

John F. Kennedy's recklessness is by now well documented, but the files' dry bureaucratic account of the president consorting with associates of the very mobsters his brother the attorney general was trying to imprison will startle even the best-read Kennedy aficionados.

There also are moments of unintentional humor, as in the case of the straight-faced FBI memo that says, "Sinatra denied he sympathized with Lenin and the Marx brothers." And the capitalized names of Marilyn Monroe, Tony Bennett, and other celebrities leaven the G-men's reports like the boldface type of gossip columns.

The files also shed light on the evolving nature of Sinatra's relationship with the FBI: He eventually joined with his would-be pursuers in the bureau in a mutually respectful common cause, when Sinatra's son was kidnapped in 1963.

In sum, the files track an iconic career whose arc seems to personify postwar America's loss of innocence: Sinatra's evolution from liberal, idealistic crooner to sophisticated, sexually liberated swinger to jaded Las Vegas headliner and friend of Republican presidents.

Was the scrutiny unfair?

The FBI twice seriously considered prosecuting Sinatra, once for denying that he was a Communist and once for denying that he partied with a mobster. But despite coast-to-coast investigations, the FBI couldn't make a case against him.

Sinatra's problem throughout his career was that he never did much to remove the taint of guilt by association, especially with the mob. Judged by the company he kept, Sinatra kept inviting more scrutiny. The FBI obliged, and its files grew until the singer became, as the journalist Pete Hamill put it, "the most investigated American performer since John Wilkes Booth."

But in many ways Sinatra wasn't so unique as a subject of FBI interest. The agency kept files on thousands of people, famous and otherwise, whenever they figured in investigations, no matter how tangentially.

According to Hoover's longtime deputy director, Cartha D. "Deke" DeLoach, the main FBI dossier on someone like Sinatra wouldn't have been kept in the agency's collection of "Central Files," which were open to virtually anyone in the bureau. Instead, most of the Sinatra material would have ended up in the "Official and Confidential" files of well-known people, which were located in Hoover's suite in two small filing cabinets behind the desk of his secretary, Helen Gandy.

There was nothing sinister in this, DeLoach maintains. In his 1995 memoir, *Hoover's FBI: The Inside Story of Hoover's Trusted Lieutenant,* DeLoach writes: "The purpose of keeping the O&C Files in an area of limited access was to protect the privacy of those about whom information had been gathered, not to maintain secret records for the purpose of blackmail."

Many a Hoover chronicler would disagree with DeLoach about the sanctity of his boss's motives, but what is undeniable is that the director often took a personal interest in the minutiae of Sinatra's life. Readers of these pages can judge for themselves why.

The FBI began compiling the dossier during one of the most charged moments in American history—the 1940s. From the start of the Second World War, Sinatra's rise to fame stirred an incredible amount of resentment and envy. The crooning heartthrob was thrilling millions of bobby-soxers, and making millions doing it, while avoiding the fate of the hundreds of thousands of other young men who forwent love and fortune to fight European fascism and Japanese imperialism.

As Sinatra himself noted, he was a surrogate to young women for "the boy in every corner drugstore who'd gone off, drafted to the war." The popular historian William Manchester put it another way: "I think Frank Sinatra was the most hated man of World War II."

And so, on the heels of pandemonium-filled appearances at New York's Paramount Theatre, a letter arrived at FBI headquarters in

Washington. Thus began the FBI's shadow biography of Frank Sinatra on August 13, 1943: A concerned citizen intimated darkly that a "shrill whistling sound" of shrieking bobby-soxers during a recent Sinatra radio broadcast might have been a devious technique "to create another Hitler here in America through the influence of mass-hysteria!"

Later, an FBI memo said that the columnist Walter Winchell gave the bureau a reader's letter asserting that the FBI was investigating whether the singer had bribed his way out of the draft. The FBI wasn't investigating any such thing, but the tip insured that it would. In February 1944, the FBI opened a "limited inquiry" that actually was far-reaching enough to dredge up records of Sinatra's 1938 arrest in New Jersey for an alleged "seduction" under a false promise of marriage—a charge that was later changed to "adultery" after it was discovered that the supposed victim was married. That matter also was dropped, and Sinatra was free to love and leave again.

As World War II ended, Sinatra charmed his fans with songs like "Put Your Dreams Away" and frothy films like *Anchors Aweigh*, with Frank playing Gene Kelly's wide-eyed, sailor-suited sidekick. But a serious film, all of ten minutes long, proved more important to the young singer's career. His heartfelt plea for racial and religious tolerance in *The House I Live In*—borne of painful memories of growing up in ethnically divided Hoboken, New Jersey—won a special Academy Award and helped debunk the singer's reputation as a frivolous, draft-dodging crooner.

The film, written by the leftist screenwriter Albert Maltz (later blacklisted), also made Sinatra a darling of the American Left and presaged the star's association with groups the FBI deemed to be Communist fronts. It wasn't long before an informant told the FBI (incorrectly) that Sinatra had "recently been admitted to the New York branch of the Communist Party."

In the conservative press, Sinatra thus became, at best, a Communist-leaning "fellow traveler." In 1946, the far-right radio commentator Gerald L. K. Smith told the House Un-American Activities Committee that Sinatra "has been doing some pretty clever stuff for the Reds," without backing up the charge. The committee never actively pursued Sinatra, but other conservative columnists, like Westbrook Pegler of the Hearst chain's *New York Journal-American* and Lee Mortimer of the *New York Daily Mirror*, picked up the red-baiting cudgel against the pro-Roosevelt singer. By 1946, Hoover himself was disdainful, scrawling this unkind comment at the bottom of a memo about Detroit schoolgirls skipping school to see the star: "Sinatra is just as much to blame as are the moronic bobby-soxers."

Later, as the bobby-soxers grew up, Sinatra's career headed into a precipitous decline—marked by a drought of hit singles from 1948 through 1952 and dreadful films like *The Kissing Bandit*. Sinatra's marriage to Nancy Barbato, whom he wed in 1939, was on the rocks, too, as he pursued affairs with a series of actresses.

Public disaffection increased after the Scripps-Howard columnist Robert Ruark denounced him in February 1947 for having flown to Havana with two members of Al Capone's Chicago gang and socializing there with the deported gangster Lucky Luciano—hard evidence of Sinatra's growing tendency to associate with tough guys.

The FBI files soon began detailing Sinatra's mob ties, and his press detractors were in high dudgeon. Mortimer, the *Mirror*'s film editor, was relentless, sarcastically opining that *It Happened in Brooklyn* "bogs down under the miscast Frank (Lucky) Sinatra, smirking and trying to play a leading man."

On April 8, 1947, Sinatra struck back, literally, socking the diminutive Mortimer when they came across each other at Ciro's nightclub in Hollywood. A month later, in one of the FBI files' most telling episodes, Mortimer met with Clyde Tolson, Hoover's right-hand man and best friend, to find out what the bureau had on Sinatra. Tolson informed Hoover by memo that he had told Mortimer he couldn't give him "any official information," yet the memo itself seems to suggest that Tolson had been helpful. Later, Mortimer reported that Sinatra had delivered $2 million in cash to Luciano in his luggage while in Havana. Often repeated, this charge isn't backed up by anything in the FBI files.

By this time, Sinatra's career was going to the dogs: He performed a canine howl on the novelty song "Mama Will Bark." In 1950, Louis B. Mayer had fired him from MGM after the intemperate star had joked too loudly that the mogul's horseback-riding injury actually resulted from falling off his mistress, Ginny Simms.

As if the draft-dodging, commie, and mob allegations weren't enough, Sinatra's marriage collapsed in the midst of a tumultuous affair with his second-wife-to-be, Ava Gardner, during which the singer attempted suicide. Coupled with his mercurial behavior, all this made Sinatra almost radioactive in show business. Performing at the Copacabana in New York while ravaged from stress, The Voice gave out as Sinatra strained to reach a high note during "Bali Hai." He'd suffered a throat hemorrhage.

Sinatra may have been desperate to relieve the pressure. On September 7, 1950, a colleague informed Tolson in a memo that a Sinatra go-between was trying to meet Hoover "with a proposition Sinatra had in mind." Since "subversive elements" with whom Sinatra had been linked "are not sure of his position," the singer "consequently feels that he can be of help as a result by going anywhere the Bureau desires and contacting any of the people from whom he might be able to obtain information." Perhaps wary of Sinatra's sincerity, Tolson scribbled at the bottom, "We want nothing to do with him," to which Hoover added, "I agree."

But Sinatra's career began a phenomenal resurgence in 1953 with his Oscar-winning turn in *From Here to Eternity*. Soon afterward, the singer tried to join a troupe traveling to Korea to entertain soldiers at Christmastime. The army, however, said no, citing his alleged Communist affiliations. Responding to suggestions that the rejection was based on information supplied by the FBI, Hoover's handwritten notation on a memo ordered subordinates to "nail this down promptly."

Agents looked into the matter and later reported on a bizarre meeting in which Sinatra tried to persuade three army generals to let him sing for the troops. One general congratulated Sinatra on his fine performance in *From Here to Eternity*—a movie that was probably more subversive than Sinatra himself ever was, for it was about infidelity, indiscipline, and brutality in the military. "I am just as communistic as the Pope," Sinatra told the generals, to no avail.

Yet the FBI persisted in trying to dig up "subversive information" on Sinatra as agents tried to prove that he lied in denying Communist affiliations to get a passport. Finally they gave up, and Hoover concluded in a memo that despite repeated "nonspecific associations" of Sinatra's name with the Communist party, "the investigation failed to substantiate any such allegation."

Not that it mattered much. By the mid-1950s, Sinatra was back on top. A collaboration at Capitol Records with the arranger Nelson Riddle was yielding the best work of Sinatra's career, albums of swing and sophistication, including *In the Wee Small Hours* (1955) and *Songs for Swingin' Lovers* (1956). He followed his Oscar success with memorable roles in, among other films, *Suddenly* (1954), in which he played a would-be presidential assassin—an eerie foreshadowing of Jack Kennedy's murder.

The FBI's interest in Sinatra might have receded but for his mob associations, which if anything were growing. In 1954 he had bought a 2 percent stake (later increased) in the Sands Hotel in Las Vegas, which reputedly had mob backers. He was seen with Joe Fischetti, one of the mobsters he had accompanied to Havana, and was especially friendly with Sam "Momo" Giancana, the Chicago mob boss who had interests in many of the clubs where Sinatra had performed.

But what really got the FBI's attention was his growing closeness to the rising young senator from Massachusetts who was running for president. Senator John F. Kennedy had even adopted Sinatra's "High Hopes" as his 1960 campaign theme song. Sinatra, for his part, badly wanted a place in Camelot. After hiring Maltz, the screenwriter for *The House I Live In,* who was now blacklisted, to do a script for another movie, Sinatra bowed to pressure from the Kennedys, first by delaying the news until after the 1960 New Hampshire primary and then jettisoning Maltz altogether.

Hoover received regular reports on all this and more. On March 22, 1960, an informant told the FBI that *Confidential* magazine was investigating a rumor that Senator Kennedy had attended "an indis-

creet party" at Sinatra's Palm Springs home. Later the FBI noted that
Sinatra and Kennedy had partied together in New York, too, and that
Confidential reportedly had "affidavits from two mulatto prostitutes in
New York." In Las Vegas, the FBI heard that "show girls from all over
town were running in and out of the senator's suite" and that
"Kennedy had been compromised with a woman."

According to FBI informers, the mob was looking for an in with
the next president of the United States. As one memo put it, the mob
wanted Sinatra to use his show-biz friendship with Kennedy in-law
Peter Lawford to get close to Jack Kennedy "so that Joe Fischetti and
other notorious hoodlums"—Sinatra's pals—"could have an entrée to
the Senator."

After the mob reportedly helped Kennedy win the election, the
FBI examined the phone records of one Judith Campbell and discovered that she was mixed up with both the president and Sam Giancana—not to mention Sinatra, who had introduced her to both men
on separate occasions. It wasn't hard to figure out that she was the
president's lover, as she later acknowledged. In early 1962, Hoover
laid out what the FBI knew for Attorney General Robert F. Kennedy,
the president's brother. It was a not-so-subtle suggestion that the president's coziness with Sinatra could destroy his presidency.

JFK got the message. In March 1962, the president distanced himself from Sinatra by canceling a scheduled stay at the singer's Palm
Springs complex, staying instead at the nearby home of Bing Crosby, a
rival crooner and a Republican at that. It must have hurt: Sinatra's
long-cultivated friendship with JFK was over, and the mob wasn't
happy. An FBI memo later noted that "Chicago sources have advised
of Giancana's disappointment in Sinatra's apparent inability to get the
administration to tone down its efforts in the anti-racketeering field."

Not that Sinatra was through hanging around with tough guys. Far
from it: He was so successful now, having just started the Reprise
record label and flying in his own private jet, that he didn't seem to
care what people thought.

He was the Chairman of the Board.

And the head of the Rat Pack. Late in 1962, he topped the bill for a week with fellow Rat Packers Dean Martin and Sammy Davis, Jr., at the grand reopening in suburban Chicago of the mob-run Villa Venice Supper Club. According to an FBI memo, the appearance by Sinatra's clan was "what can only be termed a command performance" in return for past favors from Giancana. Onstage, Dean Martin even sang parody lyrics about not getting paid for the gig.

Sinatra had the red-meat crowd roaring with a typically vicious putdown of the Hearst Broadway columnist critical of his connection to JFK: "I met many, many male finks but I never met a female fink until I met Dorothy Kilgallen. I wouldn't mind if she was a good-looking fink."

Sinatra talked the hoodlum talk, but was he walking the walk? Many in Attorney General Robert Kennedy's anti-mob Justice Department believed so. But hard evidence was elusive, as the FBI files demonstrate.

On April 24, 1963, the special agent in charge of the FBI's Los Angeles office asked Hoover to consider bugging Sinatra's home in Palm Springs. Surprisingly, Hoover promptly denied the request. "You are reminded that all misurs [microphone surveillances] must be completely justified," said the reply.

That summer, however, the FBI got a compelling new reason to keep the heat on Sinatra. At the Cal-Neva Lodge in Lake Tahoe, a casino resort in which Sinatra held a major interest, Giancana had been spotted ensconced with his girlfriend, the singer Phyllis McGuire of the McGuire Sisters. The resulting public furor—Giancana was proscribed from the casino as a known mobster—forced Sinatra to relinquish all his gambling interests in Nevada, at both the Cal-Neva and the Sands in Las Vegas.

Soon afterward, Dougald D. MacMillan, one of RFK's top mob prosecutors, arrived in Los Angeles with authority to "review all pertinent information in an effort to determine whether prosecution could be initiated against Sinatra." But his Los Angeles colleagues scoffed at his grandstanding plan to start off by grilling top stars and Sinatra friends like Dean Martin, Sammy Davis, Jr., Dinah Shore, and Eddie Fisher. "MacMillan is a boy on a man's errand," an FBI official scrawled on one memo. When Hoover found out about MacMillan's plan, he called it off.

Two months later, according to FBI memos, serious consideration was given to prosecuting Sinatra for denying in an interview with the Internal Revenue Service that Giancana had attended a two-week-long party he threw at the Claridge Hotel in Atlantic City. The FBI had evidence that Sinatra was lying—the testimony of a chorus girl at the party—but the matter was dropped as an "apparent, though minor, violation of the law." Sinatra would never have a closer brush with the FBI.

At least not in the legal sense: On December 8, 1963, two weeks after Kennedy's assassination, Frank Sinatra, Jr., age nineteen, was kidnapped from his hotel room in Lake Tahoe and held for ransom by three men, one of them an ex-schoolmate of the singer's daughter Nancy. Two days later, Sinatra paid nearly $240,000 to secure his son's release; the FBI arrested the three kidnappers days later.

The FBI agents who had worked closely with Sinatra throughout the ordeal felt they had made a breakthrough with the singer. One of them, Dean Elson, the bureau's special agent in charge for Nevada, had developed a "close personal relationship" with the star and suggested that he "might be able to induce Sinatra to help us," according to a memo.

But once again, Tolson and Hoover wanted nothing to do with Sinatra. "I do not agree," wrote Tolson in response to Elson's suggestion, to which Hoover added, "I share Tolson's views."

Still, the kidnapping episode demonstrated that Hoover and Sinatra shared at least one thing in common: an unforgiving attitude. When a Catholic prison chaplain appealed for forgiveness on behalf of two of the kidnappers, Sinatra wrote back rejecting the suggestion as "presumptuous." He informed Hoover of his exchange with the priest in a "Dear Edgar" letter. In his "Dear Frank" reply, Hoover was in an equally unmerciful mood, quoting a judge with approval: "It is not the criminals . . . that need a neuropathic hospital; it is the people who slobber over them in an effort to find excuses for the crime."

Sinatra was entering a September of his years whose bitterness belied the wistful tone of his similarly titled 1965 album. In 1966, according to an FBI memo, he hired a Washington public relations man to "determine the identity of the SOB" who "tagged" him as a "commie" in the 1940s. When asked why Sinatra still cared after all those years, the investigator told the authorities, "Sinatra is a very temperamental, vindictive and moody individual and has periods where he dwells on his past life."

Within a few years of Hoover's death in 1972, the FBI's interest in Sinatra trailed off, and little new information was added to the files.

But in 1981, after a swing to the Republicans, a retirement, a comeback, and a fourth marriage, Sinatra privately obtained his FBI dossier under the Freedom of Information Act. He turned it over to the Nevada Gaming Control Board as part of an effort to win back the gambling license he had lost thanks to Giancana in 1963.

Though the files offered plenty of reason to be suspicious of Sinatra, they proved no illegality. Perhaps that's why Sinatra got his license back. But it couldn't have hurt that he once again had friends in high places: One of his character references was President Ronald Reagan, whose inaugural gala the singer had hosted the previous month.

To many, it looked like the fix was in. As with so much else in Sinatra's life, the episode didn't so much clear up doubts about his character as illustrate them.

Less ambiguous was Sinatra's statement to an interviewer in 1963: "When I sing, I believe, I'm honest."

The FBI files presented on the following pages do not refute that.

The Life of Frank Sinatra:
Selected Highlights

1915

December 12: Birth of Francis Albert Sinatra to Martin Sinatra
and Natalie Catherine "Dolly" Garavante in Hoboken, N.J.

1935

September: As a member of the Hoboken Four, wins first prize on
Major Bowes and His Original Amateur Hour.

1938

First important nightclub gig, as a singing waiter at the Rustic
Cabin in Alpine, N.J.

Charged in Bergen County, N.J., with "seduction" under a false
promise of marriage (and later adultery, in the same case). Charges
are later dropped.

1939

February 4: Marries Nancy Barbato.

June: Joins Harry James and His Orchestra.

First recordings with the James band, including "All or Nothing
at All." James later releases Sinatra from contract so he can join the
Tommy Dorsey Band.

1940

January: Joins the Tommy Dorsey Band.

May 23: Records "I'll Never Smile Again," his first major hit,
crystallizing the yearning and despair of a generation torn apart by
World War II.

June 8: Birth of first child, Nancy Sandra.

1941

Voted Outstanding Male Vocalist by *Billboard* and *Downbeat*.
First of nearly sixty film appearances: *Las Vegas Nights*.

1942

January: First solo recordings (with Axel Stordahl arranging) on
RCA's subsidiary label Bluebird, including "Night and Day."
September: Last appearance with Dorsey band.
December 30: Appears at Paramount Theatre for the first time as
an "extra added attraction" with Benny Goodman's band.

1943

Lead singer on *Your Hit Parade* radio show (until 1945).
June: First Columbia recording session, including "Close to You."
Sinatra is backed by a vocal chorus because of a musicians' strike.
August 13: The FBI opens its first file on Sinatra, "for the purpose
of filing miscellaneous information" on the star.

1944

January 10: Birth of second child, Franklin Wayne Emmanuel.
February: The FBI opens a "limited inquiry" into whether Sinatra
had bribed his way out of the draft.
Spring: Moves family to California.
October: Columbus Day riot by fans at the Paramount.

1945

Signs with MGM and makes *Anchors Aweigh*.
Makes the film short *The House I Live In*, a plea for ethnic and
religious tolerance.
December 12: The FBI begins tracking Sinatra's alleged
Communist ties.

1946

Wins special Oscar for his role in *The House I Live In*.

1947

February 11: Flies to Havana with the Fischetti brothers of Al Capone's Chicago gang and socializes there with Lucky Luciano, father of the modern Mafia. Columnist Robert Ruark sees Sinatra with mobsters in Havana and reports about it.

February: Soon thereafter, the FBI files begin to note Sinatra's mob affiliations.

April 8: Sinatra assaults a hostile columnist, Lee Mortimer, outside Ciro's nightclub in Hollywood.

1948

June 20: Birth of third child, Christina (Tina).

1950

May: Television debut on *The Star-Spangled Revue*.

September 7: According to an FBI memo, a Sinatra go-between conveys the singer's offer to become an FBI informer.

October: First television series, *The Frank Sinatra Show*.

1951

Divorces Nancy Barbato.

August: Columnist Lee Mortimer alleges that in 1947 Sinatra delivered $2 million in cash to Lucky Luciano, a charge never proven.

November 7: Marries Ava Gardner in Philadelphia.

1952

September: Final Columbia recording session.

1953

From Here to Eternity (wins Oscar for Best Supporting Actor the following year).

Separates from Ava Gardner (and is later divorced).

April: Signs with Capitol Records and begins collaboration with the arranger Nelson Riddle.

1954

"Young at Heart" (song).

Buys a 2 percent interest (later increased) in the Sands Hotel in Las Vegas.

Army denies clearance to Sinatra to entertain troops in Korea, citing alleged Communist affiliations.

1955

The Man With the Golden Arm (Academy Award nomination for Best Actor).

Guys and Dolls (film).

September: Plays the Stage Manager in TV production of Thornton Wilder's *Our Town*, which produced the hit song "Love and Marriage."

1957

Pal Joey (film).

The Joker Is Wild (film).

"All the Way" (song).

October: Second TV series, *The Frank Sinatra Show*.

1959

Wins Grammy Awards for Album of the Year (*Come Dance With Me!*) and Best Solo Vocal Performance.

1960

Forms Reprise Records.

Ocean's Eleven (first film with the Rat Pack).

February 7: Sinatra introduces Senator John F. Kennedy to a former girlfriend, Judith Campbell, after a Rat Pack performance at the Sands Hotel in Las Vegas. They soon begin an affair.

March: Sinatra introduces Campbell to the mobster Sam Giancana at the Fontainebleau in Miami Beach. She and Giancana later had an affair.

March: FBI begins tracking Sinatra's socializing with John F. Kennedy.

1961

First Reprise album: *Ring-a-Ding-Ding*.

January: Produces John F. Kennedy's inaugural.

February: J. Edgar Hoover memo to Attorney General Robert F. Kennedy on Sinatra and the mob.

1962

The Manchurian Candidate (film).

March: JFK changes arrangements for trip to Palm Springs, staying at Bing Crosby's home rather than Sinatra's.

November 26–December 2: The Rat Pack performs at the mob-run Villa Venice in suburban Chicago, in what the FBI calls a "command performance" for Sam Giancana.

1963

January 16: The FBI interviews Sinatra about his request for a Teamsters loan to expand the Cal-Neva Lodge in Lake Tahoe, a casino in which he has a major interest.

April 24: An FBI agent proposes bugging Sinatra's Palm Springs home. Hoover says no.

Fall: Sinatra gives up his Nevada gambling license and his interest in the Cal-Neva Lodge after the mobster Sam Giancana is seen at the casino.

November 22: JFK is assassinated.

December 8: Kidnapping of Frank Sinatra, Jr.

December 12: Frankie is released on his father's birthday.

1964

June 27: A Catholic prison chaplain writes to Sinatra asking him to forgive his son's convicted kidnappers. A month later, Sinatra angrily rejects the priest's suggestion as "presumptuous" and corresponds with Hoover about the matter.

1965

November: Wins Grammy awards for Best Album of the Year (*September of My Years*) and Best Solo Vocal Performance ("It Was a Very Good Year").

November: TV special *Sinatra: A Man and His Music*, wins Emmy and Peabody awards. Laudatory CBS TV News special *Sinatra: An American Original*, hosted by Walter Cronkite.

Von Ryan's Express (film).

1966

July 19: Marries Mia Farrow.

Wins Grammys for Album of the Year (*Sinatra: A Man and His Music*) and Record of the Year ("Strangers in the Night").

"That's Life" (song).

1967

"Something Stupid" (duet with daughter Nancy).

1968

Divorces Mia Farrow.

1969

"My Way" (song).

January 24: Death of his father, Martin Sinatra.

A New Jersey commission subpoenas Sinatra to testify about organized crime in the state.

1971

March: Announces retirement.

June 13: "Final" performance at Los Angeles Music Center.

1972

House panel subpoenas him to testify about an old investment in a mob-controlled racetrack in Massachusetts.

1973
Sinatra sings "The House I Live In" at the Nixon White House. November: Ends retirement with TV show and album: *Ol' Blue Eyes Is Back*.

1974
October: The Main Event tour (televised).

1975
June 19: Giancana is murdered the night before an interview with Senate staff members about the mob's connections to the Kennedy administration and plots on Fidel Castro.

1976
July 11: Marries Barbara Marx (divorced from Zeppo). Sinatra is photographed backstage with New York mobster Carlo Gambino.

1977
January 6: Death of his mother, Dolly, in a plane crash.

1980
"New York, New York" (song).

1981
Nevada gambling license restored. President Ronald Reagan is a character reference.

1983
Receives Kennedy Center Honors Award for Lifetime Achievement.

1985
January: Produces Ronald Reagan's second inaugural.

March: Last entry in Sinatra FBI files, a death threat from a mentally disturbed woman.

May 23: Receives honorary degree from Stevens Institute of Technology in Hoboken, N.J.

May 23: Awarded Medal of Freedom. .

1988
Goes on The Ultimate Event tour with Sammy Davis, Jr., and Dean Martin (later replaced by Liza Minnelli).

1990
Launches the Frank Sinatra Diamond Jubilee tour to commemorate his seventy-fifth birthday.

1993
October: Records the album *Duets* in collaboration with well-known vocalists who tape their parts separately, including Bono of the rock group U2.

1998
May 14: Dies at the age of eighty-two.

Editors' Note

Most of the documents excerpted in this book were partly and in some cases extensively censored by the FBI, usually to comply with privacy laws and protect investigative sources. Many documents contained material that duplicated material elsewhere in the files.

For these reasons, the editors have taken some very limited liberties in a few cases. For example, the editors at times compiled portions from multiple similar memos into composites that contain the most noteworthy paragraphs from each of the originals. In those cases, the editors also excluded as much duplicative and less-noteworthy material as possible, but didn't note each and every deletion. And the transcripts of electronically monitored conversations have been edited for clarity. The editors have disclosed such techniques where appropriate in the explanatory material preceding each excerpt.

In most other cases, three asterisks (* * *) denote the deletion of whole sections of intervening text, while ellipses (. . .) indicate lesser deletions. Text blacked out (redacted) by the FBI is noted with black bars(███████████). Throughout, clearly extraneous material—such as page numbers, time-and-date stamps, numerical file references, letterheads, miscellaneous unimportant handwritten notations, and memo-routing information—has been deleted without use of the denotations mentioned above. Most errors in spelling and grammar have been corrected, too. Also, because of copyright issues, several letters from private citizens, including Frank Sinatra, have been paraphrased with only limited excerpts, in compliance with legal fair use restrictions.

Preface

Numerous documents on Frank Sinatra in the FBI files open with a short biography of the singer. Below is a typical one, from about 1950.

BIOGRAPHICAL DATA

Francis Albert Sinatra, generally known as Frank Sinatra, was born December 12, 1915 or 1916, according to his Selective Service file, and on December 12, 1917, according to public source material. He was reportedly born in Hoboken, New Jersey, the son of Martin (also reported as Anthony) and Natalie Garavante Sinatra, who were both born in Italy. His father has been a professional bantam weight boxer, boilermaker, shipyard worker during World War I, and subsequently became a Captain in the Hoboken Fire Department.

Sinatra received his public school education in Hoboken and left the Demarest High School in 1935 to work as a helper on a delivery truck for the *Jersey Observer* and contrary to publicity reports, did not serve as a sports writer for this paper. He is also reported to have taken some engineering courses at the Stevens Institute of Technology in Hoboken and in other reports is supposed to have attended the Drake Institute, dates of attendance not given.

Sinatra started his singing career in 1935 after winning an amateur contest. He subsequently won a prize on the Major Bowes Amateur Hour and toured with a unit of this company for three months. By 1939 he was singing on eighteen sustaining programs on the radio, reportedly without financial remuneration. In June, 1939, he gave up his job with a New Jersey roadhouse, The Rustic Cabin, to appear with Harry James's Band. About December, 1939, he joined Tommy Dorsey's Band and stayed with him until the summer of 1942, when he returned to radio work and personal appearances. Sinatra was the singing star of the Lucky Strike Hit Parade radio program from February, 1943, to January, 1945. During this period he began his screen work and also appeared in the Wedgewood Room of the Waldorf-Astoria Hotel in New York City.

In addition to his work as a singer Sinatra was reported in 1946 to have an interest in a race track near Atlantic City, a band, a music publishing company, and one-third interest in the Barton Music Corporation and was then considering an interest in a sports arena to be built in Hollywood, a hotel in Las Vegas, and an office building in Beverly Hills.

On February 4, 1939, he married Nancy Barbato at Jersey City, New Jersey, and they now have three children.

Sinatra registered with Local Draft Board Number 19, Jersey City, New Jersey, and received a 4-F classification on December 11, 1943.

Sinatra owned a home at 220 Lawrence Avenue, Hasbrouck Heights, New Jersey, until the spring of 1944 when he moved to Hollywood and bought a home there. He spends considerable time in New York City, but has no fixed address there.

Sinatra's Selective Service file describes him as being 5'71/2", 119 pounds, slight build, dark brown hair, and blue eyes.

* * *

The files of the Identification Division also reflect that Sinatra was fingerprinted on October 6, 1943, by the War Department as a member of the USO Camp Shows, Incorporated, and that on January 30, 1947, he was fingerprinted by the Sheriff's Office, Los Angeles, California, in connection with an application for a gun permit.

THE
SINATRA
FILES

ONE
SINATRA AND THE DRAFT

"Bugle-deaf Frankie Boy"

During World War II, Frank Sinatra generated a lot of public re-sentment and complaints largely because his first peak of stardom—marked by tumultuous appearances at New York's Paramount Theatre—had been made possible by his exemption from military service.

It turned out that the draft complaints weren't so far-fetched: As FBI documents in this chapter indicate, the young star had twice told the army he had no physical or mental disabilities, then later changed his story. His revised answer to draft doctors: He had suffered a perfo-rated eardrum at birth and was "neurotic"—afraid of crowds in partic-ular.

The ear ailment was bona fide, and Sinatra throughout his career demonstrated emotional instability. But this idol of millions of swooning teenaged girls, afraid of crowds? Could Sinatra have been pulling out all the stops to ensure a 4-F classification?

The time was one of extreme patriotism and high paranoia, as demonstrated by the first complaint received by the FBI, the earliest document in the Sinatra files. The letter, received on August 13, 1943, was from a resident of San Jose, California, who had just heard a Sinatra radio broadcast. The FBI withheld the writer's name.

Dear Sir:

The other day I turned on a Frank Sinatra program and I noted the shrill whistling sound, created supposedly by a bunch of girls cheering. Last night as I heard Lucky Strike produce more of this same hysteria I thought: how easy it would be for certain-minded manufacturers to create another Hitler here in America through the influence of mass-hysteria! I believe that those who are using this shrill whistling sound are aware that it is similar to that which produced Hitler. That they intend to get a Hitler in by first planting in the minds of the people that men like Frank Sinatra are O.K. therefore this future Hitler will be O.K. As you are well aware the future of some of these manufacturers is rather shaky unless something is done like that.

Sincerely,

███████████████████████████

Hoover's reply was perfunctory.

September 2, 1943

Dear ████████████████

This will acknowledge your recent communication.

I have carefully noted the content of your letter and wish to thank you for volunteering your comments and observations in this regard.

Should you obtain any information which you believe to be of interest to this Bureau, please feel free to communicate directly with the Special Agent in charge of our San Francisco Field Division which is located at One Eleven Sutter Building, Room 1729, San Francisco, California.

Sincerely yours,

John Edgar Hoover
Director

Complaints about Sinatra's draft exemption soon attracted the FBI's attention. One tip was passed on by a man who couldn't be ignored: the New York Mirror columnist Walter Winchell, perhaps the most influential journalist of his day, and a very close friend of Hoover. An anonymous, typed letter to Winchell prompted top FBI officials to order an investigation into Sinatra's draft record in early 1944. The letter was dated just three weeks after Sinatra was classified as 4-F (unacceptable for medical reasons) and only days after top draft officials questioned subordinates about the singer's case.

December 30, 1943

Mr. Walter Winchell
New York Mirror
235 East 45th Street
New York, N.Y.

Dear Mr. Winchell:

I don't dare give you my name because of my job but here is a bit of news you can check which I think is Front Page:

The Federal Bureau of Investigation is said to be investigating a report that Frank Sinatra paid $40,000.00 to the doctors who examined him in Newark recently and presented him with a 4-F classification. The money is supposed to have been paid by Sinatra's Business Manager. One of the recipients is said to have talked too loud about the gift in a beer joint recently and a report was sent to the F.B.I.

A former School mate of Sinatra's from Highland, N.J., said recently that Sinatra has no more ear drum trouble than Gen. MacArthur.

If there is any truth to these reports I think that it should be made known. Mothers around this section who have sons in the service are planning a petition to Pres. Roosevelt asking for a re-examination of the singer by a neutral board of examiners. You'll probably read about this in the papers within a few days unless you break the story first.

I wish I could give you my name but I would lose my job within 24 hours if I did. You'd probably recognize it immediately if I did because I have sent you numerous items in the past which appeared in your column.

In fact, the FBI had not been investigating Sinatra's draft record. But the letter became a self-fulfilling prophecy. The resulting investigation prompted this memo several weeks later to Assistant Director D. M. "Mickey" Ladd, head of the FBI's Domestic Intelligence Division. The initial inquiry into Sinatra's draft status was undertaken by the special agent in charge (SAC) for Newark, Sam K. McKee, who is reputed to have been one of the agents who gunned down Pretty Boy Floyd ten years earlier.

February 8, 1944
Call 3:10 PM.
Transcribed— 3:25 PM.

MEMORANDUM FOR MR. LADD

RE: FRANK SINATRA
SELECTIVE SERVICE

When SAC, S. K. McKee of Newark called me at the above time and date I asked him whether or not he had heard any rumors to the effect that Frank Sinatra had paid $40,000 to obtain a 4-F classification. Mr. McKee stated that he had heard nothing to this effect.

* * *

I asked SAC McKee to ascertain definitely whether Sinatra's classification was 4-F and if so, to determine why he received this classification. However, I told him that it would not be necessary at this time to make a full scale investigation or to look into the charges of $40,000 being paid the examining doctors at Newark. McKee stated that he would do this immediately and advise the Bureau of the results.

Respectfully,

G. C. Callan

McKee informed headquarters of the results of his investigation several days later, first in a telephone call with one of Ladd's underlings, Christopher Callan. McKee's report was the first hint that Sinatra had given draft officials inconsistent statements about his medical condition. And the report was spiced up with a little sex.

February 10, 1944

MEMORANDUM FOR MR. LADD

Re: FRANK SINATRA
Selective Service

SAC McKee of the Newark Office advised that Sinatra's classification appeared to be regular and that he was disqualified because of a perforated ear drum and chronic mastoiditis and that his mental condition was one of emotional instability. McKee stated that in a prior physical examination in the fall of 1943 none of these defects were noted and that in a questionnaire dated December 17, 1940, in answer to a question as to his physical condition, Sinatra

noted there were none to the best of his knowledge. He is classified
4-F as of December 11, 1943.

McKee also said it had come to the attention of one of the
Resident Agents at Hackensack, New Jersey, that Sinatra has an
arrest record and that ████████████ Hackensack County Jail,
who furnished this information, gave the Agent a photograph of
Sinatra, arrest #42799. McKee advised that Sinatra was arrested in
1938 on a charge of seduction which was dismissed and he was later
arrested on a charge of adultery.

I instructed McKee not to take any further action in this matter.
He said he would submit a letter today covering the above.

Respectfully,

G. C. Callan

*A more detailed letter to Hoover disclosed that at Sinatra's induction
physical, he left the chief clerk of his local draft board in Hudson County,
N.J., with the impression that he knew he'd be rejected. And it detailed how
many times Sinatra had denied being emotionally unstable before claiming,
in December 1943, that he was.*

February 10, 1944

Director, FBI

Re: FRANK ALBERT SINATRA
SELECTIVE SERVICE

Dear Sir:

Reference is made to the telephone message from Mr. Christopher Callan at the Seat of Government on February 8, 1944 concerning the receipt by the Bureau of an anonymous letter alleging, in effect, that $40,000 had been paid to the doctors who examined FRANK ALBERT SINATRA and thereafter gave an opinion that SINATRA had a perforated eardrum and was unsuitable for military service.

In accordance with instructions, the investigation was limited to an examination of SINATRA's Selective Service File in order to obtain from that file certain information as set forth below. On February 9, 1944, the file was examined by Special Agent ████████████████ at Local Draft Board #19 for Hudson County, Room 308, 26 Journal Square, Jersey City, New Jersey. The Chief Clerk of this board is Mrs. MAE E. JONES.

(1) PRESENT CLASSIFICATION: 4F as of December 11, 1943.

(2) REASON FOR THAT CLASSIFICATION: D.S.S. Form #221, "Report of Physical Examination and Induction," carries under Section 4, "Physical Examination Results," the following certification: "78. I certify that the above-named registrant was carefully examined, that the results of the examination have been correctly recorded in this form, that to the best of my knowledge and belief: . . . (e) FRANK ALBERT SINATRA is physically and/or mentally disqualified for military service by reason of: 1. chronic perforation [left] tympanum; 2. chronic mastoiditis."

This was supported by the stamped name, "J. WEINTROB,
Captain, M.C., Assistant Chief Medical Officer."
Immediately following

"79. . . . (b) FRANK ALBERT SINATRA was on this date
rejected for service in the Army of the United States."

This statement was supported by the typewritten name,
"R. G. WALLS, Captain, Infantry." The certification and
statement carried the place and date of Newark, New Jersey, December 9, 1943.

More detailed notations appeared in Section 4, "Physical
Examination Results," as follows:

"40. EAR, NOSE, THROAT ABNORMALITIES:
Chronic perforation lt. drum. Hist of repeated discharge
from ear—mastoid areas show coating in remaining cells
and deformity of canal. Marks sclerosis in mastoid area. . . .

"50. MUSCOLOSKELETAL DEFECTS: Fracture
deformity 3rd finger rt. *N.D.*"

"55. MENTAL: Emotional instability. *N.D.* . . .

"64. HEIGHT: 67½ inches. . . .

"65. WEIGHT: 119 lbs. . . .

"75. BLOOD PRESSURE: (a) Systolic: 122;
(b) Diastolic: 78."

(3) GENERAL APPEARANCE OF FILE, ETC.: On its face, the
file appeared to be in regular order. Mrs. Jones said that the
Local Board had been particularly careful not to afford
SINATRA special treatment and where any question of

importance arose, the Board would immediately communicate with the State Headquarters for advice in view of the "position" held by SINATRA. Mrs. Jones also said that although it had been reported over the radio and otherwise that SINATRA had had a pre-induction physical examination and knew two weeks before the date set for his induction examination that he would be rejected, no such pre-induction examination was ever given by her board for any registrant. It had been the impression of Mrs. Jones that SINATRA had had the belief that he would be rejected inasmuch as he had continued to make plans for his new radio show, but she had readily explained that to herself through the thought that he had probably had his own physician examine him.

The following inconsistencies appeared in the file: In his Selective Service Questionnaire executed December 17, 1940, under series 2, "Physical Condition," SINATRA wrote in under "Have No"—"To the best of my knowledge, I have no physical or mental defects or diseases." In an undated Current Selective Service Questionnaire which was to be returned prior to November 7, 1941 and in answer to the question, "Do you have any physical or mental defects or diseases?", SINATRA wrote "No." On October 22, 1943, in the "Extract for D.S.S. Form #221—Report of Physical Examination and Induction," SINATRA answered Question #5, "What Physical or Mental Defects or Diseases Have You Had in the Past, if any?" by the one word, "No." In answer to Question #6, "Have you ever been treated at an institution, sanitarium or asylum?" SINATRA wrote, "No." On October 22, 1943, Local Board Examining Physician A. POVALSKI, M.D., Jersey City, found that SINATRA had none of the defects set forth in Parts 1 or 2 of the List of Defects (form #220).

Independently of this investigation, it had come to the attention of Special Agent ████████████████ that FRANK SINATRA had a criminal record in Bergen County. From ███████████████████

Bergen County Jail, Hackensack, New Jersey, there was obtained an enclosed picture of FRANK SINATRA and the following information regarding the two occasions on which SINATRA was held in the Bergen County Jail: FRANK SINATRA, Arrest # 42799, Bergen County Sheriff's Office, Hackensack, New Jersey was arrested on November 26, 1938 charged with Seduction. Disposition was marked, "Dismissed." FRANK SINATRA, Arrest #42977, was arrested on December 22, 1938, charged with Adultery. The disposition on this charge was not listed. ██████████████ stated that the fingerprints taken at the time of the listed arrests were submitted to the Federal Bureau of Investigation, Washington, D.C.

The following description of SINATRA was obtained from the Selective Service File:

Name:	FRANK ALBERT SINATRA
Race:	White
Age:	28 or 29
Date of birth:	December 12, 1915 is listed in two forms; December 12, 1916, in one.
Place of birth:	Hoboken, New Jersey
Residence:	220 Lawrence Avenue, Hasbrouck Heights, New Jersey
Height:	5'7½"
Weight:	119 lbs.
Build:	Slight
Hair:	Dark Brown
Eyes:	Blue
Complexion:	Ruddy
Scars and Marks:	Scar on left side of chin below mouth

Occupation:　　　　Vocalist

Education:　　　　4 years high school, one year business
　　　　　　　　　school

Marital Status:　　Married 2-4-39, Jersey City, New Jersey

Immediate relatives:　Wife, Mrs. NANCY R. SINATRA, same
　　　　　　　　　address; Daughter, NANCY SANDRA
　　　　　　　　　SINATRA, born 6-8-40 (no record of
　　　　　　　　　second daughter appears in Selective
　　　　　　　　　Service File); Father, ANTHONY
　　　　　　　　　SINATRA, age 52, Hoboken, New Jersey;
　　　　　　　　　Mother, NATALIE SINATRA, age 49,
　　　　　　　　　Hoboken, New Jersey.

Social Security #:　138-16-0442

Nationality:　　　United States citizen . . .

This office has not received any rumors which would substantiate the allegations made in the anonymous letter.

Because of the limited investigation requested, no additional investigation is contemplated by this office.

Very truly yours,

S. K. MCKEE
SAC

McKee's discovery of an old sex case against Sinatra prompted further inquiry, even though the seduction incident was unrelated to the original draft-dodging allegation.

DATE: FEBRUARY 15, 1944
TO: MR. D. M. LADD
FROM: MR. G. C. CALLAN
SUBJECT: FRANK SINATRA—SELECTIVE SERVICE

I called SAC McKee of the Newark Office and asked if he could determine the disposition of two cases for which Sinatra was arrested, one for seduction on November 26, 1938, which was reported dismissed, and the other for adultery on December 22, 1938. The Bureau has a record of the first case but there is no record of the second case.

McKee advised that he would obtain the disposition of these cases and would advise me as soon as possible.

Handwritten notation by Hoover: "We should be certain that there is nothing irregular in this case. Note Newark's letter, which is attached. H."

The FBI withheld the complainant's name. But books by Sinatra's daughter Nancy (Frank Sinatra: An American Legend) and by Kitty Kelley (His Way: The Unauthorized Biography of Frank Sinatra) identify her as Antoinette Della Penta. Then twenty-five, she was estranged from her husband and had dated the budding singer, four years her junior. Based largely on interviews with the woman, Kelley's book reported that she had him arrested for seduction to avenge her humiliation when he reneged on a marriage proposal in favor of the woman who would become the first Mrs. Sinatra, Nancy Barbato. She withdrew that charge, the Kelley book said, after Sinatra promised to apologize to her; when he didn't, she went to his house, caused a commotion, was herself arrested, and then filed the adultery charge. She later dropped that one, too.

McKee's version of events was somewhat different.

February 17, 1944

Director, FBI

RE: FRANK ALBERT SINATRA
SELECTIVE SERVICE

Dear Sir:

Mr. William Guthrie, Clerk of the Second Criminal Judicial
District of the County of Bergen, County Court House, Hackensack,
New Jersey, furnished Special Agent ███████████████ the following
information regarding SINATRA:

Under docket #15228 of that court in the STATE vs. FRANK
SINATRA, SINATRA was charged, on November 26, 1938, by
███████████████████████████ N.J., with having committed the
following offense: "On the second and ninth days of November 1938
at the Borough of Lodi . . . under the promise of marriage
[SINATRA] did then and there have sexual intercourse with the said
complainant, who was then and there a single female of good repute
. . . contrary to and in violation of the revised statute of 1937." The
Peerless Casualty Company, 241 Main Street, Hackensack, N.J.,
went bond for SINATRA in the amount of $1500. This complaint
was withdrawn on December 7, 1938 because it was ascertained that
the complainant was in fact married. In place of that complaint and
under docket #15307, the STATE vs. FRANK SINATRA, a
complaint was filed on December 21, 1938 by ██████████████
N.J., charging SINATRA with adultery in that he, "On the second
and ninth days of November 1938 . . . did then and there commit
adultery with the said complainant, a married woman, the wife of
███████████████. SINATRA went bond for himself in the amount
of $500. On January 4, 1939, the case was remanded to the Grand
Jury by order of Judge McINTYRE.

According to Mr. Guthrie, SINATRA'S attorney was Mr.
HARRY L. TOWE of Rutherford, New Jersey, who at the present

time is the Congressman (U.S. House of Representatives) from the 7th District of New Jersey.

Under docket #18450 for the Prosecutor of the Pleas of Bergen County, it appears that a no-bill was returned on January 17, 1939 by the Grand Jury in connection with the second complaint. In accord with the no-bill the complaint was dismissed in open court of Quarter Sessions of Bergen County on January 24, 1939.

Because of the limited investigation requested, no additional investigation is contemplated by this office.

Very truly yours,

S. K. McKEE
SAC

Though there was no evidence to substantiate the allegation that Sinatra had paid $40,000 to avoid the draft, there were reasons to be suspicious. Spurred by Hoover's interest, headquarters ordered a more thorough investigation of the draft-dodging allegation. It turned out that details of the singer's emotional instability—including his supposed fear of crowds—were omitted from the official reasons for his 4-F classification to "avoid undue unpleasantness for both the selectee and the induction service."

February 24, 1944

Director, FBI

Re: FRANK ALBERT SINATRA
SELECTIVE SERVICE

Dear Sir:

Reference is made to the two letters from this office, dated February 10, 1944 and February 17, 1944, and to telephone message from Mr. CHRISTOPHER CALLAN on February 21, 1944. In accordance with instructions given by Mr. CALLAN, JOSEPH R. WEINTROB, Captain, U. S. Army Medical Corps, Chief Medical Officer, Armed Forces Induction Station, 113th Infantry Armory, Sussex Avenue and Jay Street, Newark 4, New Jersey, was interviewed by Special Agent ███████████ on February 23, 1944. The line officer in command of this induction station is Captain RAYMOND E. WALLS. Captain WEINTROB'S superior is Major FRANK GUIDOTTI, 39 Whitehall Street, New York, N.Y.

Captain WEINTROB said that he had personally examined SINATRA's ears and had rejected SINATRA against his, WEINTROB'S, wishes on the basis of a perforation of the left tympanum and chronic mastoiditis, left, either one of which would have sufficed for having rejected the registrant. The rejection was based on Mobilization Regulation #1-9, War Department, Washington, D.C., issued October 15, 1942 and amended thereafter. These regulations entitled "Standards of Physical Examination during Mobilization" set forth under Section 5, "Ears", paragraph #25, that the following defects make a registrant "not acceptable":

"(C) Perforation membrane tympani
(D) Acute or chronic mastoiditis"

Captain WEINTROB stated he had discussed this case with Major GUIDOTTI and with Colonel CHARLES E. WALSON, Chief, Medical Branch, Second Service Command, New York City, and he had, at the request of Colonel WALSON, forwarded on December 27, 1943 a true copy of the work sheet of the physical examination of SINATRA to General CHARLES C. HILLMAN, M.C., Office of the Surgeon General, War Department, Army Service Forces, 1818 H Street, N.W., Washington 25, D.C. A certified true copy of the cover letter used by Captain WEINTROB in forwarding the copy of the work sheet is enclosed with this letter. There is also enclosed a certified true copy of a letter signed by

Captain WEINTROB to Colonel WALSON on December 28, 1943
and this letter is being set forth below:

ARMED FORCES INDUCTION STATION
113th Infantry Armory
Sussex Avenue and Jay Street
Newark 4, N.Y.

28 December 1943
JW/eak
Subject: Supplementary Information, Frank A. Sinatra.

To: Commanding General, Second Service Command, Army
Service Forces, Governors Island, New York, 4, New York.
ATTENTION:

1. Supplementing the telephonic conversation of 27 and 28
December and work sheet of the physical examination of Frank A.
Sinatra, the following information is submitted:

(a) Selectee stated that at birth he sustained an injury below the
left ear, presumably from the blade of forceps. In his early childhood
he had several mastoid operations and subsequently has had frequent
and repeated attacks of "running ear" on the left side, the last having
occurred within the past several months. He also stated that he often
suffered from "head noises" on the left side.

(b) Examination of the external ear revealed that the lobule had
been removed, and there was much post auricular scarification,
including what were probably incisional scars of the previously
mentioned mastoid surgery. The external auditory canal was
narrowed and somewhat deformed and there was a considerable
quantity of inspissated wax present. The tympanum was seen to
contain a perforation. X-Rays of the left mastoid area revealed a
"sclerosing mastoiditis."

(c) During the psychiatric interview the patient stated that he
was 'neurotic, afraid to be in crowds, afraid to go in elevator, makes

him feel that he would want to run when surrounded by people. He had somatic ideas and headaches and has been very nervous for four or five years. Wakens tired in the A.M., is run down and undernourished.' The examining psychiatrist concluded that this selectee suffered from psychoneurosis and was not acceptable material from the psychiatric viewpoint. Inasmuch as the selectee was to be rejected on an organic basis, namely,

(1) Perforation of left tympanum
(2) Chronic mastoiditis, left,

the diagnosis of psychoneurosis, severe was not added to the list. Notation of emotional instability was made instead. It was felt that this would avoid undue unpleasantness for both the selectee and the induction service.

For the Commanding Officer:

In explanation of some of the medical terms used above, and in explanation of the material transmitted to Colonel WALSON by Captain WEINTROB, the latter gave the following information:

SINATRA had stated to him that he had had at least three mastoid operations in his youth. If SINATRA mentioned the name or names of the physicians involved, Captain WEINTROB was unable to recall them. The examination, according to Captain WEINTROB, seemed to verify the statement inasmuch as there were found scars behind the ear. The perforation of the drum (tympanum) was a disease perforation so far as Captain WEINTROB could tell and not the result of an incision by human hands. Captain WEINTROB stated that mastoiditis is ordinarily caused by infection of the middle ear. In SINATRA'S case, there was chronic infection of the middle ear. Such infection ordinarily causes the formation of pus, which may seek outlet through the drum causing a perforation and thereafter pus draining or running through the perforation. The pus may stop flowing in which case the perforation of the drum will ordinarily heal over until pus again causes a perforation. However, where a perforation has healed, it is possible to see that a perforation formerly existed at that spot. The diseased middle ear can spread this infection to the brain causing an abscess, or to the mastoid area. In the latter area, a diseased condition is termed "mastoiditis," which may be acute; that is inflamed, or chronic; that is more a case of a hardening of the mastoid area with the laying down of bone deposits. In adverse weather conditions and the like chronic mastoiditis may well develop into acute mastoiditis. In SINATRA'S case, his assertion that "running ear" had recently occurred was borne out by the perforation noted in the x-ray of the mastoid area, which showed that the condition was one of chronic mastoiditis. This was borne out by the appearance on the x-ray of the scelorizing or hardening of that area; that is clotting in the remaining cells of the mastoid area not removed by operations indicating that the chronic mastoiditis had had the effect of petrifying that portion of the head. Captain WEINTROB attempted to locate the x-rays of the mastoid area, but was unable to do so immediately. He said he would continue to search for them and would lay them to one side if he were able to locate them.

The Captain also stated that no one had ever attempted to influence his opinion in this case and in fact no one had discussed the SINATRA case with him prior to the actual examination. He added that within the past few weeks he has read an article by one of the New York City columnists to the effect that it was understood FRANK SINATRA'S case was not yet closed so far as induction was concerned. Captain WEINTROB stated he was satisfied in his own mind that SINATRA should not have been inducted and was willing to stake his medical reputation on his findings. He pointed to his training at the Jefferson Medical School and post-graduate work at the University of Pennsylvania Medical School as an indication of his medical qualifications.

Captain WEINTROB stated that although SINATRA was four pounds below the minimum weight for men of his height, his induction station no longer went by the rules regarding minimum weight and for that reason no mention was made of his being below minimum weight. He also stated that many men coming into the induction station are found to have known physical defects which they did not list on the questionnaire or other draft papers. Ordinarily they fail to list such defects in their draft records for fear that people will criticize them for attempting to evade the draft in that fashion.

███████████████████████████ civilian physician, at the Armed Forces Induction Station above mentioned, was likewise interviewed inasmuch as he had examined the x-rays of the mastoid area of FRANK SINATRA. ███████████████ whose residence and office address is █████████████████████████ stated that the x-rays indicated to him that SINATRA had chronic mastoiditis. He explained that the marked sclerosis or hardening of that area made that statement necessary. ████████████████ likewise indicated that he was certain that it was absolutely necessary to reject SINATRA in the induction.

Because of the limited investigation requested, no additional investigation is contemplated by this office.

Very truly yours,

S. K. McKEE
SAC

After concluding that the original allegation was unfounded, the matter was closed. Nevertheless, Sinatra later would take a beating on numerous fronts in the press. Stars and Stripes, the military newspaper, called him a coward, and the conservative Hearst columnist Westbrook Pegler derided him as "bugle-deaf Frankie Boy Sinatra." Nancy Sinatra insisted years later in one of her books that after he'd been rejected as unfit, her father "tried in vain to enlist for the next several years."

TO: Mr. D. M. LADD   DATE: 2-26-44
FROM: Mr. G. C. CALLAN
SUBJECT: FRANK ALBERT SINATRA
      Selective Service

You will recall that we inquired into the Selective Service status
of Frank Sinatra because of the receipt from Walter Winchell of an
anonymous letter which he received alleging that $40,000 had been
paid by Sinatra to procure a 4-F classification. Newark found that
Sinatra received a 4-F classification because of an ear ailment. It also
discovered that Sinatra had been arrested twice—once for seduction
and once for adultery, both arrests resulting in dismissals, and both
based on same act.

      The Director penned a notation on my memorandum to you
dated February 15, 1944, "We should be certain that there is nothing
irregular in this case," and upon your instructions, I called the
Newark Office on February 21, 1944 at 4:45 p.m. and instructed
ASAC [Assistant Special Agent in Charge] R. W. Bachman to have
the physician who examined Sinatra interviewed. The Newark
Office has complied with these instructions and there is attached
hereto Newark's letter of February 24, 1944 which indicates very
definitely that Sinatra was properly rejected because of a perforation
of the membrana tympani and acute or chronic mastoiditis. During
the course of the interview, it was ascertained from the examining
physician, Dr. Joseph R. Weintrob, Captain, U.S. Army, Medical
Corps, that Sinatra stated he had, in his early youth, been operated
on on several occasions for mastoiditis. X-ray pictures have borne out
Sinatra's statements in this regard. Captain Weintrob said the scar
tissue which was the result of the operation was readily perceptible
and in this connection the operational scars very clearly appear on
the left profile photograph taken on the occasion of one of Sinatra's
arrests by the Sheriff's Office at Hackensack, New Jersey. Either the
perforation of the tympani or the mastoid condition is, as Captain
Weintrob points out, cause for rejection of a registrant under War
Department regulations.

It therefore appears that Sinatra was properly rejected from military service and there is no indication that the statements made in the anonymous letter above referred to have any foundation. Consequently, in the absence of further instructions, no additional inquiries will be conducted in this matter.

TWO

SINATRA, THE FBI, AND THE PRESS

"Mr. Mortimer was appreciative."

Frank Sinatra had a tempestuous and at times complicated relationship with both the FBI and the press. Little did he know that the two institutions were sometimes collaborating with each other against him.

They needed each other. As FBI agents delved into every aspect of the star's life, they depended on obvious sources of information like press reports as well as confidential informants. The FBI files now make clear that some of the journalists who wrote those reports were in effect FBI informants as well, providing unsubstantiated rumors for the bureau to run down—including Walter Winchell's tip about the draft covered in chapter 1. The FBI returned the favor on occasion, helping journalists digging for dirt on the singer.

In 1946, the ultraconservative Hoover demonstrated that he was no fan of the singer when Louis B. Nichols, one of his top aides, reported disapprovingly on a stop in the star's nationwide tour, attaching a fairly innocuous press clipping as supporting material.

TO: Mr. Tolson   DATE: May 14, 1946
FROM: L. B. Nichols

As a symptom of the state of mind of many young people I wish to call to your attention the following incident that occurred in Detroit on last Wednesday.

Frank Sinatra arrived in Detroit around midnight and a group of bobby soxers were waiting for him at the airfield. He eluded them and they then congregated at the stage door of the Downtown Theater where he was scheduled to give his first performance around 10:00 a.m. on Thursday morning. The line started forming at around 2:00 a.m. The police started challenging girls who appeared to be under 16 and tried to send them home. However, I have been told, there was a long line of mere kids, many of whom carried their lunches, and they remained in line until the theater opened. Truant Officers started checking the lines early in the morning and were berated by the girls. There was widespread indignation on the part of numerous individuals that I came in contact with and a severe indictment of parents of the girls. One individual went so far as to state that Sinatra should be lynched. I am attaching hereto a page from The Detroit Times showing some of the girls.

Handwritten notation by Hoover: Sinatra is as much to blame as the moronic bobby-soxers. H.

A year later, Sinatra was taking a beating in the press for his association with alleged mobsters, his draft record, and his political activities, which some considered left-leaning enough to be Communist.

Things boiled over at Ciro's restaurant in Hollywood on April 8, 1947, when he was arrested for slugging his biggest press nemesis—the Hearst columnist Lee Mortimer. The singer later said the muckraking scribe had been "needling me" for two years with blistering columns. Nancy Sinatra has written that Mortimer held a grudge against her father for rejecting a song he'd written.

Press clippings in the FBI files included speculation that a recent Mortimer piece about Sinatra's association with the mobster Lucky Luciano had infuriated the singer. But one article pointedly noted that the Luciano story actually was broken by Robert Ruark, a "6-foot, 200-pound columnist." Mortimer weighed about 120 at the time.

At Ciro's that night, Sinatra claimed Mortimer had goaded him by calling him a "dago." Mortimer insisted that Sinatra's attack was unprovoked. Sinatra later settled the case by paying Mortimer $9,000 and withdrawing the slur accusation.

Mortimer wasn't through with Sinatra, though. A month after the Ciro's incident, the FBI's Nichols wrote this memo to Clyde A. Tolson, Hoover's top aide and closest friend, to prepare the director for a planned meeting with the aggrieved columnist. This memo clearly shows that the FBI was inclined to help Mortimer.

May 12, 1947

MEMORANDUM FOR MR. TOLSON

RE: FRANK SINATRA

In view of the Director's conference with Lee Mortimer tomorrow it would appear that there are three specific problems that have been raised on which the Director desires information. The following is being submitted:

1. Mr. Mortimer said he had a picture of Sinatra getting off a plane in Havana with a tough-looking man whom he has been unable to identify. He believes he is a gangster from Chicago.

Observation: It is suggested that this picture be exhibited to Agents who have worked on the reactivation of the Capone gang in

Chicago, as well as to Agents in the Newark Office who have been working on criminal work, in view of the known contacts that Sinatra has had with New York hoodlums. It is entirely possible that in this way the unidentified picture might be identified. If we identified the individual we could secure a picture of the person identified and furnish that to Mortimer and then in turn let him go out and verify the identification in such a way as to remove the Bureau from any responsibility of furnishing information.

2. Mortimer stated that Sinatra was backed when he first started by a gangster in New York named Willie Moretti, now known as Willie Moore.

Observation: It is well known that Willie Moretti of Hasbrouck Heights, New Jersey, controls gambling in Bergen County, New Jersey, and is a close friend of Frank Costello. According to Captain Matthew J. Donohue of the Bergen County Police, Moretti had a financial interest in Sinatra. In this connection, Sinatra resides in Hasbrouck Heights.

The Los Angeles Office has reported that a boxing show was being sponsored by Sinatra together with Henry Sanicola and Larry Rummans. According to reports, they incorporated, formed a company and sold stock to raise money to build "a little Madison Square Garden Arena" in Los Angeles. At the same time it was reported that Sinatra was interested in purchasing a hotel and gambling establishment that was being built in Las Vegas, Nevada. He was assisted by an attorney named Herbert Pearlsen. Sanicola and Rummans were not further identified. It is known that Bugsy Siegel went to Los Angeles on December 18, 1946, to contact Lana Turner, Jimmy Durante and Frank Sinatra for the purpose of having them attend the opening of the Flamingo Hotel. Sinatra, however, did not attend either the opening on December 26, 1946, or December 28, 1946, which was attended by several stars including George Raft, Brian Donlevy, June Haver, Lucille Ball, Sonny Tufts and others. It is likewise known that Mickey Cohen, well-known gambler and racketeer who operates out of Los Angeles, has been in contact with Sinatra on occasions.

In August, 1946, the New York Office was advised by Frances Duffy, clerk of the Local Selective Service Board #180, New York City, that she resides at 424 Second Street, Brooklyn, New York, in a home owned by Mrs. Mary Fischetti. Miss Duffy stated that Sinatra, accompanied by Charles Fischetti, visited the home of his mother and spent the evening there in about June of 1946.

The Chicago Office advised that on August 8, 1946, a request was made of Charles Fischetti to get in touch with his brother Joe for the purpose of contacting Frank Sinatra in New York to expedite hotel reservations around November 7, 1946. It was indicated that the reservations for the hotel were desired by the Fischettis as they intended to attend the Notre Dame–Army football game. Fischetti is a Chicago hoodlum who was a subject in the Bureau's investigation on the Re-Activation of the Capone Gang.

An informant in Chicago advised ███████████████████ Joe Fischetti met Charles Baron and furnished the information to the effect that both Joe Fischetti and Charles Baron had purchased two dozen shirts and forwarded them to Frank Sinatra in Hollywood. The shirts were boxed in two separate boxes and a card was placed in each box, one from Joe Fischetti and the other from Charles Baron. Baron apparently is associated with a Ford agency on South Michigan Avenue in Chicago.

The Washington News on April 10, 1947, carried a story datelined Hollywood, April 10, which carried the following statement:

> "Frankie explained he took out the permit two months ago to 'protect personal funds.' Shortly thereafter he went to Cuba, where he met Gambler Lucky Luciano. Their alleged friendship was blistered in Mr. Mortimer's column and was believed to be the spark for Tuesday night's fracas.
>
> "(Frankie's 'friendship' with Luciano was first revealed by Robert Ruark, 6-foot, 200-pound columnist for the News and other Scripps-Howard papers.)"

If Lee Mortimer has not already done so, he might contact Robert Ruark. Ruark personally told me that he has been investigating Sinatra and it is entirely possible that Ruark might have uncovered some information that may be of assistance. There is attached hereto Mr. Ruark's column of February 20, 1947. Also, Mortimer might check with law enforcement contacts in Bergen County and endeavor to secure the information from Captain Donohue which he has on Moretti and Sinatra.

3. Mortimer also desires Bureau information on Sinatra's arrest on a sex offense.

Observation: The records of the clerk of the Second Criminal Judicial District of the County of Bergen, Hackensack, New Jersey, reveal the following information: Docket 15228 in the State vs. Frank Sinatra reflects that Sinatra was charged on November 26, 1938, by ███████████████████████ New Jersey, as follows: "On the second and ninth days of November, 1938 . . . under the promise of marriage he (Sinatra) did then and there have sexual intercourse with the said complainant who was then and there a single female of good repute. . . ." The Charles Casualty Company, 214 Maine Street, Hackensack, New Jersey, made Sinatra's bond of $1,500. On December 7, 1938, the complaint was withdrawn when it was ascertained that the complainant was in fact married.

Docket 15307 in the case of State vs. Frank Sinatra reveals a complaint was filed on December 21, 1938, by ████████████████ ████████████████████████████ New Jersey, charging Sinatra with adultery in that he ". . . on the second and ninth days of November, 1938 . . . committed adultery with the said complainant, a married woman, wife of ██████████████". Sinatra made his own bond of $500 on January 4, 1939, and the case was remanded to the jury by order of Judge McIntyre.

Docket 18540 for the prosecutor of the bills, Bergen County, reveals that a no-bill was returned on January 17, 1939 by the grand jury and the complaint charging adultery was dismissed in open court for quarter sessions on January 24, 1939. Sinatra was then represented by Harry L. Towe of Rutherford, New Jersey. Towe is now a member of Congress and the Director may recall meeting him at my house prior to the Shrine Dinner in Alexandria.

4. Conceivably the New York Mirror might have access to the records at Local Board #19 for Hudson County, Room 308, 26 Journal Square, Jersey City, New Jersey. In February of 1944, the chief clerk of this board was Mrs. Mae E. Jones. On the detailed notations appearing in section 4, physical examination results, (made by Captain J. Weintrob, M.C., Assistant Chief Medical Officer), appears the following observation: "55—Mental: emotional instability, N.D." When interviewed later, Captain Weintrob furnished us with a copy of a communication which he had addressed to the commanding general wherein paragraph C reads as follows:

"During the psychiatric interview the patient stated that he was 'neurotic, afraid to be in crowds, afraid to go in elevator, makes him feel that he would want to run when surrounded by people. He had somatic ideas and headaches and has been very nervous for four or five years. Wakens tired in the A.M., is run down and undernourished.' The examining psychiatrist concluded that this selectee suffered from psychoneurosis and was not acceptable material from the psychiatric viewpoint. Inasmuch as the selectee was to be rejected on an organic basis, namely,

(1) Perforation of left tympanum
(2) Chronic mastoiditis, left,

the diagnosis of psychoneurosis, severe was not added to the list. Notation of emotional instability was made instead. It was felt that this would avoid undue unpleasantness for both the selectee and the induction service."

There is attached hereto a more detailed summary memorandum prepared in Mr. Rosen's division on February 26.

Tolson ended up meeting with Mortimer the following day. He later briefed Hoover on the visit, all the while insisting that he had not given the columnist any "official assistance," when in fact it appeared that he had been helpful.

TO: DIRECTOR   DATE: May 13, 1947
FROM: CLYDE TOLSON

I talked this afternoon to Mr. Lee Mortimer, of the New York Daily Mirror, who wanted to ask some questions concerning Frank Sinatra. I told Mr. Mortimer that, of course, he realized that we could not give him any official information or be identified in this matter in any manner, which he thoroughly understands.

He left a photograph taken of Frank Sinatra in Cuba and asked whether we could identify one individual shown in the picture. Copies of this photograph are being made and an effort will be made to determine whether any of our Agents are acquainted with the person in question.

Secondly, he was interested in the association between Sinatra and Willie Moretti of Hasbrouck Heights, New Jersey. I told Mr. Mortimer in this connection that his best bet would be to make appropriate contacts with the Bergen County Police and possibly with a Captain Donohue.

Also, Mr. Mortimer was interested in Sinatra's arrest on a sex offense. He had practically all of the information concerning this charge and I merely indicated that he might secure information as to the ultimate disposition of the charge by contacting the prosecutor of the bills, Bergen County, New Jersey.

Also, Mr. Mortimer had already learned of the contents of the selective service file pertaining to Sinatra and knew the location of the board in Jersey City. He indicated that while he had secured the contents of this file on an informal basis, he understood that these records were not subject to subpoena.

Mr. Mortimer had already contacted Robert Ruark, who has written several derogatory articles concerning Sinatra.

Mr. Mortimer told me that he understood that Colonel Fain D'Orsey, alias Charles Conley, was arrested in the spring of 1946 for smuggling narcotics from Mexico to the United States and at the

time of his arrest was driving a station wagon which belongs to
Sinatra. He indicated that Sinatra has made no effort to secure
repossession of this station wagon but he has learned that possibly
D'Orsey will furnish enough information to the Narcotics Bureau to
include Sinatra in a conspiracy charge. He stated he planned to have
the Hearst Office arrange for him to see Mr. Anslinger, of the
Narcotics Bureau, in an effort to run this down. I am trying to
ascertain whether we have a criminal record of this person on the
basis of the information furnished.

Mr. Mortimer was appreciative of the opportunity to talk to me
and thoroughly understood we could not be of any official assistance
to him in this matter.

*In an open letter to the public issued in the spring of 1947, Sinatra
denounced "certain unscrupulous newspapermen" who were attacking him
and thanked the journalists standing by him, including Winchell, who had a
role in touching off the Sinatra draft investigation in 1944. And years later,
Winchell evidently passed on another damaging and unsubstantiated
allegation to the FBI, as evidenced by this excerpt from a memo sent by the
Los Angeles FBI office to Hoover.*

The Bureau by letter to Springfield dated July 11, 1951, captioned
██████████████ INFORMATION CONCERNING, furnished a
photostatic copy of a letter written by ██████████████████
Peoria, Illinois, dated July 23, 1950, addressed to Mr. WALTER
WINCHELL. A copy of this letter was confidentially furnished to
the Bureau. The letter contains quotations from a booklet written by
KENNETH GOFF entitled "Confessions of Stalin's Agent." One of
the quotations describes SINATRA as "one of the outstanding Reds
in Hollywood." According to ████████████████ letter, the booklet
also includes other allegations concerning SINATRA.

Another reporter, Bill Davidson of Look *magazine, asked the FBI for
derogatory information on Sinatra in 1957. His January 20 letter to Louis
Nichols, a Hoover aide, cited "constant allegations" circulating about Sina-*

tra: Had Sinatra been arrested for rape or assault in Jersey City or Hoboken in the early 1930s? the journalist wanted to know. Had his mother been arrested and charged as an abortionist? And had two of Sinatra's uncles been arrested for bootlegging during Prohibition?

In response, the FBI official immediately ordered up a synopsis of the Sinatra files (below) that included specific replies to Davidson's inquiries. Later that year, Davidson wrote an award-winning series on Sinatra for Look *magazine, prompting libel and invasion-of-privacy lawsuits from the singer, which were eventually dropped.*

TO: Mr. Nichols   January 23, 1957
FROM: M. A. Jones
SUBJECT: FRANCIS ALBERT SINATRA
            AKA. FRANK SINATRA

SYNOPSIS:

Frank Sinatra was born December 12, 1915 or 1916, at Hoboken, New Jersey, of Italian-born parents. He left high school in 1935 to obtain employment and during that year, began his singing career in night clubs and road houses in the northern New Jersey area. He was married in 1939 to Nancy Barbato and has three children by that marriage. He divorced her in 1951 and married actress Ava Gardner, from whom he was separated after approximately two years of marriage. Allegations concerning his contacts with the Communist Party and numerous communist front groups came to the Bureau's attention for a number of years and were included in a memorandum sent to the State Department in December, 1954, on their request for a name check on Sinatra. In view of a sworn affidavit, executed by him on January 10, 1955, in connection with his application for a passport, to the effect that he had never been a member of the Communist Party or of any organization of a subversive character, the State Department requested an investigation by the Bureau to determine whether prosecution was warranted against Sinatra for making a false statement in the application. The investigation developed no evidence connecting Sinatra with the Communist Party or any of its front groups aside from his membership in the Independent Citizens Committee of the Arts, Sciences, and Professions in 1946. This organization was cited by the California Committee on Un-American Activities as a communist front and included a number of other prominent citizens in its membership. In 1948, Sinatra allegedly took part in an appeal to the voters of Italy to vote against the communist ticket in the elections then being held in that country. Material has appeared in the press linking Sinatra with known hoodlums, and in February, 1947, he was alleged to have spent four days in the company of Lucky Luciano, the deported Italian criminal who was prominent in the narcotics traffic in America. His name has also been prominently linked with Joseph and Rocco Fischetti, members of the Capone gang, Willie Moretti, former underworld boss of Bergen County, New Jersey, James Tarantino, an associate of Benjamin "Bugsy" Siegel, and other hoodlums on the west coast. As recently as 1955, he was seen frequenting an after-hours bottle club in New York frequented by known hoodlums and is reputedly one of the twelve major stockholders in the Sands Hotel, a gambling establishment in Las Vegas allegedly controlled by Abner "Longy" Zwillman and Joseph Stacher, both notorious gangsters from New Jersey. . . . Sinatra's mother, Mrs. Natalie Sinatra, was arrested in November, 1937, on a charge of abortion. No disposition is given for this case. Lawrence Garavente, said to be an uncle of Sinatra. ■■■■■■■■■■■■ ■■■■■■■■■■■■■■■■■■■■■■■■■■■ Bureau files do not verify his relationship to Sinatra. In 1944, columnist Frederick C. Othman, in a syndicated article, quoted Sinatra as saying that he received a letter from the Bureau concerning an applicant in which he was requested to return four autographed photographs for the girls in Mr. Nichols' office. When contacted, Sinatra denied the story but stated that he had received a letter of that kind from the office of the Adjutant General and would have Othman correct the matter. In September, 1950, through an intermediary, Sinatra offered his services to the Bureau, and the Director noted his agreement with Mr. Tolson's comment that we "want nothing to do with him."

*   *   *

SPECIFIC INQUIRIES MADE BY DAVIDSON

In his letter, Davidson stated that he planned on doing a definitive, three-part profile on Sinatra for "Look" magazine and was concerned about several items which he had come across since the manner in which they were resolved would help in "pitching" his article. . . .

Davidson asked for verification of the following:

1. That Sinatra was arrested for rape in Jersey City or Hoboken around 1934. The charge is supposed to have been reduced to seduction and then thrown out by the Grand Jury. (Westbrook Pegler has reported this several times in his columns.)

> COMMENT: The records of the clerk of the Second Criminal Judicial District of the county of Bergen, Hackensack, New Jersey, reveal the following information: Docket 15228 in the State vs. Frank Sinatra reflects that Sinatra was charged on November 26, 1938, by ████████████████████████ New Jersey, as follows: "On the second and ninth days of November, 1938, . . . under the promise of marriage, he (Sinatra) did then and there have sexual intercourse with the said complainant who was then and there a single female of good repute. . . ." The complaint was withdrawn when it was ascertained that the complainant was in fact married. Docket 15307 in the case of the State vs. Frank Sinatra, indicates a complaint was filed on December 21, 1938, by ████████████ ████████████████████████ New Jersey, charging Sinatra with adultery in that he ". . . on the second and ninth days of November, 1938, . . . committed adultery with the said complainant, a married woman and wife of ████████████." . . .
>
> Docket 18540, for the Prosecutor of Bills, Bergen County, reveals that no bill was returned on January 17, 1939, by the grand jury, and the complaint charging adultery was dismissed in open court for quarter sessions on January 24, 1939. . . .

2. That Sinatra was arrested and convicted of assault around the same time (presumably the 1930's).

COMMENT: There is no information in Bufiles [bureau files] or the records of the Identification Division to substantiate such an arrest. News articles, however, reflect that Sinatra was arrested on April 9, 1947, in Hollywood on a battery warrant based upon a complaint by Lee Mortimer, New York columnist. Sinatra entered a plea of not guilty and was released on a $500 bail. No disposition of this case appears in the file.

3. That Mrs. Natalie Sinatra, his mother, was arrested 6 or 7 times for operating an abortion mill in Hoboken between the years 1930 and 1950 and that she might have been convicted once.

COMMENT: "Time" magazine, . . . a copy of which is attached, reported that Sinatra's mother, known generally as Dolly Sinatra, started out as a practical nurse and helped her husband run a little barroom at the corner of Jefferson and Fourth in Hoboken. She allegedly was active in Democratic ward politics and acted as a midwife at a number of neighborhood births. According to the article, she was a "power" in her part of town, and in 1909 was made a district leader. In 1926, the Mayor of Hoboken appointed her husband to a captaincy in the fire department. The records of the Identification Division contain a single card reflecting a criminal arrest on November 15, 1937, of Mrs. Natalie Sinatra, with alias Dolly Sinatra, on a charge of abortion. Her residence was given as 841 Garden Street, Hoboken, New Jersey, and the card was received from the Hoboken, New Jersey, Police Department. No disposition of the case is given, and the incident is not mentioned in Bufiles. . . .

4. That Sinatra's uncles, Champ and Lawrence Garavente, were arrested and perhaps convicted of bootlegging in Hoboken in the 1920's and early 1930's.

COMMENT: There are no references in Bufiles or the records of the Identification Division identical with Champ Garavente. There is no information in Bufiles to the effect that Lawrence Garavente is related to Frank Sinatra.

Not all journalists were treated well by the FBI. In this excerpt from a heavily censored memo dated September 17, 1963, the Los Angeles office reports to the director on information provided by a "sensationalist" journalist, whose name the FBI blotted out. The memo recounts threats the journalist received that invoked the name of the reputed mobster Sam Giancana, a Sinatra friend. The journalist also mentions an encounter he'd had with Sinatra at the restaurant the singer owned in Beverly Hills with the actor Peter Lawford, Jack Kennedy's brother-in-law, and other investors.

▮▮▮▮▮▮▮▮▮▮ said that SINATRA does not like him as he had written up some articles unfavorable to SINATRA several years ago at a time when SINATRA was a part owner of Puccini's Restaurant. ▮▮▮▮▮▮▮▮▮▮ stated he had a date one night and his girl friend insisted on going to Puccini's and he finally agreed to reluctantly. While ▮▮▮▮▮▮▮▮▮▮ was at the restaurant SINATRA came in and surveyed the customers and thereafter ▮▮▮▮▮▮▮▮▮▮ was paged to the telephone. When he answered the telephone it was dead and as he hung it up SINATRA appeared and called him all kinds of dirty names.

▮▮▮▮▮▮▮▮▮▮ told SINATRA in effect, "I am not going to hit you since I see you have a number of your hoodlum friends around you. Give me my check and I will get out of here." SINATRA allegedly replied, "I don't want your money . . . it is dirty money."

Three years later, the same journalist contacted the FBI again, as re-counted here in an excerpt from a heavily censored Teletype.

TELETYPE
FBI LOS ANG.
7:07 PM PDST URGENT 5/9/66
TO: DIRECTOR
FROM: LOS ANGELES
INFORMATION CONCERNING
CAPTIONED INDIVIDUAL TELEPHONICALLY CONTACTED
THE OFFICE AT ELEVEN THIRTY A.M. THIS DATE AND ADVISED
THAT HE HAD BEEN BEATEN BY FOUR INDIVIDUALS WHOM HE
SUSPECTS AS BEING FRANK SINATRA'S MOB. HE REQUESTED
FBI ASSISTANCE IN IDENTIFYING THESE INDIVIDUALS.

 RELATED
TO SINATRA'S DIFFICULTIES WITH MEXICAN AUTHORITIES.
█████████ WENT ON TO STATE THAT ON
████████████████████████ WHEN HE DROVE HIS CAR
████████████████ HE WAS GRABBED BY FOUR THUGS AS HE
LEFT THE CAR AND WAS SEVERELY BEATEN. HE SAID HE
IMMEDIATELY NOTIFIED THE HOLLYWOOD DIVISION OF THE
LOS ANGELES PD WHO IS INVESTIGATING.
    HE SAID HE IS CERTAIN IN HIS OWN MIND THAT THE FOUR
THUGS WHO COMMITTED THE BEATING WERE MEMBERS OF
SINATRA'S GROUP. HE SAID HE BELIEVES THIS SINCE SINATRA
THREATENED HIM IN THE PAST ████████████████████████
    IT IS NOTED IN LOS ANGELES FILES THAT BY LETTER DATED
SEPTEMBER SEVENTEEN, NINETEEN SIXTY-THREE, THE BUREAU
WAS ADVISED OF A CONTACT WITH ████████████ AT
WHICH TIME HE SPOKE OF AN ALLEGED THREAT MADE BY

SINATRA WHILE ███████████ WAS DINING AT PUCCINI'S
RESTAURANT, OF WHICH SINATRA IS REPORTEDLY PART
OWNER.

███████████ REQUESTED THAT THE FBI IMMEDIATELY
MAKE AVAILABLE TO HIM PHOTOGRAPHS OF SINATRA'S
HOODLUM ASSOCIATES SO THAT HE, ███████████, MIGHT
VIEW THEM IN AN EFFORT TO IDENTIFY THE INDIVIDUALS
WHO BEAT HIM.

███████████ WAS TACTFULLY ADVISED THAT THIS WAS
NOT A MATTER WITHIN THE INVESTIGATIVE JURISDICTION OF
THE FBI, AND THAT IT WAS PURELY A MATTER FOR LOCAL
POLICE AUTHORITIES. AT THIS POINT ███████████ BECAME
VERY ARROGANT AND OBNOXIOUS AND DEMANDED THAT
THE FBI ENTER HIS CASE. IT SEEMED THAT ███████████
WAS MAKING EVERY ATTEMPT TO STAMPEDE THE FBI INTO HIS
CASE.

AFTER CLEARLY POINTING OUT THE POSITION OF THE FBI IN
A MATTER SUCH AS THIS, THAT WE WILL COOPERATE WITH
LOCAL POLICE AUTHORITIES IN EVERY WAY POSSIBLE, THAT IT
IS A MATTER FOR POLICE INVESTIGATION THE CALL WAS
TERMINATED IN WHAT APPEARED TO BE A FRIENDLY TONE.

THREE
SINATRA AND COMMUNISM

"Mrs. Roosevelt in pants"

For many years, the FBI was much more concerned with combating the then ominous-seeming threat of communism than with fighting organized crime, the very existence of which Hoover questioned until the late 1950s. From the dawn of the cold war, the FBI intensively monitored the domestic activities of not only the Communist party, but also groups deemed too left-wing by Senator Joseph McCarthy, the House Un-American Activities Committee (HUAC), and conservative Sinatra antagonists in the press like Lee Mortimer and Westbrook Pegler.

Sinatra was among the first of many entertainment figures whose patriotism was thrown into doubt by the red-baiting of the anti-Communists. His ardently liberal New Deal politics, of course, made him an obvious target. And Sinatra wasn't shy about collaborating with outspoken leftists, including Albert Maltz, the screenwriter for Sinatra's acclaimed pro-tolerance film short *The House I Live In* (1945). The film, which won him a special Academy Award, was a mixed blessing at cold war's outset: It made him a darling of the American left.

It is clear, however, that the FBI was overstating the case when, in internal reports from the period, it referred to Sinatra as a "communist sympathizer" or a "CP fellow traveler." In the end, it had nothing on him but the ordinary activities of a liberal celebrity.

Moreover, the singer was more nimble than Maltz and others who were blacklisted; he at first belittled charges that he was a Communist sympathizer, then confronted them head-on. And at one point an intermediary told the FBI that Sinatra was willing to spy on certain groups for the bureau. Thus Sinatra emerged from the McCarthy era with his career, if not his reputation, more or less intact.

A few months after World War II ended and just after the release of The House I Live In, *Sinatra made headlines trying to diffuse racial tensions in Gary, Indiana, where white high school students were boycotting classes to protest a desegregation effort.*

Confronting a rowdy and antagonistic audience in the school auditorium, Sinatra stood center stage, his arms folded, staring down the crowd for two anxious minutes until the catcalls and stomping gave way to absolute silence. Then he stepped up to the microphone and announced, Hoboken-style, "I can lick any son of a bitch in this joint." Hostility gave way to cheers, but his impassioned plea for tolerance ended up insulting some locals and failed to end the strike. It also cemented the boyish singer's status as a hero to American liberals of every stripe, including Communists.

This excerpt, from a 1950 report in the FBI files, summarized the incident.

GARY, INDIANA, SCHOOL STUDENTS STRIKE INCIDENT, NOVEMBER 1, 1945

On October 18, 1945, the white students at the Froebel School in Gary, Indiana, went on strike for a second time. The first walkout occurred during September, 1945, when several hundred white students demanded that the school be made an all white school. The Indianapolis Office reported that the trouble between the white and colored races at this school dated back at least to the spring of 1944 when there had been an attempt to establish an all white Parent Teachers Association in opposition to the Association then functioning under the presidency of Beatrice Lawrence, wife of Howard Lawrence, a Communist Party organizer for Lake County, Indiana. This move was defeated and the PTA, including both white and Negro members, continued with Mrs. Lawrence as President. On November 1, 1945, Frank Sinatra appeared at the Memorial Auditorium in Gary, Indiana, at which time he made an appeal to end the school strike. During his speech Sinatra charged that the strike had been fomented by adults under the leadership of Joseph Lach, a prominent citizen and undertaker in Gary, Indiana. Sinatra referred to Lach as a small time politician who had never been elected to office. Sinatra also attacked Julius Danch and referred to him as a man of shady character, opposed to whites and Negroes associating together, and said that he would personally ask the Mayor to throw Danch out of his office as City Hall Custodian. Sinatra also said that he had talked with the student strike leader, Leonard Levenda, who had refused to meet with him, but that he would try again to talk with Lavenda before leaving Gary. Levenda reportedly denied Sinatra's charge and claimed that he had talked with Sinatra before the meeting and told him that Lach and Danch had no part in the school strike.

Danch was identified as the Editor of a monthly Catholic bulletin, the president of the Hungarian Political Club in Gary, and City Hall Custodian since January, 1943.

As a result of Sinatra's attack on Lach and Danch, Father Lawrence T. Grothaus, Pastor of the Saint Anthony's Church and Director of the Catholic Youth Organization in Gary, left the stage in disgust. Father Grothaus told Sinatra's manager, George Evans, that Sinatra should not have delved into personalities. Evans reportedly replied that Sinatra's information was in part, at least, received from the confidential files of the FBI. He later stated that he could not recall who had made the statement regarding FBI files; however, Evans' statement pertaining to FBI files was witnessed by Police Captain Peter Billick and Patrolman ▆▆▆▆▆▆▆▆ of the Gary, Indiana Police Department.

Relative to Sinatra's source of information, Captain Billick advised that a check of Sinatra's contacts from the time he arrived until he left the same evening revealed that Sinatra had no opportunity to obtain the information concerning Lach and Danch while he was in Gary.

The meeting on November 1, 1945, which was addressed by Frank Sinatra had been arranged by the Anselm Forum. It was said that many of the leaders of the Anselm Forum were CIO leaders and "so-called liberals." The Indianapolis Office advised that they had no record of this group. No evidence was developed from informants of the existence of any subversive activities in connection with the

Froebel School strike which, in the opinion of Captain Billick, was brought about by the students acting on their own. He further reported that Julius Danch viciously fought the Communists: however, the Communists did seize upon this strike to charge that it was a plot by the steel mill interests in Gary to divide the colored people against the whites and thereby cause friction between the unions and the mills, in order to defeat a wage increase which the CIO was then demanding. The Communists also charged in a Daily Worker article on September 29, 1945, that Julius Danch had started the move two years ago when he attempted to form an all white PTA. In addition, the American Youth For Democracy organization in Gary distributed pamphlets on one occasion concerning the strike situation. . . .

It was reported that there had been indications that the appearance of Frank Sinatra at Gary, Indiana, on November 1, 1945, "was perhaps induced by the AYD or by the Communist Party. . . ."

But an unidentified outside source reported that Frank Sinatra paid his own expenses in coming to Gary.

Six weeks following the Gary incident, the special agent in charge (SAC) of Philadelphia told Hoover that an informant had identified Sinatra as a Communist.

TO: Director, FBI　　　　　　　　DATE: December 12, 1945
FROM: SAC, Philadelphia
SUBJECT: FRANK SINATRA
　　　　　　SECURITY MATTER—C

Recently, Confidential Informant ██████████████████ advised that while attending ██████████████████ ████████████████████████████ that FRANK SINATRA, well known radio and movie star, is a member of the Communist Party. He was told that SINATRA formerly held membership in the American Youth for Democracy organization of New Jersey but has recently been admitted to the New York branch of the Communist Party.

███████████ advised that the reason SINATRA was discussed was because of the recent article which appeared on him in "Life" magazine, setting forth his position on racial hatred and showing SINATRA talking before a Gary, Indiana, high school group.

On November 25, 1945 a full page article appeared in the Sunday "Worker" on FRANK SINATRA. This article was written by WALTER LOWENFELS, Philadelphia correspondent for the "Worker".

In the Sunday "Worker" dated December 2, 1945 under "Pennsylvania News" the following item appeared: "FRANK SINATRA is going to get a gold medal and a silver plaque at the Broadwood Hotel, December 10. He will receive the first annual Golden Slipper Square Club Unity Award for his contribution to racial and religious tolerance."

This information is being furnished for whatever action is deemed advisable.

Hoover months later asked for the first full report on what the FBI had in its files on Sinatra. It was forwarded to Hoover by a top bureau official, Edward A. Tamm, later a federal judge. It contained information about his draft and alleged mob ties, but the bulk was an extraordinarily detailed accounting of his political activities. (The excerpts here have been compiled from two drafts of the same memo; some entries have been deleted to avoid duplication with material elsewhere in this book.)

TO: THE DIRECTOR   DATE: 2-26-47
FROM: Mr. Edw. A. Tamm

The attached memorandum concerning Frank Sinatra is obviously most poorly and improperly arranged and I am again having it done over.

In view of the length of time since you requested it, however, I thought it might be of some current value to you in its present form.

Attachment

ASSOCIATION WITH COMMUNISTS AND
COMMUNIST FRONT GROUPS

Bureau files contain numerous references which allege that Sinatra has made speeches for, written articles for, or attended or supported rallies sponsored by organizations dominated by Communist groups. Information in this regard which is of particular interest follows.

It has been ascertained that William Dieterle, a motion picture director in Hollywood and reliably reported to be a strong supporter of the Communist party and the Soviet Union, was in receipt of a letter from Frank Sinatra postmarked at New York City June 26, 1945. On the evening of September 2, 1946, Frank Sinatra was a guest artist at a concert held at Los Angeles, California by the Hollywood Independent Citizens Committee of the Arts, Science, and Professions which has been reliably reported to have been one of the main Communist political pressure and propaganda groups existing. It has been reliably reported that an unknown person conferred with Lionel Berman, Communist party member and celebrity contact man for the Communist party in New York City, relative to the possibility of getting Frank Sinatra to speak at an inter-racial meeting to be held at Corona, Long Island. It has been reliably reported that Frank Sinatra was scheduled for appearance on a program sponsored by the Paramount Studio Club in Los Angeles, California, held on February 12, 1946. One of the scheduled speakers at this meeting was identified as Earl Robinson, a member of the Communist party in that area.

Gerald L. K. Smith, who was called before the Congressional Committee investigating un-American activities, petitioned the Committee to investigate the activities of Frank Sinatra who, he stated, seems to be a highly paid, emaciated crooner but who recently gave support to a meeting of the American Youth for Democracy which held an elaborate banquet at the Hotel Ambassador in Los Angeles, December 16, 1945.

The Daily Worker under date of September 15, 1945 reported that Frank Sinatra would be a sponsor of the World Youth Conference to be held in London October 31 to November 9, 1945.

An unusually reliable source informed that a yearbook to be published by the American Youth Division of the Communist Party will reportedly contain contributions by Frank Sinatra.

In the September 6, 1945 issue of "The Witness," an article written by Edward Harrison entitled "The Church's Joint Support of Republican Spain" reflected that the Church League for Industrial Democracy has joined with a large number of organizations in sponsoring a rally on behalf of Republican Spain which rally would be held in Madison Square Garden the evening of September 24, 1945 and speakers would include Frank Sinatra.

In the Daily Worker dated January 2, 1945 an article headed "Yugoslav Relief Opens 1946 Drive" sets out that the American Committee for Yugoslav Relief opened its activities for 1946 with a Town Hall Benefit Concert organized by the Greenwich Village Chapter. The concert was sponsored by individuals including Artie Shaw and Frank Sinatra.

An article in the Daily Worker dated May 21, 1946 quoted Frank Sinatra as denying charges that he was crooning American bobby soxers into the hands of the Comunists. The article states that a representative of the Knights of Columbus alleged that Sinatra, a Catholic, had aligned himself with Communists when he spoke at a Red Rally of 16,000 left wingers in New York's Madison Square Garden. Sinatra stated it was a rally sponsored by the Veterans Committee of the Independent Citizens Committee of Arts, Science and Professions urging the passage of legislation to provide housing for veterans. Sinatra was quoted as saying, "The minute anyone tries to help the little guy he is called a Communist."

It is reliably reported that Frank Sinatra sent $100 to the Joint Anti-Fascist Refugee Committee in response to a telegraphic request for a donation. In addition a request was made of Sinatra to appear as a guest at a dinner given by the organization on December 4, 1944 in honor of William Gropper, a contributor to the Daily Worker.

The Daily Worker for January 16, 1946 reported that Sinatra received an award at the "New Masses" dinner held at the Hotel Commodore, New York for his courageous fight on behalf of all minorities.

It has been reliably reported that Frank Sinatra was selected as a vice chairman of the Board of Directors Independent Citizens Committee of the Arts, Science and Professions, Incorporated at a meeting held February 10, 1946. This group has been reported to be a Communist Party front group and several of its officers are reported Communists or fellow travelers.

An article appearing in the Baltimore Afro-American dated April 10, 1945 reflected that Frank Sinatra was to give a talk on racial harmony. It stated that Sinatra was reported to have beaten several southern cafe owners who refused to serve negro musicians in his party.

On May 3, 1946 Phil Schatz, a reported Communist and member of the National Executive Board and Executive Secretary of the American Youth Division, Detroit, Michigan, made arrangements for an affair for Sinatra to be held at the Jewish Community Center in Detroit on May 13, 1946. It is reported that this rally was held to combat Anti-Semitism and all religions were invited to participate. The American Youth Division was among the sponsoring groups.

On March 13, 1945 Francis Damon of the American Youth for a Free World contacted Captain Orest Shevtzov, a Red Army officer and representative in the United States for the Youth Fascist Committee in Moscow, at which time he was advised that a picture would be taken of him in his uniform along with Frank Sinatra.

A technical surveillance on the National Maritime Union, Baltimore, Maryland revealed that Florence Schwartz, chairman of the finance committee of the Communist Political Association of Baltimore endeavored to get Sinatra, Orson Welles, and several others to appear in behalf of the committee on November 3, 1944.

The Baltimore Afro-American on April 10, 1945 reported that Sinatra was to give a talk on racial harmony.

The same paper also reported that Sinatra allegedly beat several southern cafe owners who refused to serve negro musicians in his party.

According to the weekly intelligence summary submitted by the New York Division on May 16, 1946, Sinatra was one of the speakers at the Veterans American Rally, a Communist infiltrated group which held a meeting at Madison Square Garden on that date. Other speakers included Senator Claude Pepper and Ralph Ingersoll, who was editor of the newspaper PM.

On May 20, 1946, according to a technical surveillance, the Russian Consulate at Los Angeles was advised that Mr. and Mrs. Frank Sinatra could not attend the Consulate party on that date.

An article appeared in the Narodni Glasnik (National Herald), an organ of the Croatian Communists in the United States, which reflected that an open letter was sent to the lodges of the Croatian Beneficial Brotherhood of the IWO concerning "I Am An American Day." The article announced that a publication entitled "The Idea of Americans," by Frank Sinatra, could be purchased at the rate of sixty cents for one hundred copies. In the same publication, for October 18, 1944, an article stated that Sinatra gave $7,500 to the Political Action Committee at a banquet held in the Women's Department of the Political Action Committee. It also stated that Sinatra donated $5,000 for himself and $2,500 for his wife.

Intrigued, Hoover asked for additional information on three seemingly innocuous items in the memo.

TO: Mr. E. A. Tamm   DATE: April 19, 1947
FROM: A. Rosen
SUBJECT: FRANK ALBERT SINATRA, with alias
           MISCELLANEOUS—INFORMATION
           CONCERNING

PURPOSE

To set out the information available relative to three allegations concerning Sinatra's activities in reply to the Director's query: "Are the paragraphs marked with ink provable?"

ANALYSIS

1—The AYD Year Book will contain a contribution by Frank Sinatra.

Facts: ASAC [Assistant Special Agent in Charge] A. H. Belmont of the New York Division advised that Bureau Agents had obtained a copy of the AYD Year Book published in the fall of 1946 and also the first issue of "Youth" magazine, a bimonthly publication of the American Youth for Democracy, 150 Nassau Street, New York City, dated April 19, 1947, and neither of these books make any mention of Frank Sinatra. Mr. Belmont advised that Sinatra's name is not mentioned in either of the books and he did not contribute any article.

The information that Sinatra intended contributing an article to the Year Book was developed through the technical surveillance on the American Youth for Democracy, New York City, which revealed that on March 22, 1946, ███████████████ called an unidentified man who was obviously a representative of Sinatra and inquired concerning a 500-word article on "Discrimination" which Sinatra was to prepare for the American Youth for Democracy Year Book. Mr. Sinatra's representative inquired of ███████████████ if the American Youth for Democracy was not the former Young Communist League, pointing out that Sinatra's political beliefs do not run "toward social beliefs—towards Communism."
███████████████ advised that the AYD was not the former Young Communist League and stated the AYD was made up of persons of all religious and racial beliefs. Mr. Sinatra's representative then indicated that Sinatra would prepare the desired article. ASAC Belmont advised that there was no information in the files concerning the reasons Sinatra did not contribute the article.

2—Newspapers reported that on January 14, 1946, Sinatra was one of twenty-two Americans who received awards at the New Masses dinner held at the Commodore Hotel January 14, 1946.

Proof: ASAC Belmont of the New York Division advised that this affair was not covered by Agents or informants and there was no proof of Sinatra's personal attendance at the affair other than that indicated in the <u>Daily Worker</u> and other New York papers. The article in the <u>Daily Worker</u> reflected that Sinatra was given the award "for his courageous fight on behalf of all minorities."

3—On May 3, 1946, Phil Schatz, a reported Communist and member of the National Executive Board and Executive Secretary of the American Youth for Democracy, Detroit, Michigan, made arrangements for an affair for Sinatra to be held at the Jewish Community Center in Detroit on May 23, 1946. It is reported that this rally actually took place on May 16, 1946, its purpose being to combat Anti-Semitism, and all religions were invited to participate. The American Youth for Democracy was among the sponsoring groups.

Proof: The technical surveillance on the American Youth for Democracy, Detroit, Michigan, reflected that Phil Schatz spent considerable time arranging for this affair. ███████████ FBI confidential informant, reported that Sinatra, who was then playing an engagement in a local Detroit theater, personally appeared at the rally and was presented with a scroll of appreciation for his contribution to the Youth of America.

Another FBI document offered more details on one of the things that caught Hoover's eye, and should have established once and for all that Sinatra was no Communist sympathizer. It didn't.

Advertisements issued by the American Youth for Democracy during 1946, concerning a yearbook which it intended to publish, entitled "Youth," claimed that Frank Sinatra would contribute an article to it on the subject of discrimination.

Detroit Informant
███████████ on or about
5/23/46.

New York Informant
███████████ 6/14/46.

The New York Office obtained a copy of the AYD yearbook which was published in the Fall of 1946. Sinatra's name is not mentioned in this book.

> Memorandum from Mr. A. Rosen
> to Mr. E. A. Tamm, dated April
> 19, 1947, Re: "Frank Albert
> Sinatra."

In this connection, however, on March 22, 1946, an unidentified representative of Frank Sinatra was requested by an AYD representative to contribute a 500-word article on discrimination for the AYD yearbook, "Youth." Sinatra's representative inquired for information about the nature of the AYD, asking if it wasn't a continuation of the former Young Communist League, which was denied, although the AYD representative did admit that there were some Communists in the organization.

Sinatra's representative explained that he wanted to be sure of the type of organization he was dealing with since Sinatra and his "political beliefs don't run towards Communism" and added, "If they are strictly out-and-out Communists we don't fight them, we don't have any cause to question their rights—they can do as they believe, but it doesn't mean that we necessarily have to be active and further the principles of an organization with which we have nothing in sympathy." He also pointed out Sinatra had "recently" been criticized by one of the columnists for his connection with the American Youth for Democracy.

In conclusion, Sinatra's representative stated that, "We'll manage to get a story to you." He had previously admitted having had some dealings with the AYD in the past.

The FBI's interest in Sinatra wasn't limited to his political activities. In April 1947, Sinatra was in New York to receive an award at the Waldorf-Astoria for fighting racial and religious intolerance. Two days before the award ceremony, a woman visited Sinatra's room at the hotel. The en-

counter was deemed important enough to warrant this memo to Tamm from Alex Rosen, another headquarters official. (Bernard "Toots" Shor, the renowned New York City restaurateur mentioned here, was friendly with both Sinatra and Hoover.)

TO: Mr. E. A. Tamm   DATE: April 17, 1947
FROM: A. Rosen   5 p.m.
SUBJECT: FRANK SINATRA, with aliases
            MISCELLANEOUS INFORMATION CONCERNING

Assistant Special Agent in Charge A. H. Belmont advised that ███████████████ well-known prostitute, stated through arrangements made by "Toots" Shor, she paid a professional visit to Sinatra at his room in the Waldorf-Astoria on April 11, 1947. She advised, however, that due to her drunken condition, she was unable to fill her engagement, but nevertheless expected to be paid a fee of $100.

BACKGROUND
███████████████ was interviewed by Bureau Agents in connection with the Crime Survey program and during the interview it was observed that she had in her possession an address card containing the notation, "Room 5H, Waldorf, 2:30." Questioned concerning this, she advised that on April 11th, she had received a call from "Toots" Shor instructing her to make a professional visit to Sinatra to this room which he was occupying at the Waldorf-Astoria. She stated that when she arrived there, she found Sinatra in the company of ███████████████ and during the course of the visit became so drunk that she did not engage in sexual relations with Sinatra. She expressed the hope, however, that despite this, he would pay her the fee of $100 for her engagement.

Handwritten notation at the bottom: Director advised.

The FBI came upon other indications that Sinatra consorted with prostitutes.

██

████████████████████████ was arrested by the Los Angeles
Police Department on December 1, 1947. At that time her "call
house customer book" included the name of Frank Sinatra.

> Los Angeles Crime Survey,
> 4-15-48.

A New York Crime Survey Report of April 15, 1949, reported
that various prostitutes operating on their own as call girls
maintained address books which included the names of many
Hollywood personalities including that of Frank Sinatra.

> New York Crime Survey report of
> 4-15-49.

*Meanwhile, Sinatra was coming under attack in Washington at hearings
of the House Un-American Activities Committee and in California, where
state senator Jack B. Tenney, a virulent anti-Communist, led HUAC's
counterpart panel in the legislature. FBI reports excerpted and summarized
testimony by Gerald L.K. Smith, the far-right radio commentator, and
other like-minded citizens regarding Sinatra.*

On 1/30/46, GERALD L. K. SMITH testified before the HUAC
Committee, which was headed by Honorable JOHN W. WOOD,
Chairman. Page 17, paragraph 1, of this testimony contained a
petition filed with the committee by SMITH. This petition was
entitled, "A Petition for Redress of Grievances and for an
Investigation into Promoted Terrorism, Denial of Civil Liberty,
Conspiracy Against Freedom, Organized Character Assassination,
Corrupt Practice, Organized Rioting, etc." The part of SMITH's
petition pertaining to SINATRA is quoted as follows:

"I petition this committee of Congress to investigate the activities of FRANK SINATRA who, on the surface seems to be just a highly paid emaciated crooner, but who recently gave support to a meeting of the American Youth for Democracy which held an elaborate banquet at the Hotel Ambassador in Los Angeles and which organization was recently branded by J. EDGAR HOOVER as the successor to the Young Communist League and one of the most dangerous outfits in the nation."

Page 46 of SMITH's testimony is as follows:

"SMITH:

Shortly after that, the Youth for Democracy, which is the successor of the Young Communist League, held a banquet at the Ambassador Hotel in Los Angeles.

"Mr. ADAMSON:

Is that the American Youth?

"SMITH:

The American Youth for Democracy, successor to the Young Communist League. The most conspicuous personality used in advertising this meeting was the much publicized crooner, FRANK SINATRA. Then SINATRA entered into a campaign to exonerate these children who had been leaders in this organization for truancy. At this same meeting, the much publicized movie star, INGRID BERGMAN appeared and spoke. At this banquet, were the most outstanding Communists of the state.

"Mr. THOMAS:

You wouldn't say FRANK SINATRA was a Communist, would you?

"SMITH:

He may not be that intelligently, but he certainly is being used by the CP because when you take a man that is publicized as he is and then direct the spotlight that leads right to a young Communist banquet, you overtake millions of young people unprepared for that sort of persuasion and lead them to believe that Communism is respectable.

"Mr. THOMAS:

Would you say he was sort of a Mrs. ROOSEVELT in pants? (laughter)

"SMITH:

Well, I would not want to represent myself as an authority on that, but I would say this, Congressman, that I am convinced that FRANK SINATRA is not a naïve dupe. He has been appearing recently and frequently at meetings known to be set up by the CP.

"Mr. THOMAS:

He and I live in the same county in New Jersey.

"SMITH:

Well, of course you must consider the SINATRA vote. I don't think they are for you."

Page 47, Paragraph one, of SMITH's testimony before the HCUA is quoted as follows:

"There is a cabal in California which includes Congressman PATTERSON, HELEN GAHAGAN, ORSON WELLES, FRANK SINATRA, and INGRID BERGMAN who are playing with STALIN's first line."

Page 54 of SMITH's testimony is as follows:

"SMITH:

Here is a copy of a telegram I sent to Miss BERGMAN and I think I sent a copy to this committee.

"Mr. ADAMSON:

What is the date of it?

"SMITH:

1/12/46." (The telegram mentioned above is quoted as follows:)

"It is reported that on December 16 you participated in a program held under the auspices of the American Union for Democracy at the Ambassador Hotel, Los Angeles, together with FRANK SINATRA and others. About the same time, J. EDGAR HOOVER, speaking before the Catholic Youth Organization of New York City, asserted this organization was successor to the Young Communist League and was positively organizing a campaign to undermine our American government. Did you appear at this banquet with an intelligent understanding of its sponsorship, or were you the innocent victim of a slick program committee? A copy of this telegram has been forwarded to the Congressional Committee to Investigate Un-American Activities and to J. EDGAR HOOVER."

"I received no reply or recognition to that."

More than once Sinatra decried the insinuations. In late 1947, he joined Hollywood in opposing HUAC, according to this item in the FBI files.

ACTIVITIES IN CONNECTION WITH HCUA
INVESTIGATION OF COMMUNISM IN HOLLYWOOD
According to a November 21, 1947, news article, Sinatra was one of a group of movie personalities who were scheduled to participate in a radio broadcast on November 22, 1947, entitled "Hollywood Fights Back." This broadcast, which had been arranged by the Committee for the First Amendment, was part of a program protesting the investigation of Communism in Hollywood by the HCUA.

The Committee for the First Amendment was described as "a recently created Communist front in the defense of Communists and Communist fellow travelers" in the 1948 report of the California Committee on Un-American Activities.

The House committee was keeping tabs on the singer, according to this FBI summary of the committee's Sinatra files.

The following information was contained on indices cards in the general index of the House Committee on Un-American Activities. No attempt was made to check the information with the periodicals or other sources from which it was taken. It is noted that all these cards were entitled, FRANK SINATRA:

(1) Singer—Action for Palestine Rally from the People's World, September 27, 1947, Page 3.

(2) Committee for the First Amendment, signer of statement attacking the Committee on Un-American Activities from People's Daily World, October 29, 1947, page 3.

(3) Supported broadcast against hearings on Un-American Activities in the motion picture industry from the Worker, November 2, 1947, page 5.

(4) Progressive Citizens of American Film, "The House I Live In" to be shown 11/21/47 at Bret Harte School, from People's Daily World, 11/21/47, page 4.

(5) Daily Worker, 1/7/46, page 11, columns one and two. New Masses awards for greater interracial understanding, received award, honored at dinner, Hotel Commodore, New York City, 1/14/46.

(6) Hollywood Independent Citizens Committee of the Arts, Sciences, and Professions. FRANK SINATRA was listed as Vice-Chairman of this on a letterhead dated 5/28/46 and 12/10/46.

(7) New Masses Second Annual Awards Dinner; received award for contribution made to promote democracy and interracial unity from New Masses dated 11/18/47, page 7.

(8) American Society for Cultural Relations with Italy. Member of the Board of Directors from the L'Unita del Popolo, 3/8/47.

(9) Defended by MIKE GOLD, Daily Worker, 4/12/47, Page 6.

Carrying such monitoring efforts to the extreme, the FBI in September 1950 created a detailed chart plotting Sinatra's affiliations with allegedly Communist groups.

REPORTED ASSOCIATION WITH
OTHER COMMUNIST FRONT ORGANIZATIONS

Organization	Citation	Nature of Association
Action Committee to Free Spain Now	(1)	Listed as a speaker for dinner at Henry Hudson Hotel, N.Y.C., 5-9-46 but sent telegram of support and regret at not being able to attend.
Veterans of Abraham Lincoln Brigade	(1)	
American Committee for Spanish Freedom	(1')	
American Committee for Yugoslav Relief	(1)	Sponsor per "Daily Worker," 1-2-46 of a concert, N.Y.C., 1-1-46 Sponsor per letterhead stationery, 4-8-46 Wife named Chairman of Yugoslav Children's Food Drive, 1946
American Crusade to End Lynching	(3)	Sponsor, 1946
American Society for Cultural Relations With Italy, Inc.	(4)	Member, Board of Directors, 1947. Sinatra denied authorizing use of his name.
Committee for a Democratic Far Eastern Policy	(1)	Sent message of congratulations to dinner held at Hotel Roosevelt, N.Y.C., 4-3-46
Free Italy Society, aka Free Italy Movement	(2)	Accepted invitation to speak at annual ball and dinner in Los Angeles, 2-23-46
Independent Citizens Committee of the Arts, Sciences and Professions	(2)	Elected as one of the vice chairmen 2-10-46, N.Y.C.; speaker, rally in Los Angeles, 2-25-46, arranged by Music Division, Hollywood ICCASP, and presented with a document signed by Abraham Lincoln for his work re: Racial Tolerance. Elected as one of the vice chairmen of

the Hollywood ICCASP, 4-14-46
Speaker, Veterans Emergency Rally,
N.Y.C., 5-16-46. In publicly denying that
this rally was a subversive meeting
Sinatra stated: "It was a rally sponsored
by the Veterans Committee of the
ICCASP. The Committee was urging
passage of legislation to provide houses
for veterans. I was trying to help the
veterans to get homes to live in. If that is
a subversive activity, I am all for it."
Participant, concert in Hollywood Bowl,
9-2-46.

International Workers Order	(1)	IWO distributed copies of a pamphlet highlighting excerpts from an address allegedly made by Sinatra at a World Youth Rally 3-21-45 on racial and religious discrimination.
Joint Anti-Fascist Refugee Committee	(1)	Contributor, $100 in 1944 Scheduled to be a speaker at a mass rally to be held 9-24-45, N.Y.C. No record that he appeared. Scheduled to speak at JAFRC dinner to be held 5-7-46, N.Y.C. No record of his appearance.
Mobilization for Democracy	(2)	Gerald L. K. Smith charged Sinatra co-operated with organization in organizing a picket line protesting Smith's appearances in Los Angeles.
"Narodni Glasnik"	(2)	Printed and distributed the 1946 Croatian National Almanac which contained an article by Sinatra.
"New Masses"	(5)	Received award "for his courageous fight on behalf of all minorities" at dinner held 1-14-46, N.Y.C.
Southern Conference for Human Welfare	(5)	Master of Ceremonies, dinner, N.Y.C., 12-16-46

The code for the numerals appearing under the column "Citation" is as follows:
1 – Attorney General
2 – 1948 report, California Committee on Un-American Activities
3 – Military Intelligence
4 – Informants and Newspaper Articles
5 – House Committee on Un-American Activities.

A subsequent memo went on for pages and pages about the singer's sup-posedly subversive affiliations. Just a few entries give the gist and flavor.

ALLEGATIONS OF AFFILIATION
WITH THE COMMUNIST PARTY

Frank Sinatra was scheduled to make three appearances at Italian-American meetings in New York City in connection with an election campaign, one of which had been arranged by the Communist Political Association for November 1, 1944. However, Sinatra did not appear at this meeting. No reason was given for his absence by members of the Party, but they were considerably agitated because he did not attend.

*　　*　　*

An informant advised, exact date not reported, that Sam Falcone, identified as a Communist Party member and Chairman of the Legislative Committee of UE Local 301, proposed that a UE campaign committee have Frank Sinatra come to Schenectady to put on a program inasmuch as Sinatra was an old member of the Young Communist League and would come for the Communist Party at a nominal rate.

*　　*　　*

The March, 1944, issue of "Spotlight," monthly publication of the AYD, featured a statement issued by Frank Sinatra which it claimed was issued by him in response to their request. The statement answered a charge which this magazine said had been made in April, 1944, by Artur Rodzinski, Conductor of the New York Philharmonic Orchestra, that "jive" was responsible for juvenile delinquency and that Sinatra was as responsible as anything or anyone for delinquency among the younger generation.

*　　*　　*

In this regard, it was reported that Artur Rodzinski's charge that jazz contributed to juvenile delinquency resulted in a running debate in the public press and that the "New York Evening Sun," date not given, ran a three-column front page article on the Sinatra-Rodzinski feud.

* * *

The program for the Second Annual AYD dinner, which was held at the Ambassador Hotel in Los Angeles on December 16, 1945, reflected that Frank Sinatra received an award which was presented to him by a Rabbi Max Nussbaum. An informant who attended the dinner reported, however, that Sinatra was not present and the award was made to him through Mrs. Sinatra.

* * *

Robert W. Kenny, former California State Attorney General, appeared as a defense witness at the trial of Harry Bridges on January 31, 1950. During his testimony, Kenny admitted sponsoring an AYD dinner in Los Angeles during December, 1945, and added that he had attended same with Frank Sinatra.

* * *

It was learned on May 23, 1946, that one of the AYD members had interviewed Frank Sinatra when he was in Chicago and had asked him about "red-baiting" in the AYD. Sinatra reportedly replied that he had received a letter from one of the AYD members in the Tom Paine Club asking him if it were true that the AYD was a "Red" organization. Sinatra said he had not answered the letter. The AYD member, in explaining this to other club members, expressed confidence that Sinatra would answer the letter in the right way.

* * *

On May 16, 1946, a group of Detroit Youth Clubs, including the AYD, held an Inter-Cultural Rally at the Jewish Community Center, Woodward and Holbrook Streets, Detroit, to honor Frank Sinatra, who was then playing an engagement at a downtown theater in Detroit. Erma Henderson, AYD President, acted as Chairman of the rally which was attended by about 250 people. Sinatra was presented with a scroll of appreciation for his contributions to the youth of America.

*   *   *

On May 5, 1946, Philip Schatz, AYD Executive Secretary, said that the rally honoring Frank Sinatra represented a good opportunity for them to set up a permanent organization of which the AYD would be a part and that through such an organization the AYD could gain a great deal of prestige.

On April 1, 1948, AYD members at Chicago, mentioned that Frank Sinatra had gone to Italy and that he would do more for Italian Communists than anybody else could do.

*   *   *

According to the "Daily Worker" of March 17, 1945, Frank Sinatra accepted an invitation to address the World Youth Week Rally at Carnegie Hall, New York City on March 21, 1945. This rally was sponsored by the American Youth for a Free World with the cooperation of various racial groups. A report concerning the March 21, 1945 meeting, however, does not make any reference to Frank Sinatra being present.

*   *   *

The program for a dinner held on May 9, 1946, at the Henry Hudson Hotel in New York City, which had been sponsored by the Action Committee to Free Spain Now, the Veterans of the Abraham Lincoln Brigade and the American Committee for Spanish Freedom, listed Frank Sinatra as a speaker. Sinatra did not attend this dinner, but did send a telegram of support and expression of regret for being unable to be there.

*   *   *

Frank Sinatra was named as one of several artists who sponsored a Town Hall benefit concert arranged by the Greenwich Village

Chapter of the American Committee for Yugoslav Relief on January 1, 1946.

The American Committee for Yugoslav Relief has been cited as a subversive and Communist organization by the Attorney General.

* * *

Another governmental agency conducting intelligence investigations reported on September 13, 1946, that Frank Sinatra was one of the sponsors of the "American Crusade to End Lynchings" for which Paul Robeson was chairman. This organization supported a pilgrimage to Washington, D.C., on September 23, 1946. A parade was scheduled to be held on September 23, 1946, which was to be led by colored and white veterans who were to march to the Lincoln Memorial where a national religious ceremony would be held and persons who escaped lynching mobs were to be presented to the audience.

* * *

According to a news release, Frank Sinatra was scheduled to speak against racial intolerance as the guest of honor at the Free Italy Society's annual ball and dinner to be held February 23, 1946, at the Kastritta Hall, 3220 North Broadway, Los Angeles, California. This news article identified said organization as an anti-Fascist group.

Sinatra was quoted as follows: "I will be happy to join with my fellow Italian-Americans in the cause of true democracy."

It was announced that the theme of the affair would be to fight domestic Fascism as personified by Gerald L. K. Smith.

* * *

Westbrook Pegler reported in his column in November, 1947, that after Sinatra had appeared at a show held under the auspices of the ICCASP in New York City during May, 1946, his manager, George Evans, said that Sinatra had "put himself under the political guidance of two reporters who are experts on Communism, and agreed not to mess around with any outfit which they disapproved."

* * *

Frank Sinatra was identified as one of the artists who participated in a concert held in the Hollywood Bowl on September 2, 1946, which had been arranged by the Hollywood Independent Citizens Committee of the Arts, Sciences and Professions. The principal guest speaker at this affair was Senator Claude Pepper, who spoke on relations between the United States and Soviet Russia. This fund, raising meeting is estimated to have collected between forty and fifty thousand dollars.

* * *

In connection with Sinatra's activities with the ICCASP, it has been reported that in 1943 he supported the Hague political machine in New Jersey and, in 1944, actively campaigned on behalf of former President Franklin D. Roosevelt. He is reported to have visited the White House in September, 1944, in company with Toots Shor, New York restaurateur, at which time he conferred with the President. Considerable adverse publicity is reported to have resulted from this visit and as a consequence, according to this particular report, Sinatra became incensed and donated $7,500 to the Democratic cause and became an active member of the Independent Voters Committee of the Arts and Sciences for Roosevelt which reportedly subsequently merged with the ICCASP.

* * *

CONTACTS WITH RUSSIAN CONSULATE OFFICIALS

On March 13, 1945, Francis Damon of the American Youth for a Free World, supra, contacted Captain Orest Shevtzov, representative in the United States for the Youth Anti-Fascist Committee in Moscow, who was then at the Russian Consulate in New York City, and informed her that all pictures would be taken the following day. The Captain was advised that she should be in her office at 11:15 A.M. in uniform and that the first picture would be taken with Newbold Morris, President of the City Council of New York, and the second picture would be taken with Frank Sinatra at 2:30 P.M. on March 14, 1945.

On May 20, 1946, the Russian Consulate in Los Angeles was advised that Mr. and Mrs. Frank Sinatra and others who were named would not be able to attend the party at the Consulate that night.

Even Sinatra's dentist turns up in the files as a subject in a spying investigation.

Frank Sinatra's dentist, Dr. Abraham Benedict Weinstein, has been investigated by the Bureau in connection with the Gregory case investigation and is also the subject of a pending Security Matter–C case, New Haven Office of Origin. Elizabeth Terrill Bentley, informant in the Gregory case, named an individual known to her as "Charlie" as a contact of Jacob Golos. . . . Dr. Weinstein was not identified by Miss Bentley as the individual known to her as "Charlie" but many of the characteristics of "Charlie" as named by her closely parallel those of Dr. Weinstein. . . .

Investigation by the New Haven Office reflects that Weinstein was born on September 18, 1900, at New York City, where he is a practicing dentist; further, that for many years he has associated with top functionaries in the Communist Party such as John Williamson, Gus Hall, Irving Potash and Carl Winter, as well as several individuals known to be Communist Party sympathizers such as Anna Louise Strong, Leon and Barney Josephson and others. He is known to have been in contact with Ralph Bowman, suspected Russian espionage agent, and has been in the company of individuals named as Russian espionage agents by Elizabeth Bentley. . . .

It is known that Dr. Weinstein is quite friendly with Sinatra's manager, George Evans. On one occasion, a Sam Bronstein, connected with the Motion Picture Industry, requested Dr. Weinstein to use his influence on George Evans to get Sinatra to make a picture and that if successful Dr. Weinstein would receive a fee of $25,000 for his services. Information was furnished reflecting that Evans and Dr. Weinstein met on several occasions to discuss this proposition.

The author of another lengthy FBI memo detailing Sinatra's activity during this period either had a sense of humor about the matter or simply was careless in identifying Sinatra's alleged political soul mates.

The 4/19/47 issue of the "New York Daily Mirror" carried an article by Jack Lait entitled "All in the Family." The article pertained to Charlie Chaplin and Frank Sinatra, who had held press conferences that week during which Sinatra denied he sympathized with Lenin and the Marx brothers.

By 1950, with his career in decline, his marriage to Nancy Barbato on the rocks, and a tempestuous affair with Ava Gardner under way, Sinatra was anxious to counter suggestions in the press that he was a draft-dodging subversive. An intermediary contacted FBI agent Paul J. Mohr with an extraordinary offer. Mohr passed on the offer in a memo to Tolson.

TO: MR. TOLSON   DATE: September 7, 1950
FROM: J. P. MOHR
SUBJECT: FRANK SINATRA

███████████████ called at my office today after having endeavored to arrange an appointment to see the Director. I explained to ███████████████ that the Director was extremely busy, that he was fully committed and would be unable to see him. ███████████████ stated that he had been requested by Frank Sinatra to contact the Director with . . . a proposition that Sinatra had in mind. ███████████████ said he was a friend of Sinatra, that he considered him to be a sincere individual and that he has known him for six years. ███████████████ described Sinatra as a "Dago who came up the hard way" and said he is a conscientious fellow who is very desirous of doing something for his country. ███████████████ stated that Sinatra feels he can do some good for his country under the direction of the FBI.

███████████████ stated that Sinatra is sensitive about the allegations which have been made concerning his subversive activities and also his draft status during the last war. Sinatra feels that the publi-

city which he has received has identified him with subversive
elements and that such subversive elements are not sure of his position and Sinatra consequently feels that he can be of help as a result
by going anywhere the Bureau desires and contacting any of the
people from whom he might be able to obtain information. Sinatra
feels as a result of his publicity he can operate without suspicion.

██████████████ stated Sinatra is a Catholic but is not a
practicing one. He also stated that Sinatra denies any subversive
affiliations or interests on the part of himself and ███████████ is
sure that Sinatra is truthful, otherwise ███████████ stated he
would not bother the FBI with this matter.

██████████ stated that Sinatra was desirous of getting this
project before CIA. However, ████████████ said he told Sinatra
that CIA was not the proper place to make the approach. However,
██████████████ did contact a friend in CIA who told
████████████ that he should take the matter up with the FBI
since we were primarily charged with domestic intelligence
activities.

████████████ stated that Sinatra's principal contacts are in
the entertainment field in Hollywood and New York City.
██████████ further advised that he didn't know whether
Sinatra has any current information with respect to subversives. He
said that Sinatra understands that if he worked for the Bureau in
connection with such activities it might reflect on his status and his
standing in the entertainment field but he is willing to do anything
even if it affects his livelihood and costs him his job.

██████████ said that Sinatra is willing to go "the whole way."
██████████ stated that Sinatra can, of course, be reached
through his residence in Hollywood but that he is presently living in
the Hampshire House in New York City and that he is looking for an
apartment in New York City since he is starting a television show on
ABC on Saturday, October 7, 1950, and consequently will be in New
York City for the next year.

I told ████████████ that I wasn't aware of Sinatra's activities
other than what I had read in the papers. I told him further that I

wasn't aware of Sinatra's possibilities and that that was something we would have to analyze and determine. I further told ████████████ that we would not ask Sinatra or any other individual to engage in any activities that would reflect on the individual and that any action taken by the individual would have to be a voluntary decision on his part. ████████████ was also informed that I was not aware of the fact that Sinatra could be of use to us but that I would call to the Director's attention ████████████'s visit to me and that we would consider Sinatra's request and that if he could be utilized we would communicate with him.

The Security Division has been requested to prepare a memorandum for the Director concerning information appearing in our files with respect to Sinatra.

Handwritten notation by Tolson: We want nothing to do with him. C.

Handwritten notation by Hoover: I agree. H.

Sinatra had entertained troops overseas at the end of World War II. In 1954, his career rejuvenated by his Oscar-winning turn in From Here to Eternity, *he offered to go to Korea to do so again. The army, however, wasn't interested, as this exchange of memos shows. The first is an army document that ended up in the FBI's files; the others track the FBI's involvement in the matter.*

17 September 1954

MEMORANDUM FOR THE RECORD:

SUBJECT: Clearance of Mr. Frank Sinatra to accompany an entertainment group to the Far East during the Xmas Holiday period.

1. In response to a request made by Mr. Frank Sinatra for an appointment to discuss the matter of his clearance for a Xmas

Holiday entertainment tour to the Far East, a meeting was arranged in the office of The Adjutant General at 1300 hours, 16 September 1954. Participants were:

Major General John A. Klein, TAG
Major General Gilman C. Mudgett, Chief of Info.
Brig. Gen. Alfred E. Kastner, Asst to the Asst
   Chief of Staff, G-2
Mr. Sinatra

2. General Klein opened the discussion with remarks to the effect that all present were aware of the purpose of Mr. Sinatra's visit. He then asked General Kastner to outline the basis upon which Mr. Sinatra's request for clearance was denied.

3. General Kastner explained that over a period of years many items had appeared in the public press, including The Daily Worker and kindred publications, which reflected adversely on Mr. Sinatra, and which to a considerable degree identified the latter with the communist line. He pointed out that as a result, serious question existed as to Mr. Sinatra's sympathies with respect to communism, communists, and fellow travelers. He stated that particularly in view of recent events and actions hinging on the matter of subversives, the Army could not grant clearance to any individual about whom the slightest doubt existed.

4. Mr. Sinatra stated that he hated and despised everything that pertained to communism; that he had never been a member of a communist inspired organization, nor had he ever made contribution to such organizations. He attributed the unfavorable press items to irresponsible individuals who preyed on those in "entertainment." He said that he considered these writings so absurd that he had not even undertaken to refute them. He related that he had responded to a reporter's question regarding his attitude toward communism with the remark: "I am just as communistic as the Pope." He said that the reporter informed him that such a quote was not printable. He emphasized the point that he was most eager to provide entertainment for service personnel in the Far East; that he had

specified Far East because he thought our largest forces were located there, but that he was willing to perform anyplace else including the continental United States; that a pressing moving picture engagement had precluded him from making a similar tour some two years ago. He stated that he would carry matters to the Attorney General in order to clear his name, and that he would engage counsel to represent him. (General Kastner had previously indicated to Mr. Sinatra that it was his privilege as a civilian to take his case to the Attorney General and had made suggestion regarding the desirability of counsel.)

5. General Mudgett advised Mr. Sinatra that from an entirely impersonal point of view, the Army, circumstances being as they are, could not at this time risk granting him a clearance. He digressed to congratulate Mr. Sinatra on his fine performance in "From Here to Eternity." Generals Klein and Kastner expressed similar sentiments. General Klein also expressed appreciation for Mr. Sinatra's generous offer to provide entertainment for our troops overseas.

6. After Mr. Sinatra's departure, those remaining agreed that in similar cases arising in the future, requests for appointments should be refused unless there exist compelling reasons to the contrary; that in any instance where an appointment is granted, The Assistant Chief of Staff, G-2, The Chief of Information, and The Adjutant General, or their representatives, should meet jointly with the individual concerned; further, that the place of meeting should be other than in the office of the Assistant Chief of Staff, G-2.

> T. J. MARNANE
> Colonel, AGC
> Executive Officer, TAGO

TO: Director, FBI   DATE: 10/18/54
FROM: SAC, NYC
SUBJECT: FRANK SINATRA
             MISCELLANEOUS INFORMATION
             CONCERNING

JEROME DOYLE, former Agent and presently a member of the
firm of Cahill, Gordon, Zachry and Reindel, NYC, today provided
the following data which Mr. Doyle received from HENRY JAFFE,
attorney for Frank Sinatra:

Frank Sinatra allegedly was being booked to go to Korea this
Christmas as part of a USO entertainment group, consisting of
various show people, and to the surprise of Sinatra and Henry Jaffe
the Army denied clearance to Sinatra. Allegedly Sinatra and/or Jaffe
went to Washington to talk to the Army to determine just why
clearance was denied to Sinatra, and allegedly the Army advised that
it had information from the FBI which prompted the Army to deny
clearance to Sinatra. This information allegedly was that Lee
Mortimer in a newspaper column stated that Sinatra was a
Communist. This is the information which allegedly came from the
Bureau's files. The Generals in question are: Major General John A.
Klein, Adjutant General; Major General John C. Mudgett, Chief of
Information; and Major General A. G. Trudeau, Chief of
Intelligence.

Mr. Doyle stated he was advising this office so the above
information could be furnished to the Bureau since he believes Jaffe
will be writing to the Bureau regarding this matter.

Handwritten notation by Hoover: Nail this down promptly. H.

TO: MR. A. H. BELMONT   DATE: October 22, 1954
FROM: MR. R. R. ROACH
SUBJECT: FRANK SINATRA
         MISCELLANEOUS—INFORMATION
         CONCERNING

Reference is made to a letter from the SAC, New York, dated
October 18, 1954, in the above-captioned matter in which the
Bureau was advised by Jerome Doyle, former Bureau Agent,
concerning information he had received from Henry Jaffe, attorney
for Frank Sinatra. Allegedly, Sinatra and/or Jaffe went to
Washington to talk to the Army to determine why clearance was
denied to Sinatra, who had been booked to go to Korea for
Christmas as part of a USO entertainment group, and allegedly the
Army advised that it had information from the FBI which prompted
the Army to deny clearance to Sinatra. This information referred to
allegedly was that Lee Mortimer in a newspaper column stated that
Sinatra was a Communist; that this information allegedly came from
Bureau files.
   The Director noted "Nail this down promptly. H."
   Colonel W. A. Perry, Chief of Security, G-2, furnished Liaison
Agent ████████████ a copy of a memorandum prepared by
Colonel Marnane, Executive Officer to the Adjutant General,
concerning the conference which Sinatra had with the Army in the
Office of the Adjutant General on September 16, 1954, and for
which Colonel Marnane prepared the minutes. In essence, this
memorandum advises that, pursuant to a request by Frank Sinatra to
be advised why he had been denied clearance, an appointment had
been made for him to appear in the office of Major General John A.
Klein, the Adjutant General, on September 16, 1954. Present
besides the Adjutant General were Major General John C. Mudgett,
Chief of Information; and former Brigadier General Alfred Kastner,
formerly Deputy Assistant Chief of Staff, G-2. At the outset of the
conference, General Klein asked General Kastner to outline for Mr.
Sinatra the basis upon which Mr. Sinatra's request for clearance had

been denied. General Kastner explained that over a period of years many items had appeared in the public press, including the "Daily Worker," and kindred publications, which reflected adversely on Mr. Sinatra and which, to a considerable degree, identified Sinatra with the Communist Party line and, as a result, is serious evidence as to Mr. Sinatra's sympathies with respect to Communism, Communists, and fellow travelers.

General Klein advised Sinatra that, in view of such evidence, the Army could not grant clearance to any individual about whom the slightest doubt existed.

Sinatra then went on to state that he hated Communism, had never been a member of a Communist organization, had no contact with Communists or Communist organizations, and the irresponsible accusations made against him had been so absurd that he had not refuted them. He went on to relate that he was eager to provide entertainment for the troops anywhere in the Far East, Europe or the Continental United States. He further stated that he would carry this matter to the Attorney General in order to clear his name, and he would engage counsel to represent him.

General Mudgett then informed Sinatra that, from an entirely impersonal point of view, circumstances being as they were, the Army could not risk at this time giving a clearance to Sinatra.

Colonel Marnane advised ▓▓▓▓▓▓▓▓▓▓ that he was at the conference and prepared the minutes of same. He stated that the officers mentioned above were present also, General Kastner representing G-2 for General Arthur G. Trudeau. He advised that General Kastner, other than the statements attributed to General Klein and General Mudgett, carried the entire conversation for the Army. General Kastner restricted his comments concerning Sinatra's Communist connections in their entirety to newspaper clippings, and at no time did he ever mention files of the FBI or any other organization. As a matter of fact, Colonel Marnane stated that the G-2 file prepared for this conference merely consisted of newspaper clippings, and it was agreed that if Sinatra pressed G-2 for the source of their information, General Kastner was going to present the file to Sinatra so that he could read it.

Colonel Marnane advised that the name Jaffe is unknown to him but advised that Sinatra was accompanied to General Klein's office by an individual, whose name he could not recall, who was introduced to him as an agent of some sort. This individual remained in the outer office during the conference.

Bureau files reflect that in answer to a name check request from the U. S. Air Force (OSI) a summary of information concerning Sinatra was furnished to that Agency on January 22, 1952, and a Photostat of the summary was furnished G-2 on February 19, 1952. This summary advised that no investigation had been conducted concerning Sinatra. However, information from public sources and reliable informants concerning his affiliation with numerous Communist front groups, as well as association with known criminals and hoodlums, was furnished. Information was also furnished from a confidential informant ███████████ (described as reliable) that in December, 1945 ████████████████████████████████ ████████████████████████████████████ ██████████████████████████████ advised him that Frank Sinatra, the well-known radio and movie star, was then a member of the Communist Party. The informant stated he was told that Sinatra formerly held membership in the American Youth for Democracy (cited by the Attorney General) in New Jersey but had recently been admitted to the New York branch of the Communist Party.

The summary furnished to OSI and G-2 did not include any reference to Lee Mortimer or to the information which Lee Mortimer allegedly used in his newspaper column, namely, that Sinatra was a Communist, which information was reported to have come from Bureau files.

RECOMMENDATION:
For your information.

*Blocked from traveling overseas to entertain the troops, Sinatra applied
for a passport a couple of months later, shortly before heading to Australia
for a three-week tour. In applying for the passport, he gave the government
certain assurances, according to this excerpt from a later FBI report on the
matter.*

On January 10, 1955 FRANK SINATRA executed the following
affidavit for the Passport Division of the Department of State:

"In connection with my application for a passport, I make
the following statements under oath:

"I am not now nor have I ever been a member of the Communist Party, any so-called Communist Front organizations, or
any other group or organization of a subversive character; I am
not now nor have I ever been affiliated with any organization
which has been engaged in subversive activity of any kind
whatsoever."

*The FBI and others in the government suspected Sinatra was lying,
prompting a full-fledged year-long investigation of the singer's veracity, involving FBI offices across the country, and some very old accusations
against Sinatra.*

TO: Mr. L. V. Boardman   DATE: February 21, 1955
FROM: Mr. A. H. Belmont
SUBJECT: FRANCIS ALBERT SINATRA
              SECURITY MATTER—C
              FRAUD AGAINST THE GOVERNMENT

On 12-14-54 a name check request concerning Sinatra was
received from the State Department in connection with a passport
application. On 12-30-54 the Department of State was advised that
the FBI had conducted no active investigation of Sinatra. Also the
memorandum provided information received by the FBI concerning
Sinatra which is in summary: Sinatra has allegedly been connected

with varying degrees such as sponsorship and/or membership with 13 Communist front groups or activities in Los Angeles, Detroit, and New York City. One informant alleged in 1945 that he had been told that Sinatra had recently been admitted to membership in the New York Branch of the Communist Party. This informant was described as confidential and reliable. Sinatra's association with numerous gangsters and hoodlums including Lucky Luciano and Willie Moretti were set out. It was also noted that in 1948 Sinatra was scheduled to transcribe an anti-Communist broadcast for Italian consumption and that as of 1951 Sinatra was listed as a participant in an anti-Communist rally.

On 1-10-55 Sinatra executed a sworn affidavit for the Passport Division of the State Department at New York County, New York, stating that he was not then and had never been a member of the Communist Party, any so-called Communist front organizations or any other group or organization of a subversive character. As of 2-17-55 the Washington Field Office was advised in confidence that the Passport Division of State Department was sending two copies of the above affidavit to the Department "with request for investigation to determine whether criminal proceedings against subject for apparent violation of 18 USC 1542 warranted." Section 1542 is "false statement in application and use of passport." Los Angeles and New York were advised of this information. Sinatra is the well-known singer and motion picture actor.

RECOMMENDATION:

That the FBI conduct no investigation in this matter at this time. This is in accordance with established policy in passport fraud matters since the State Department directed their request to the Justice Department. We will, of course, act immediately on request from either Justice or State Departments.

Handwritten notation by Clyde Tolson at the bottom: I suggest a complete summary be prepared on Sinatra. C.
Handwritten response by Hoover: Yes. H.

The resulting summary, drafted a week later, included recent informa-
tion indicating that Sinatra was anything but a Communist, according to
this excerpt:

The "Daily Worker" an east coast Communist newspaper, of April
10, 1951, contained an article captioned "Where Are the Big Stars
Who Once Opposed the Un-Americans?" The article mentioned
Frank Sinatra as one who had at one time made strong statements
against the HCUA but was now silent.

The New York "Daily News" of April 27, 1951, reported that on
the preceding day the Stop-Communism Committee was launched
to fight against "Red influence in the entertainment world." Sinatra
was listed as participating in a rally sponsored by the Committee.

Nevertheless, a top Justice Department official asked the FBI to look
into the passport matter.

TO: Director,   DATE: March 7, 1955
      Federal Bureau of Investigation
FROM: William F. Tompkins, Assistant Attorney General, Internal
        Security Division
SUBJECT: FRANCIS ALBERT SINATRA a.k.a. Frank Sinatra
          SECURITY MATTER—C
          FRAUD AGAINST THE GOVERNMENT

Information has recently been received from the Department of
State to the effect that the captioned subject in attempting to secure
a passport filed with that Department an affidavit dated January 10,
1955 in which he stated that he had never been a member of the
Communist Party or any Communist front organizations. This
Division has also been advised that the Department of State received
information from your Bureau which indicates that the subject has
been affiliated with a number of Communist front organizations and
that it has also been alleged that he was a member of the Communist
Party.

Inasmuch as the statements contained in his affidavit, if false, would constitute a violation of Title 18, U.S.C., Sections 1001 or 1542, it would be appreciated if you would conduct an appropriate investigation to determine whether sufficient evidence exists to warrant prosecution under the statutes.

For your information and assistance there is transmitted herewith a photostatic copy of the affidavit executed by the subject.

And Hoover in a March 18, 1955, memo authorized a major investiga-tion, ordering agents in Los Angeles and seven other cities onto the case. Memos poured in from FBI offices across the country, as agents combed their files for "subversive" information about Sinatra and re-interviewed sources who previously had tied Sinatra to Communist party groups. They didn't come up with much, as reflected in the samples below.

From New York:

The files of the New York Office contain the following subversive information on the above-captioned subject:
    ▆▆▆▆▆▆▆ BEANIE (C. B. BALDWIN), Executive Vice Chairman of the National Citizens Political Action Committee, who very recently in Washington's Willard Hotel conducted an intensive four-day course in practical politics under the sponsorship of the NCPAC, about the "September 2nd thing." The "September 2nd thing" ▆▆▆▆▆▆▆ was a big concert in the Hollywood Bowl on that date. It was expected to draw 23,000 people. ▆▆▆▆
▆▆▆▆▆▆▆▆▆▆▆▆▆▆▆▆▆▆▆▆▆▆▆▆▆▆▆▆▆▆▆
▆▆▆▆▆▆▆▆▆ it would feature ROBINSON (perhaps EDWARD G. ROBINSON), GREGORY PECK and FRANK SINATRA. ▆▆▆▆▆▆ RUBINSTEIN would do a concerto, PAUL ROBESON might sing, and the symphony orchestra would consist of 100 pieces. ▆▆▆▆▆
    The New York Office is not in possession of any information that would indicate that SINATRA attended this affair.

From Newark:

On 3/31/55 at East Orange, N.J., SAS [Special Agents] ██████████ and ██████████ contacted ██████████ former security informant whose identity must be protected, and who is described as having furnished reliable information in the past. ██████████ has in the past exhibited a definite reluctance to testify. This informant stated he recalls that FRANK SINATRA, the famous vocalist, had contributed to Communist youth organizations in the early 1940s. However, he did not know if SINATRA was a member of the CP or any CP dominated or infiltrated organization or a member of the CP or of a CP youth group. He stated he recalls that information regarding SINATRA'S contributions and sponsorship, if any, appeared in some CP publications such as the "Daily Worker" or the Sunday "Worker," but at this time he cannot recall where. This was all the information he had regarding SINATRA.

On 4/13/55, SA [Special Agent] ██████████ contacted ██████████ and ██████████, whose identities must be protected, and who should be described as having furnished reliable information in the past. They advised that they know of no subversive information pertaining to FRANK SINATRA.

The New York office also provided new, though perhaps not important, information about Sinatra's dentist.

On 4/11/46, ██████████ who has furnished reliable information in the past, advised that Dr. ABRAHAM B. WEINSTEIN contacted FRANK SINATRA and an appointment was made for SINATRA to come to Dr. WEINSTEIN for a dental appointment at 5:00 pm on that date.

ABRAHAM BENEDICT WEINSTEIN is a dentist who maintains his offices at 20 E. 53rd St., NYC.

On 1/18/55 ██████████ Brooklyn, NY (who requests that her identity be concealed) ██████████ [advised] that certain of

Dr. WEINSTEIN'S patients and acquaintances were believed by her to be members or sympathizers of the CP.

███

███

███████████████████████████████████████

Investigation on Dr. ABRAHAM WEINSTEIN was instituted on 12/7/45 when it was ascertained through a physical surveillance of JOSEPH GREGG and PETER RHODES that they were observed to enter the office of Dr. WEINSTEIN, 20 E. 53rd St., NYC. Both GREGG and RHODES were mentioned as members of an espionage group who were operating in Washington, D.C. at that time, by ELIZABETH BENTLY, an admitted former Communist courier. . . . ████████████████ who has furnished reliable information in the past, advised SA [Special Agent] ███████████████ on 12/10/46 that FRANK SINATRA, the singer, contacted Dr. WEINSTEIN at his office and advised him that he had made reservations for the Dr. and his wife at the Wedgewood Room at the Waldorf Astoria on the following Friday.

New York also offered exculpatory evidence.

In a clipping from the "NY Mirror" dated 4/5/48, in an article captioned, "SINATRA TO STAGE RADIO PLEA TO ITALY FOR DEFEAT OF REDS," by LOUELLA PARSONS. This article is quoted in part as follows:

"An appeal broadcast directly to the Italian people to vote against the Communist ticket at the 4/18/48, election is being arranged for by FRANK SINATRA. His guests will be JIMMY DURANTE, JOE DIMAGGIO and ALIDA VALLI. The hour long show will be in Italian.

"SINATRA, who returned from NY today, was asked by Washington officials to get together a show with famous guests of Italian parentage, and FRANKIE gladly accepted the assignment to help fight Communism. Twenty-seven recordings will be made and played in various parts of Italy in an effort to reach even the most remote parts of that troubled nation. FRANKIE told me Washington also had requested that CLARK GABLE and TYRONE POWER appear on the show, even though they are not of Italian descent and do not speak the language."

The Los Angeles office on October 11, 1955, told Hoover that it had serious doubts about the case.

Considerable investigation has been conducted by the Los Angeles Office and other Bureau offices in connection with the instructions outlined in referenced letter. A review and analysis of the results of the investigation fails to develop any positive evidence connecting SINATRA with the Communist Party or the Communist Party movement.

In view of the foregoing, it is believed that the submission of a regular investigative report setting forth the results of the many interviews undertaken would be preferable to the preparation of a prosecutive summary due to the absence of the calibre of information which should logically be incorporated in a prosecutive summary report.

It is noted that the miscellaneous information furnished by informants in years past, and which was summarized by the Bureau in memorandum form dated 9/30/54, is essentially hearsay, most of which, even if true, would have little probative value.

*   *   *

Several former Communist Party members in Hollywood, who have furnished reliable information in the past, and who normally would have been in a position to know if SINATRA were connected with the Communist Party or the Communist Party movement, advised that they had no information that SINATRA was a member of the CP nor did they ever hear him referred to as such in Party circles, or as being connected with the Communist movement.

Because of the foregoing, the Los Angeles Office contemplates the submission of a regular investigative report in this matter unless instructed by the Bureau to the contrary. Such report will be prepared and submitted to reach the Bureau within thirty days.

Los Angeles filed a twenty-eight-page report on the investigation to head-quarters on November 4, 1955.

Investigation conducted developed no evidence connecting FRANK SINATRA with the Communist Party (CP) or the CP movement aside from his membership in the Independent Citizens Committee of the Arts, Sciences, and Professions in 1946, an organization described by the California Committee on Un-American Activities as a "Communist front." In 1946 he was being considered by the Los Angeles County Communist Party as a potential Party recruit. In 1948 he was indicated to have arranged an anti-Communist radio program for broadcast in Italy. Results of investigation set forth.

*   *   *

RESULTS OF INVESTIGATION

The following organizations, which have been referred to in this report, have been designated by the Attorney General of the United States pursuant to Executive Order 10450: Communist Party, Communist Political Association, Young Communist League, American Youth for Democracy, Labor Youth League, International Workers Order, and Action Committee to Free Spain Now.

*   *   *

AT PHILADELPHIA, PENNSYLVANIA

The above informant was a former member of the District Committee of the CP in Pennsylvania. ███████████ advised in the latter part of 1945 that . . . he was informed by ███████████ . . . that FRANK SINATRA, the well-known radio and movie star, was then a member of the CP. ███████████ was told that SINATRA formerly held membership in the American Youth for

Democracy (AYD) in New Jersey and had recently been admitted to
the New York Branch of the CP.

███████████ was reinterviewed on September 12, 1955 and
stated that he had a vague recollection of [a meeting] possibly
sometime around November 1945 in ████████████ which was
attended by ████████████ and many others. At this meeting . . .
Informant recalled that at the above CP meeting, ████████████
told him that SINATRA was an old line member of the CP and had
come up from the YCL. Informant also recalled having been told
essentially the same thing by some unknown woman . . . who was
also present at the above CP meeting. Informant further recalled
███████████ and the unknown woman telling him that
SINATRA had been admitted to the CP in New York City.

Informant advised that he could furnish no information which
would corroborate the above allegations and, further, that he had no
personal knowledge that would connect SINATRA with the CP or
the CP movement. He advised that he did not know SINATRA
personally and had never attended any affairs at which SINATRA
was present.

AT CHICAGO, ILLINOIS
███████████████████

The above informants, who are familiar with some phases of CP
activities in the Chicago area, advised in June 1955 that they had no
information concerning FRANK SINATRA.

AT DETROIT, MICHIGAN
███████████████████

Detroit, Michigan
The above individual, who is a self-admitted member of District
7, CP, USA, . . . advised on March 4, 1955 that to her knowledge
FRANK SINATRA was never active in the CP or any related front
groups in the State of Michigan.

*   *   *

███████████████████████

The above informants, who are familiar with CP and related CP front group activities in the State of Michigan, advised in March 1955 that FRANK SINATRA is unknown to them in connection with the CP movement.

AT NEWARK, NEW JERSEY
███████████████████

Above informant advised on March 31, 1955 that he had a recollection of the Communist press occasionally carrying information indicating that FRANK SINATRA had contributed to the Communist youth organizations in the early 1940's. Informant did not recall any specific publications or issues and had no personal knowledge or other information concerning such allegations. Informant stated that he also had no information connecting FRANK SINATRA with the CP or the CP movement.

*   *   *

AT NEW YORK, NEW YORK
████████████████████

Informant furnished a pamphlet on July 28, 1947 reflecting that it was written by FRANK SINATRA and bearing the title "Thoughts of an American," published by the International Workers Order (IWO). This pamphlet, in part, refers to the "pushing around" SINATRA received while attending school in New Jersey. The pamphlet was directed at racial tolerance and read, in part, as follows:

> "It is up to all of us to lay aside our unfounded prejudices and make the most of this wonderful country—this country that has been built by many people, by many creeds, nationalities and races in such a way that it cannot be divided . . . and can never

be conquered . . . but will always remain the United States . . .
one nation, indivisible, with liberty and justice for all."

██████████████

New York, New York
The above individual was a member of the CP in New York . . .
He served as an informant for the FBI and subsequently . . . On May
19, 1955 he furnished a signed statement . . . which reads, in part, as
follows:

> ". . . I do recall in 1944 during the Roosevelt campaign for
> re-election Frank Sinatra appeared at a rally which was spon-
> sored by the Upper West Side Citizens Committee, which was a
> communist front organization. The rally was held at St.
> Nicholas area 66th St and Columbus Ave. NYC. This rally was
> held to promote the re-election of President Roosevelt.
> "Frank Sinatra appeared and sang two songs, made no speech
> and left the hall immediately. He was contacted by ████████,
> who was a member of the James Connolly Branch of the Com-
> munist Party, to sing at this rally. I do not know whether Sinatra
> had any knowledge of the Communist Party membership of
> ██████████."

*   *   *

AT SALT LAKE CITY, UTAH
██████████████

The above informant, who has some knowledge of CP activities
in the State of Utah, advised on March 21, 1955 that he has no
information relative to FRANK SINATRA.

AT LAS VEGAS, NEVADA
██████████████

The above informants, who are in a position to learn of some CP
activities in the Las Vegas, Nevada, area, advised on April 20, 1955

that they have no information connecting FRANK SINATRA with the CP or the CP movement.

AT LOS ANGELES, CALIFORNIA

███████████████████

Above informant advised on January 18, 1946 and on reinterview April 25, 1955 that he was present at the above-described "Welcome Home Joe" dinner. He reported that the award for FRANK SINATRA was presented during the affair to a woman who was introduced as Mrs. FRANK SINATRA. The award was given as a result of SINATRA's performance in the motion picture "The House I Live In," a racial tolerance production. Informant advised on April 25, 1955 that he had never heard of FRANK SINATRA or Mrs. FRANK SINATRA in connection with the CP or the CP movement.

███████████████

Hollywood, California

The above individual was a member of the CP in the Los Angeles [area] . . . [but she] advised . . . on April 7, 1955 that she never heard of FRANK SINATRA in connection with the CP movement nor had she ever heard of him making any contributions to the CP. She pointed out that individuals connected with the motion picture industry were found to be extremely generous when asked for donations to various causes. Because of this she felt it altogether possible that SINATRA could have, at one time or another, donated to causes sponsored by the Party, although such fact, if true, had never come to her personal attention.

* * *

███████████████

Beverly Hills, California

The above individual joined the CP in New York . . . [and] was a member of the CP within the film industry . . . He advised SA [Special Agent] on April 1, 1955 that he does not know FRANK

SINATRA personally and has never heard of him in connection
with the CP movement.

*   *   *

███████████████

Los Angeles, California

The above individual was a member of a Hollywood cultural club
of the LACCP. . . . He advised . . . on October 28, 1951 that he
recalled one of the CP members in his group, ████████████████
having remarked at Party meetings that she knew NANCY
SINATRA, wife of FRANK SINATRA. ████████████████ indicated
that she had received contributions from NANCY SINATRA for
one or more Party "causes." ████████████████ advised that he never
heard any comments in Party circles, however, connecting FRANK
SINATRA or his wife with the CP or the CP movement. He stated
that FRANK SINATRA had made a recording of the song, "The
House I Live In," and on which a motion picture was subsequently
based. ████████████████ advised that this song was written by EARL
ROBINSON.

*The Los Angeles FBI report included what is probably the most eloquent
statement attributed to Sinatra regarding red-baiting.*

"Hollywood on Trial—The Story of the Ten
Who Were Indicted" by GORDON KAHN,
published by Boni and Gaer, Inc.,
New York, Copyright 1948

The following, attributed to FRANK SINATRA, appeared at
page 19 in the above book:

> "Once they get the movies throttled how long will it be
> before the Committee goes to work on freedom of the air? How
> long will it be before we're told what we can and cannot say into
> a radio microphone? If you make a pitch on a nation-wide

network for a square deal for the underdog, will they call you a
Commie? . . . Are they gonna scare us into silence? I wonder."

The above book pertained to the so-called "Hollywood Ten,"
previously referred to in this report.

A month and a half later, Hoover finally put the investigation to rest.

TO: Assistant Attorney General   DATE: December 21, 1955
     William F. Tompkins
FROM: Director, FBI
SUBJECT: FRANCIS ALBERT SINATRA
          SECURITY MATTER—C
          FRAUD AGAINST THE GOVERNMENT

Enclosed for your information is one copy of the report of Special
Agent ██████████████ dated November 4, 1955, at Los Angeles,
California, in captioned matter.
    Information concerning Sinatra's execution of an affidavit for the
Passport Division of the Department of State on January 10, 1955,
appears on page seven of the enclosed report. In his affidavit, Sinatra
denied past or present membership in the Communist Party or in any
group or organization of a subversive character.
    Information beginning on page 18 of the enclosed report reflects
that "The Independent" dated February 13, 1946, published by the
Independent Citizens Committee of the Arts, Sciences and
Professions, listed the name of one Frank Sinatra among ten names
under the heading "Vice Chairmen." The California Committee on
Un-American Activities report for 1948 on page 262 describes the
Independent Citizens Committee of the Arts, Sciences and
Professions as a "Communist front."
    For your further information, the above-mentioned issue of "The
Independent" also listed among the ten vice chairmen of the
Independent Citizens Committee of the Arts, Sciences and
Professions such individuals as Joseph E. Davies, Fiorello H.

LaGuardia, Archibald MacLeish and Dr. J. Robert Oppenheimer. Included in the list of some 30 members of the Board of Directors appeared the name of James Roosevelt.

A copy of the above report has been furnished to the Department of State. No further investigation will be conducted in this matter in the absence of a specific request from you.

Nevertheless, the FBI continued to file away information about Sinatra's alleged ties to Communists, no matter how absurd, as shown in this entry in a later summary of the files.

On 1/11/56 ██████████████ furnished information regarding a conversation she overheard which indicated that ██████████████ and ██████████████ might be operating a ham radio.

██████████████ stated that a conversation which she overheard on 6/9/55 suggested possible plans for the evacuation of communists from Wisconsin in the event of enemy attack on the West Coast. In the event of an air attack some communists would be able to find refuge at the homes of Frank Sinatra and Tony Martin.

Marilyn Monroe even turned up in one entry.

██████████████ that Marilyn Monroe, the actress, arrived in Mexico on 2/19/62 and associated with members of the American communist group. Her entry into Mexico was reportedly arranged by Frank Sinatra through former President Miguel Aleman. Marilyn was much disturbed by Arthur Miller's marriage on 2/20/62 and was very vulnerable because of her rejection by her former husband.

A decade after being cleared of charges that he lied about his political leanings to get a passport, Sinatra was still seething over suspicions that he was a Communist, according to this memo from one FBI official to another. (The bitterness expressed by Sinatra here stood in contrast to his tone in recording his classic "Strangers in the Night" less than two weeks hence.)

TO: W. C. Sullivan   DATE: 3/31/66
FROM: D. J. Brennan, Jr.
SUBJECT: FRANCIS ALBERT SINATRA,
      AKA Frank Sinatra
      SECURITY MATTER—C

On 3/30/66, Colonel John R. Elting (U.S. Army), G-2, Military District of Washington, advised that on 3/25/66, Joseph F. Goetz (Colonel, U. S. Air Force, Retired), a public relations man located at 1500 Massachusetts Avenue, Washington, D.C., contacted him and informed him that he had been commissioned by Frank Sinatra, the entertainer, to determine the identity of the "S.O.B." who had "tagged" Sinatra as a "commie."

Colonel Elting explained that in 1950, 1952, and 1954, Sinatra had offered his services for entertainment of military troops overseas. In each instance, he was not cleared by Army because of his reported affiliation with subversive organizations. Elting added that Sinatra was later cleared in 1962 to entertain troops overseas, but that this clearance expired in 1966 without the clearance having been used.

Elting furnished the attached intra-Army memorandum setting forth the details of a conference between representatives of Army and Sinatra in response to a request made by Sinatra for an appointment to discuss the matter of his clearance for a Christmas holiday entertainment tour to the Far East in 1954. During this conference, Brigadier General Alfred E. Kastner, Assistant to the Assistant Chief of Staff, G-2, informed Sinatra that over a period of years, many items had appeared in the public press which reflected adversely on Sinatra and which, to a considerable degree, identified Sinatra with the communist line. Sinatra, at the time, stated that he hated and despised everything that pertained to communism; that he had never been a member of a communist-inspired organization, nor had he ever made contributions to such organizations. He attributed the unfavorable press items to irresponsible individuals who preyed on those in entertainment. He related that he had responded to a reporter's question regarding his attitude toward communism with the remark "I am just as communistic as the Pope."

Inquiry was made of Colonel Elting by Liaison Agent as to why Sinatra, at this late date, wanted to pursue this matter. According to Elting, Goetz stated that Sinatra is a very temperamental, vindictive and moody individual and has periods where he dwells on his past life. Goetz added that he has known Sinatra for many years and he had noted several occasions where Sinatra, in retrospect, has made derogatory comments concerning individuals who have hurt him in the past. Elting advised that he gave Goetz no satisfaction other than to state that Sinatra was recently cleared to entertain troops overseas. Goetz informed Elting that he was going to counsel Sinatra to drop the matter.

FOUR

SINATRA AND THE MOB— THE EARLY YEARS

"Has this relationship been strictly social?"

Ever since his days in Hoboken, New Jersey, as the self-centered only child of an indulgent mother, Frank Sinatra found it useful to associate with people who could get things done for him.

It was a habit that the star carried with him into the entertainment and nightclub business, which had more than its share of thugs in those days.

In February 1947, Sinatra's habit became public knowledge. The Scripps-Howard columnist Robert Ruark happened to be in Havana at the same time Sinatra was. The singer had flown to the Cuban capital in those free-wheeling pre-Castro days with Joe (Joe Fish) Fischetti and his brother Rocco, members of Al Capone's Chicago gang. He was seen socializing there with Lucky Luciano, exiled father of the modern Mafia, at a casino, a racetrack, and parties.

Within days, Ruark reported these facts in a column headlined "Sinatra Is Playing with the Strangest People These Days." The singer's public image would never be the same.

The FBI was paying attention, too. Days after Ruark's story appeared, reports of Sinatra's alleged mob ties began turning up in the bureau's files. At the time, the FBI was primarily interested in Sinatra's supposedly Communist affiliations, as shown in the files excerpted in chapter 3. But as the red scare faded, the FBI's focus shifted.

Sinatra always defended his friendships with alleged mobsters as benign: He was just being cordial to admirers, however unsavory, who frequented the saloons where he performed, or who had a financial stake in them. Yet as Sinatra himself bought stakes in nightclubs and casinos, first in the Sands Hotel in Las Vegas in 1953 and then in the Cal-Neva Lodge in Lake Tahoe in 1961, he increasingly was judged by the company he kept. The FBI suspected the mob had interests in both establishments.

FBI summaries of Sinatra's suspect activities suggest a rogues' gallery of early associations, though many of the reports were unsubstantiated. (Most of the material below comes from a September 29, 1950, compilation, though some entries have been deleted and relevant entries from other documents have been included.)

ASSOCIATION WITH CRIMINALS AND HOODLUMS
A. Ralph Capone

According to an informant of unknown reliability, Frank Sinatra is a nephew of Ralph Capone, well-known Chicago gambler, being a son of one of Capone's sisters. According to this informant, the Capones brought Sinatra out of obscurity by buying him a nightclub job and paying representatives of the press for favorable publicity.

> ██████████████, who
> claimed to have connections
> with Ralph Capone.
> Milwaukee letter dated
> October 21, 1947,
> Re: "Capga"

B. Charles "Lucky" Luciano

In February, 1947, a newspaper columnist reported that Frank Sinatra had been in Havana, Cuba, for four days during the past week and "his companion in public and in private was Luciano, Luciano's body guards, and a rich collection of gamblers and highbinders. The friendship was beautiful. They were seen together at the race track, the gambling casino and at special parties."

> Column by Robert C. Ruark
> in the "Washington News," of
> February 20, 1947.

Luciano is the notorious underworld character who was deported from Cuba to Italy in the spring of 1947.

In connection with the above story concerning Sinatra's association with Luciano, Robert Ruark personally advised Mr. Nichols that he had been investigating Sinatra.

> Memorandum from Mr.
> Nichols to Mr. Tolson dated
> May 12, 1947,
> Re: "Frank Sinatra"

* * *

C. Mickey Cohen

An informant obtained Mickey Cohen's personal address and telephone book from a highly confidential source and it is to be noted that Frank Sinatra was listed in this book together with his address, 10051 Valley Springs Lane, North Hollywood.

> General Crime Survey, April,
> 15, 1947, Los Angeles Field
> Division

On December 23, 1946, Mickey Cohen asked Jimmy Tarantino to get Frankie Sinatra to come over to the Cohens' house for ten minutes in order to meet the 14 year old daughter of a Frank Minitti of Cleveland, Ohio, where he was engaged in the excavating business, and asked Tarantino to ask Frankie "to do it for me." Later it was arranged that Cohen and the Minittis attend one of Sinatra's broadcasts and sit on the stage and apparently they did meet him.

It was further reported that, since January 7, 1947, Sinatra and Cohen have consulted several times, apparently about some fighters that Sinatra had under contract. Further, that on one occasion Cohen accused an unknown individual of having threatened Frank Sinatra, which was denied.

██████████

> Los Angeles report dated
> January 17, 1947.
> RE: "Benjamin 'Bugsy' Siegel,
> was.;
> Miscellaneous Information
> Concerning,
> Crime Survey"

D. Charles Fischetti, Joseph Fischetti and Rocco Fischetti

In his column entitled "Broadway" which appeared in the "Washington Times Herald" of February 28, 1947, Danton Walker stated "Frankie Sinatra was the Miami Beach house guest of the Fischetti boys of Chicago—Rocky, Charlie and Joe—and flew with him to Havana, which is how he happened to meet Lucky Luciano, which is expected to get bigger as time goes on."

The Fischetti brothers are well-known underworld characters in the Chicago area, who have been reported by other sources to be closely acquainted with Frank Sinatra. The Fischettis are reported to be cousins of the late Alphonse Capone. This may possibly account for Sinatra's connection with them, if it is true, as reported above, that he is a nephew of Ralph Capone, the brother of the late Al Capone.

Joseph Fischetti, born in May, 1910, Brooklyn, New York, is considered more or less a public relations contact for his two brothers, Rocco and Charles, and is known to have contacts throughout the country among the underworld, as well as with individuals in the entertainment field. It is believed that he is associated with his brothers in handbook operations in Chicago and, according to reports, the brothers operate a gambling concession at the Chez Paree night club in Chicago, which is reported to be operated under the protection of Joseph Arvey and Arthur X. Elrod, Democratic politicians in Chicago.

> Chicago report dated
> November 18, 1946,
> Re: "Capga"

Charles Fischetti, who claims to have been born in Brooklyn, New York, on March 24, 1901, was reported, in 1948, by police informants to be the nation-wide contact man for the Chicago Syndicate and to own several gambling houses on the wealthy Chicago North Shore. Rocco Fischetti has been the business manager of the Fischetti gambling houses.

> General Crime Survey,
> Chicago Office,
> October 15, 1948
> Chicago report November 18,
> 1946,
> Re: "Capga"

As of October, 1948, the Fischetti brothers resided at the Barry Apartments, 8100 Sheridan Road, Chicago. In addition, they reportedly spend considerable time in Miami, where they are also reported to operate their gambling interests.

Additional evidence of Sinatra's association with the Fischetti brothers is noted below:

Through the assistance of former members of the Chicago Police Department, a photograph was located which had been taken in Havana, Cuba, in September, 1947, which shows Frank Sinatra getting off of an airplane preceded by Joseph Fischetti and followed by Rocco Fischetti.

> General Crime Survey,
> Chicago Office,
> October 15, 1948

During May, 1947, an informant reported observing Frank Sinatra in the company of Joseph Fischetti several times, during the period that Sinatra had been in Miami Beach, at that time. The informant added that he believed the two men had made a trip together to Havana, Cuba. This informant further stated that either Joseph Fischetti had made a statement to the effect that he had a financial interest in Sinatra, or that someone had repeated this remark as having been made by Joseph Fischetti.

>  May 17, 1947.
> Miami letter dated May 28, 1947,
> Re: "Joseph Fischetti,
> Miscellaneous, Crime Survey."

Information was received that when Joseph Fischetti returned to Chicago on July 23, 1946, he was in touch with Frank Sinatra, who was then entertaining at the Copacabana in New York City, and arrangements were made for the men to visit together.

Sometime between August 16 and August 23, 1946, exact date not given, Frank Sinatra's secretary, Bobby Burns, contacted Joseph Fischetti from Los Angeles to explain that Sinatra expected to be in New York about September 5, and arrangements were made with Fischetti for them to get together in New York City for three or four days.

> Technical Surveillance on the Fischetti brothers, 3100 Sheridan Road, Chicago.

The Chicago Field Office advised that Charles Fischetti was requested to get in touch with his brother, Joe Fischetti, for the purpose of contacting Sinatra in New York to expedite room reservations for a football game to be played around November 7, 1946. It was indicated that the reservations for the hotels were desired by the Fischettis as they intended to take in the Notre Dame–Army football game. In addition, it was reported that Fischetti forwarded two dozen shirts to Frank Sinatra in Hollywood.

Charles Fischetti, accompanied by Frank Sinatra, visited Fischetti's mother at 424 2nd Street, Brooklyn, New York, about May or June, 1946. It was the informant's impression that Sinatra was a very close friend of Charles Fischetti, since he visited Charles Fischetti and Fischetti's mother for approximately three hours, during this particular visit.

> Frances Duffy, 424 2nd Street, Brooklyn, New York, a clerk at LDB, 180, Brooklyn, New York.
> New York report 10-15-46, Re: "Capga"

It was reported on April 15, 1947, that Joseph Fischetti had been in telephonic communication with Frank Sinatra at least once a week.

> General Crime Survey,
> Chicago Office,
> April 15, 1947.

E. Don Junior

On August 9, 1948, Don Junior, a Los Angeles gambler and associate of Johnny Meyer, entered the apartment of Allen Smiley and during the course of his visit related a story of a party which he had attended the past week-end at Balboa with Bill Cagney, brother of James Cagney the movie actor, Frank Sinatra and their girl-friends. At this particular time, Junior was attempting to locate a house with Smiley to start a gambling establishment. Meyer and Smiley are identified hereinafter.

> ██████████████
>
> Los Angeles letter dated
> August 13, 1948,
> Re: "Aaron Smehoff, was,
> Falsely Claiming Citizenship;
> Perjury"

It was also learned that Don Junior had attended a party on the night of August 16, 1948, with William Cagney and Frank Sinatra.

██████████████

F. Willie Moretti

During the course of inquiries made by the Newark Field Division in connection with the crime survey program, information was received from Captain Matthew J. Donohue of the Bergen County Police, Hackensack, New Jersey, that Willie Moretti of Hasbrouck Heights, New Jersey, has a financial interest in Frank Sinatra. It should be mentioned that Frank Sinatra's residence is also in Hasbrouck Heights, New Jersey. Willie Moretti is the leader of a gang known as the Willie Moretti Gang operating in Bergen County, New Jersey. Moretti is reported to control the numbers rackets, horse racing, and gambling throughout Bergen County, New Jersey. The Newark Office has advised that Moretti is a close associate of Frank Costello, well-known gambler of New York City, and that during 1933 Moretti, while visiting the Arlington Hotel, Hot Springs, Arkansas, was in the company of Lucky Luciano.

> Captain Matthew J.
> Donohue,
> General Crime Survey,
> May 13, 1944,
> Newark Field Division

On February 6, 1948, Moretti was interviewed by Bureau Agents from Newark Office under suitable pretense at which time he admitted among other things his association with Frank Sinatra.

An informant "recently" related an incident concerning Frank Sinatra, who prior to the time he went into the movies ███████████████ worked for Pete LaPlaca and others in Bergen County, New Jersey. Pete LaPlaca was identified as Willie Moretti's bodyguard. The informant stated that when Sinatra was "recently" separated from his wife, a cousin of Sinatra's wife who is related to a key member of the Moretti mob, contacted Willie Moretti regarding Sinatra's marriage difficulties and as a result Willie Moretti personally instructed Sinatra to go back and live with his wife. Sinatra immediately obeyed the orders of Moretti. Informant stated that Sinatra and Lou Costello, the movie and radio comedian, both "kick in" to Moretti.

General Crime Survey,
April 15, 1948.
Newark Division

Lee Mortimer reported that Frank Sinatra was backed when he first started by a gangster in New York named Willie Moretti, with alias Willie Moore.

Memorandum for Mr. Tolson
from
Mr. Nichols dated May 12,
1947,
Re: "Frank Sinatra"

G. Aaron Smehoff, w.a., Allen Smiley
On June 13, 1948, Allen Smiley, notorious Los Angeles underworld character who was with "Bugsy" Siegel the night he was murdered, claimed to know Frank Sinatra quite well.

Westbrook Pegler has made reference to Sinatra's associations with Smiley in editorials which he had written criticizing the Department of Justice for not prosecuting its case against Smiley with greater vigilance.

Column by Westbrook Pegler
in the "Washington Times
Herald," and "New York
Journal American," 10-3-47.

Smiley was born in Russia on January 10, 1907, and came to Canada seven years later with his parents where his father became a citizen of Canada. Smiley subsequently entered the United States, assertedly at Detroit, in 1922, and since that time has been in this country without an immigration visa or passport. He was arrested by the FBI on November 21, 1947, charged with falsely claiming citizenship and with perjury. On August 1, 1949, he was sentenced to one year in jail and fined $1,000 for twice falsely claiming he was a United States citizen. He appealed his case and the Ninth Circuit Court of Appeals rendered a decision on April 13, 1950, upholding the District Court's finding of guilty.

The Los Angeles District Office of the Immigration and Naturalization Service issued an order May 12, 1949, that Smiley be deported to Canada and if that country would not accept him then to Russia. Service of this order was pending the outcome of Smiley's prosecution. Smiley's hearing was re-opened by INS on August 1, 1950, for the sole purpose of including in the record of Smiley's conviction in the U.S. District Court at Los Angeles on charges of falsely claiming citizenship.

On May 6, 1948, Jack Dragna, Los Angeles hoodlum, called at the apartment of Allen Smiley and asked for a list of names of persons to be invited to the wedding of his, Dragna's, daughter. Smiley listed about 45 persons for Dragna including Frank Sinatra and others who were mostly racketeers, gamblers, bookmakers or otherwise closely associated with the underworld.

███████████████

Los Angeles letter dated
May 14, 1948,
Re: "Aaron Smehoff, w.a.,
Allen Smiley, USTA,
Racketeering Activities,
Crime Survey in Los Angeles,
Falsely Claiming
Citizenship—Perjury"

H. James Tarantino

Westbrook Pegler made reference to Tarantino's association with Frank Sinatra in his column which appeared in the "Washington Times Herald" on October 3, 1947, in which he stated "Tarantino is a swipe and hustler who used to hang around Jacobs' Beach, a stretch near Madison Square Garden where the fighters, managers, and racketeers gather. He has a <u>cheap</u> police record in Newark and he has been a friend and protégé of Frank Sinatra."

Pegler further stated in this article that George Evans, Sinatra's press agent and manager, had denied that Sinatra had anything to do with Tarantino. In contradiction of this, Pegler reported that on February 4, 1946, Frank Sinatra's name was signed first under the signature of a "Citizens Committee" to a wire to Fred Howser, Prosecuting Attorney of Los Angeles County, demanding police protection for Tarantino and his wife and children who had been "threatened and harassed by political gangsters." Pegler also reported that Sinatra had called the meeting of this "Citizens Committee."

Pegler further reports that Evans had specifically said Sinatra did not finance Tarantino's paper.

"Washington Times Herald"
10/3/47

James Tarantino, Editor and Publisher of the magazine, "Hollywood Nite Life," a scandal sheet published in Hollywood, California, was interviewed at his request by the San Francisco Office on May 18, 1949. He claimed at that time to have learned of an alleged plot by William Clinton Wren, Managing Editor of the San Francisco "Examiner" to "blast him" on a trumped up extortion charge, and said he wanted the Bureau to have all the facts in case the complaint was made against him.

Tarantino advised that the magazine, "Hollywood Nite Life," was incorporated in California in 1945 by Barney Ross, former welterweight champion, Henry Sanicola and himself. He reported that Sanicola is a very good friend of Frank Sinatra and that Sinatra had helped finance the deal with $15,000. This group operated the magazine for approximately six months, after which time Tarantino said he acquired full ownership.

> San Francisco Crime Survey
> Report

On November 10, 1949, Inspector Frank J. Ahern, San Francisco Police Department, advised the Los Angeles Office that he believed that Tarantino's publication was sponsored by Frank Costello's criminal syndicate and that Tarantino had been invaluable in infiltrating political machines in order to allow Costello's mobsters to operate with the co-operation of such politicians and officials.

Tarantino specializes in sensationalism and during 1949 featured a so-called "expose" of the narcotics traffic in Hollywood which allegedly involved Judy Garland, Actress, and Actor Robert Mitchum. He is reported to take orders from Michael "Mickey" Cohen, Los Angeles' leading hoodlum, and was friendly with the late Bugsy Siegel.

> Memorandum from A. Rosen
> to Mr. Ladd,
> Re: ████████████
> dated June 1, 1949.
>
> Los Angeles letter,
> November 21, 1949,
> Re: "Hollywood Nite Life."

ALLEGATIONS THAT SINATRA IS A DOPE RACKETEER

███████████████████████████████████████

██████████████████████████████████████ directed a letter
to the Attorney General under date of June 10, 1947, wherein he
stated that he had quite a bit of information concerning vice rackets,
narcotics and jewel thieves which he thought might be of interest to
the Department of Justice. This letter was referred to the Bureau on
June 20, 1947, and ████████████████ was subsequently interviewed
by Bureau Agents at the ████████████████

██

After being assured that his information would be kept in strict
confidence, he related among other things that Frank Sinatra
handled dope on the West Coast for Bugsy Siegel, Allen Smiley and
George Raft. ████████████████ alleged that Sinatra maintained his
headquarters in one of the bigger hotels in Hollywood, either the
Roosevelt or Hollywood Hotels, and further reported that he had
heard that the bell hop at this hotel was in on the deal.

> Atlanta letter August 20,
> 1947.
> Re: "████████████████ with
> alias;
> Information Concerning"

REPORTED INTEREST IN GAMBLING ESTABLISHMENTS

It was reported in April, 1946, that Frank Sinatra was sponsoring
one of the groups who were then planning on promoting boxing
shows in Los Angeles. Sinatra, together with a Henry Sanicola and
Larry Rummans, incorporated and sold stock to raise money to build
a "Little Madison Square Garden" arena in Los Angeles, California.
Sinatra was further reported to be then completing plans to organize
a stable of boxers to be managed by Henry Sanicola. Sanicola was
identified as a lifelong associate of Frank Sinatra who has managed
his business interests over a great many years. Sinatra was also
reported to be interested in a new hotel and gambling establishment

then being built at Las Vegas, Nevada. It was reported that this
enterprise was being financed by Sinatra and an attorney named
Albert Pearlsen.

> General Crime Survey,
> 4-15-46,
> Los Angeles Office.

With regard to Sinatra's reported interest in a hotel and gambling
establishment at Las Vegas, it was reported that on August 13, 1946,
"Bugsy" Siegel met with two other men, Bones Remmer and an
attorney named Austin White, at which time Siegel complained that
16 weeks of work and two million dollars had been put into the hotel
at Las Vegas which was then 75 percent completed, but now a stop
order had been issued. He further complained that Sinatra had put
an O.K. on a $1,500,000 building in the South. It developed from
their conversation that, according to Siegel, the approval for the
hotel building at Las Vegas had been given and the stop order issued
by a man named Bender, who was head of the Civilian Production
Administration in San Francisco.

Bones Remmer has been identified by the San Francisco Office as
Elmer M. Bones Remmer who resides in Orinda, California, and is a
well known local gambling boss who owns interests in several
gambling establishments in the vicinity of California and Nevada.

The reference to the hotel under construction at Las Vegas,
Nevada, may possibly have reference to the Flamingo Hotel in which
Siegel had an interest.

> Technical surveillance on
> Bugsy Siegel,
> San Francisco teletype, dated
> 8/13/46,
> Re: "Benjamin 'Bugsy'
> Siegel."

Bugsy Siegel, a prominent hoodlum operating on the west coast was reported to have gone to Los Angeles on December 18, 1946 to contact Lana Turner, Jimmy Durante, and Frank Sinatra for the purpose of having these individuals attend the opening of the Flamingo Hotel operated by Siegel.

A June 8, 1964, FBI summary on Sinatra gives the flavor of some of the raw, often unsubstantiated but nevertheless tantalizing tips and innuendos the bureau was collecting regarding the singer's mob affiliations. The summary also includes a reference to the columnist Lee Mortimer's 1951 report that Sinatra served as a money courier for Lucky Luciano, which the FBI files do not corroborate. (Some less-noteworthy entries have been deleted.)

During the period Sept. 20 through Oct. 8, 1946, various informants furnished information regarding Joseph Fischetti. Included was information that Fischetti and Charlie Baron, a Ford automobile dealer, 2223 South Michigan, Chicago, sent two dozen shirts to Frank Sinatra in Hollywood. On 10/8/46, Baron asked Charlie Fischetti to have his brother, Joe Fischetti, contact Frank Sinatra and have him expedite room reservations in connection with a football game to be played around 11/7/46. Baron probably had reference to the Army and Navy game to be played in NY on 11/9/46. The Fischetti brothers were key figures in the Chicago crime syndicate.

(Delicate confidential
source)

On 10/15/46 the Newark Office advised that Al Silvani, Frank Sinatra's bodyguard, flew to NJ and took charge of Tami Mauriello's training before his fight with Joe Louis. (no date)

On 6/6/50 the Miami Office advised that a reliable informant (not identified) advised that Joe Fischetti, prominent underworld figure, had been in Miami Beach during the 1946–47 winter season accompanied by Frank Sinatra. They stayed for a period at the Grand

Hotel and had taken a trip to Havana, Cuba. The informant stated it was rumored among the underworld that Fischetti owned a percentage of Sinatra's contract (not described).

On 1/10/47 the Los Angeles Office advised that Mickey Cohen was attempting to open a gambling joint in Los Angeles and had imported five hoodlums from Cleveland, Ohio. He had been in contact with Frank Sinatra on some sort of a deal and had introduced Sinatra to the Frank Minnitis, who were staying at the Ambassador Hotel. The Cleveland Office had advised that Minniti was Vice-President of the Standard Excavating Company of Cleveland, and a close friend of Frank Milano, reputed syndicate head in Cleveland.

On 7/31/47 Los Angeles Confidential Informant ████████████████ advised that Joe Lynch, a crooked fight promoter tied in with the corrupt State Athletic Commission, was a good friend of Mickey Cohen of the Mafia. Informant stated that Cohen double-crossed Lynch at a Madison Square Garden fight in NY where Lynch had arranged for Frank Sinatra and other celebrities to be present.

In the latter part of 1950, ██████████████████████████ Philadelphia (protect identity), advised in connection with Robink that he had heard a rumor that an American had delivered $1,000,000 in cash to Lucky Luciano in Italy, presumably to effect the re-entrance of Luciano into the US. It was mentioned that Frank Sinatra had recently travelled abroad. ████████████████ appeared surprised and immediately asked if the FBI knew anything definite that Sinatra was the underworld contact.

He claimed that Sinatra was the person named in the above described rumor. It was noted that the name of Sinatra was not volunteered by ████████████████ and the information might have been conjecture on his part. The story was highly unlikely because of probably legal restrictions regarding the removal of large amounts of cash from the US.

On 4/15/54 the NY Office furnished a summary memorandum concerning Joseph A. Doto, commonly known as Joe Adonis, which listed numerous hoodlums with whom he had been associated. The list included Frank Sinatra.

On 1/10/55 the Chicago Office furnished a copy of "The Juke Box Racket" written by Virgil W. Peterson, Operating Director, Chicago Crime Commission, Sept., 1954. The report, marked confidential, made reference to the close relationship existing between the underworld and many stars in the entertainment field, for example, Frank Sinatra's close association with notorious gangsters. Sinatra owned an interest in the gambling casino called The Sands in Las Vegas, Nev. His business associates included Malcolm Clarke, once a partner of the notorious Capone gangster, Charles Gioe, in a Chicago Loop gambling pay-off establishment. A New Jersey investigator had informed the Chicago Crime Commission that Sinatra had Willie Moretti as his mentor and manager.

On 3/29/51 the NY Office advised in connection with the Kefauver Committee to Investigate Organized Crime In Interstate Commerce that Frank Sinatra had been interviewed at NYC and had denied any knowledge of the whereabouts of missing witnesses, Charles and Rocco Fischetti. He stated his last contact with them was in Miami a year ago. Approximately six weeks before he had seen Joe Fischetti, their brother, in NYC but did not know his address there. Sinatra denied that the Fischettis had any financial interest in any of his enterprises.

This reference sets out lengthy information regarding Frank Sinatra, who with Joe DiMaggio and several other individuals, on 11/5/54 attempted to raid an apartment in Hollywood which was occupied by Sheila Stewart, a friend of Marilyn Monroe who was about to obtain a divorce from DiMaggio. It was reported that DiMaggio was attempting to find derogatory information against Marilyn Monroe. The California State Senate Committee and the Los Angeles Grand Jury conducted an investigation regarding the matter.

Records of the Sheriff's Office, Clark County, Las Vegas, Nev., revealed that on 8/28/58 Eugene Warner was observed in a friendly conversation with Frank Sinatra and former baseball player, Joe

DiMaggio, at the Sands Hotel. The nature of the conversation and extent of friendship were unknown.

It was noted that Warner was suspected of ████████████ at the Sands Hotel and Gambling Casino, Las Vegas. Sinatra was part owner at the Sands and appeared there annually as an entertainer.

████████████████████████ made available a manuscript regarding members of the "Mafia" which was prepared in 1951 by someone in the employ of the Federal Narcotics Bureau. The manuscript had been loaned to a person in Los Angeles and the source desired that the document be treated as confidential. Background information was set out concerning Frank Sinatra as follows:

He was a front for the "Big Mob," and the principal contact with Jorge Pasqual who represented the "Big Mob" in Mexico. Sinatra was "discovered" by Willie Moretti after pressure from Frank Costello and Lucky Luciano.

The Fischetti boys in Chicago owned a part of Sinatra. On one occasion Sinatra delivered $2,000,000 to Luciano in Cuba. The Mob reportedly forced Tommy Dorsey to release Sinatra from a contract. The owners of Sinatra were to hold a meeting in Las Vegas on 8/19/51 which would follow a meeting of the grand council of the Big Mob which was to be held in Cleveland, Ohio, 8/15–17/51. The meeting was said to be the most important meeting in modern times. "(See Mortimer story; Sinatra Confidential)"

On 1/24/56 ████████████ of the NY Office, advised that singer Frank Sinatra was originally backed by top hoodlum, Joe Adonis.

This reference is a NY summary memorandum dated 3/15/56 regarding Anthony Strollo, who with other hoodlums was involved during the raid on the Gold Key Club, NYC, on 2/10/56.

Frank Sinatra visited the Gold Key Club regularly when in NYC. He appeared to prefer the company of these hoodlums, and their admiration for him appeared to be mutual. During the winter of 1955, Vincent Mauro, a henchman of Strollo, gave an elaborate party for Sinatra at the Club on the occasion of his departure for a personal appearance tour of Australia.

This tour followed an appearance by Sinatra at the Ciro Club at Miami where the group thought his presence might be required to pull that establishment out of a hole. It was alleged that Sinatra appeared at the Club as a favor to Mauro for a salary far below the payment he usually received for night club appearances.

Miami letter, 3/21/58, stated that ████████████████████ ████████████████████████████ advised that Frank Sinatra who appeared at the Fontainebleau Hotel, came to Miami through the friendship and persuasion of Joseph Fischetti. Sinatra and Lauren Bacall planned to stay at Fischetti's home in North Bay Village but due to last minute changes they stayed at the Fontainebleau.

████████████████████

████████████████████████████ furnished confidential information that Frank Sinatra was among the group of Americans who were putting up ten million dollars for the construction of the Monte Carlo Hotel and gambling casino in the Barlovento development in Havana.

████████████████████████████████

████████████ former PCI, (protect identity) advised that on 8/10/58 Frank Sinatra was met at Midway Airport, Chicago, by Joe Fischetti, a former Chicago hoodlum, then residing in Miami, and taken to the Ambassador Hotel. After lunch, Sinatra, Fischetti and Dean Martin, a well-known entertainer who was also in Chicago, were taken by ████████████████ of the Chicago PD to the River Forest residence of Anthony Accardo where they gave a "command performance."

During the period ████████████████████████████ advised that racketeers continued to "muscle in" on the entertainment field. He stated that Frank Costello (not identified) took over Frank Sinatra when he was struggling to be recognized, promoted him financially, and was responsible for his present success.

On 4/4/60 a Bureau Agent advised that in the summer of 1959 there was a large gambling setup at Gurney's Inn, Montauk, NY, and that Frank Sinatra was among the customers.

████████████████████████████ advised that Dominick Bruno, reported to have Mafia connections, had attempted unsuccessfully to get Frank Sinatra to appear at his Three Rivers Inn, Three Rivers, NY. Sinatra would only appear at a Las Vegas club (believed to be the Dunes), an Atlantic City club owned by an old friend who started him in the entertainment business, (not identified) and the Copacabana in NY, where he had obligations. Informant explained that these obligations dated from Sinatra's "emancipation" from Tommy Dorsey who once owned Sinatra to the extent that Sinatra only received 10% of his gross income. Sinatra got Frank Costello, nationally known racketeer, to obtain his release from Dorsey for $150,000. As a result Sinatra was obligated to the Sinatra syndicate and therefore worked at the Copacabana. Sinatra was reputed to be a possible runner for Lucky Luciano during his overseas visits and a couple of years ago they had been pictured together in newspapers in Cuba. Informant was of the opinion that if Dominick Bruno had any top syndicate or Mafia connections he would have been able to get Sinatra to appear at Three Rivers Inn.

██████████████████████████████████

██ (protect identity) advised that David Gerson, deceased, formerly proprietor of the City Grill at 1432 Market St., Philadelphia, had owned 32 shares of stock identified by Inft. [informant] as "Cal-Neva." Herman Taylor, Philadelphia fight promoter, apparently "fronting for the mob" at Philadelphia, attempted to purchase the shares but because of his associations, the Nevada Gambling Commission intervened. Paul D'Amato, operator of the 500 Club in Atlantic City, withdrew an offer to buy the shares because he learned that the Nevada Gambling Commission was having an investigation conducted on him. Inft. believed that because of these failures Frank Sinatra was approached. Sinatra bought 28 shares and Dean Martin purchased the remaining shares.

The above informant believed Sinatra was "closely aligned with the rackets" and as an example stated that when Sinatra played at the 500 Club in Atlantic City in 1960 he was a constant companion of Joseph Fischetti, alleged former lieutenant of Al Capone. Fischetti would allow no one to see Sinatra without his sanction. During that time Sinatra also associated with Paul D'Amato and Felix John De Tullio.

On 1/6/60 ███████████████████████████████████ ███████████████ (protect identity) advised that Joe Valeno, a singer whose true name was Joe Poleno or Poliano, had allegedly made numerous recordings for an unnamed company in NYC next to or near Radio Corporation of America studios. The records had been suppressed because he would not voluntarily participate in "drug traffic." One of Valeno's arrangements, "Garden of Eden," was allegedly taken by Frank Sinatra who recorded it as his own, and the record was now being sold. Sinatra allegedly paid Valeno $10,000 for this song plus a two percent "pressure fee," not further defined.

███████████████████████████████ Central Intelligence Squad, NYC PD [Police Department], advised that on the evening of March, 28, 1960, Generoso Salvatore Del Ducca was stricken with a heart attack at the Fontainebleau Hotel, Miami Beach, Fla. At the time he was stricken he was seated at a table in the company of Frank Sinatra. A [listening device] revealed that various prominent hoodlums attended his funeral in NYC on 4/4/60.

NOTE: It's not clear if the below entry relates to the same incident.

████████████████████ at which time they discussed the current illness of ███████████████ (not identified), who had suffered a recent attack which resulted in his being hospitalized. █████████████████ that Frank Sinatra was responsible for causing █████████████ to drink more heavily than he ordinarily did and was having him run around with a lot of young broads, which had resulted in ████████████████ sustaining this attack. Informant stated that though ██████████████ [has] always been a drunk, he hated to see Sinatra cause more trouble than he had already caused.

On 9/15/61 the Miami Office advised that ████████████████ ██ (protect identities) and ██████████████ were carefully scrutinizing the ownership of Puccini's Restaurant, Miami, Florida. It had been reported to each of these sources that this restaurant was backed by Frank Sinatra. It was reported that arrangements were being made to make a test case to determine if a duplex apartment building adjoining the restaurant could be opened as a casino for illegal gambling. The Beverage Commission planned that the restaurant would be permitted to open and then action would be taken against the management.

██████████████ advised that he learned from ████████████ ███ 500 Club at Atlantic City, NJ. ██████████████████████ ██████████████████████████████████████ but Joe Fischetti, a well known hoodlum, and Frank Sinatra had an interest in the Club. Sinatra also had an interest in a number of substantial crap games operating in the Philadelphia area, and was presently entering into an enterprise in Las Vegas which involved the building of a $10,000,000 gambling casino. ██████████████ was confident that Fischetti and other underworld figures would have an interest in this undertaking.

██████████████████████████████████ is aware of the fact that SINATRA enjoys surrounding himself with hoodlums and believes that SINATRA would give up his show business prominence to be a hoodlum himself if he had the courage to do so.

In 1959, an agent for the Internal Revenue Service questioned Sinatra under oath in Los Angeles during an investigation of possible mob skimming at clubs where Sinatra performed. In his testimony, Sinatra denied that the Chicago mob boss Sam Giancana was present at a string of nightly parties he threw that summer during an extended engagement at the Claridge Hotel in Atlantic City. But he did acknowledge recently becoming acquainted with the mobster. Sinatra's friendship with Giancana would grow in the coming years and figured prominently in the singer's life as he grew close to a rising young senator from Massachusetts, John F. Kennedy.

Set out herein is the affidavit in question:

"Q. Are you acquainted with a Mr. Sam Giancana?
A. I am.
Q. How long have you known the gentleman?
A. A couple of years. A little under a couple of years.
Q. Approximately when did you first meet Mr. Giancana?
A. March 11, I think, 1958.
Q. Where did this meeting take place?
A. In the Fontainebleau Hotel.
Q. Miami Beach, Florida?
A. Yes.
Q. Have you ever had any business dealings with Mr. Giancana?
A. None.
Q. Has this relationship been strictly social?
A. Yes.
Q. Has Mr. Giancana ever approached you in connection with any financial business proposition?
A. No.
Q. When was the last time you saw Mr. Giancana?
A. Sometime early in August.
Q. 1959?
A. At the Chicago Airport, 1959.
Q. Mr. Sinatra, in regard to the previous interview which we had with you on November 6, 1959, at your attorney's office, at that time you supplied information substantially as follows: That your relationship with Mr. Giancana was strictly friendly; that you had seen him approximately 6 to 10 times, several of these meetings having taken place at the Sands Hotel, Las Vegas, Nevada, where you were appearing at the time.
A. Yes.
Q. That you had considered Mr. Giancana more or less a fan of yours; that you possess no knowledge as to Mr. Giancana's business activities; that you have never been approached by Mr. Giancana with a financial proposition. Is that correct?

A. That is absolutely correct.

Q. Do you have any way of knowing at this time how Mr. Giancana would have come into possession of your unpublished home phone number, CR 4-2368, listed to you at 2666 Bowmont Drive, Beverly Hills, California? Can you give us information as to how he may have come—

A. I gave it to him.

Q. Was there anything specific that you recall with reference to giving him this phone number?

A. Not at all. I give my phone number to many people.

Q. Would this likewise be true of your CRestview 5-4977, Oxford Publications, Inc., the unpublished number, TExas 0-8701, your unpublished phone at Metro Goldwyn Studios?

A. Yes.

Q. Was there any specific purpose that you had given these numbers to Mr. Giancana?

A. None.

Q. Mr. Sinatra, information has come to our attention that during the period July 25, 1959 to August 2, 1959, you were staying at the Hotel Claridge, Atlantic City, New Jersey, and at that time you had rented numerous rooms at this hotel and had given a party which was attended by Mr. Giancana. Is that correct?

A. No.

Q. Were you staying at the Claridge at that time?

A. Yes.

Q. Has Mr. Giancana attended any parties given by you, Mr. Sinatra?

A. No.

Q. With reference to the last interview, at that time you supplied information that the occasion of your last meeting with Mr. Giancana was in Chicago and at that time you had contacted Mr. Giancana for the purpose of making arrangements to have him transfer your luggage from the airport to the train in Chicago. Is that correct?

A. I guess so, except one little thing. I don't remember calling
   him because I don't know where to call him. Apparently—I
   have to guess, but apparently he called me; that is probably
   what happened. I don't remember calling him. I wouldn't
   know where to call him.
Q. Have you ever had occasion to visit Mr. Giancana at his
   residence in Chicago?
A. No.
Q. Do you know where he lives?
A. No."

*Much later, the FBI would decide that Sinatra had probably made a false
statement in the affidavit: An informant, a chorus-line dancer at the same
party, apparently contradicted the singer's account. The alleged lie would be
discovered as the bureau closed in on Sinatra, aspirant to royal status in
JFK's Camelot.*

FIVE

SINATRA, THE KENNEDYS, AND THE MOB—THE COURTSHIP

"Some sort of indiscreet party."

Sinatra met the actor Peter Lawford in April 1944, at a party given by the boss of MGM, Louis B. Mayer. Ten years later, Lawford married Patricia Kennedy, younger sister of John F. Kennedy. Sinatra's friendship with Lawford blossomed into a friendship with Kennedy, whose stay at the singer's home would later be memorialized by a bronze plaque on the door to its guest room.

By 1960, Sinatra and his Rat Pack colleagues had taken Las Vegas by storm, and the Massachusetts senator had become their golfing pal—and their candidate for president. On stage with Sinatra at the Sands one night, Dean Martin called the boyish politician in the audience "one of my best buddies"—and then cracked up the senator by turning to Sinatra and saying, "What the hell is his name?" All the while, mobsters like Chicago boss Sam "Momo" Giancana and Johnny Roselli lurked in the background, seeking to use Sinatra to gain political influence.

Memos about the overlapping exploits of Sinatra, Kennedy, and alleged mobsters soon swelled the FBI's files.

The FBI first became interested in Sinatra's friendship with Kennedy in early 1960 as the Massachusetts senator's campaign was touring the country blaring its theme song—Sinatra's specially reworked recording of "High Hopes." On March 23, 1960, the special agent in charge (SAC) of the New Orleans FBI office gave Hoover an early indication of Sinatra's role in the campaign and the mob's interest in its outcome. It also provided evidence of Kennedy's weakness for the ladies—including an as-yet-unidentified woman he met at the Sands in Las Vegas. She would become quite significant later.

TO: DIRECTOR, FBI
FROM: SAC, NEW ORLEANS
SUBJECT: SENATOR JOHN F. KENNEDY
            INFORMATION CONCERNING

On 3/22/60, ███████████████ who operates a ███████████████ in New Orleans, La., furnished the following information:

███████████████ stated that among ███████████████ are JERRY WALD, Hollywood motion picture producer, and PHILLIP FRANK KASTEL, New Orleans top hoodlum. ███████████████ stated that ███████████████ KASTEL and other clients, he travels frequently to Las Vegas, Nev., Hollywood, and Miami, Florida. He said that ███████████████ KASTEL's ███████████████ he has met a number of well known hoodlums, such as MEYER LANSKY, whom he described as a gambler operating in Miami and Havana, Cuba, and JOE FISCHETTI, aka. JOE FISH, who ███████████████ believes is the dominant figure in the racketeering element in the Miami area. ███████████████ claims that as a result of his contacts with these individuals, he has met socially a number of their associates, whose identities are not known to him, and whom he has not sought to identify, feeling that inquisitiveness on his part might be detrimental to his·relationship with KASTEL.

In this connection, ███████████████ stated that on occasions he has overheard conversations between these individuals concerning their activities, some of which have no significance to him. He pointed out that he has never exhibited any inquisitiveness concerning these conversations because he felt "it would not be healthy for him." ████████████ related that within the past week he has returned from the Miami area and while there he learned from individuals, whom he declined to identify, but whom he claims are members of the underworld element, that FISCHETTI and other unidentified hoodlums are financially supporting and actively endeavoring to secure the nomination for the Presidency as democratic candidate, Senator JOHN F. KENNEDY. He stated as evidence of this fact, FRANK SINATRA is going to campaign for KENNEDY in several of the primaries. ████████████ stated he has known SINATRA personally since the latter has been connected with motion pictures in Hollywood and he knows that SINATRA is a nephew of JOE FISCHETTI. SINATRA is only booked to appear after clearance is obtained with FISCHETTI.

He advised that in addition to SINATRA, a song writer named JIMMY VAN HEUSEN is in Miami writing campaign songs for KENNEDY. ████████████ advised that VAN HEUSEN is SINATRA's song writer and at the present time, VAN HEUSEN's secretary is rooming with an airline hostess of National Airlines named BARBARA JEAN GALL.

████████████ advised that BARBARA JEAN GALL is a native of Miami Springs, Fla. and in the past has associated with various hoodlums in the Miami area. ████████████ stated that it is his opinion that SINATRA and VAN HEUSEN are being made available to assist Senator KENNEDY's campaign whereby FISCHETTI and other hoodlums will have an entre to Senator KENNEDY.

████████████ advised that Senator KENNEDY's brother-in-law, PETER LAWFORD, a well known movie actor, has been cultivated by SINATRA and they are now apparently close associates. He advised that it is Las Vegas gossip that LAWFORD has a financial interest in the Sands Hotel in Las Vegas.

████████████ claimed that the controlling interest in the Sands Hotel is owned by DOC STACHER, although the latter's name does not appear as an owner. He advised that it is his understanding that LAWFORD has an interest of one half of one per cent in the hotel.

██████████████ stated when in Miami he had occasion to overhear a conversation which indicated that Senator KENNEDY had been compromised with a woman in Las Vegas, Nevada. He stated that he knows that Senator KENNEDY was staying at the Sands Hotel in Las Vegas about 6 or 8 weeks ago during the filming of a movie entitled "Ocean 11," starring DEAN MARTIN. He stated that he observed Senator KENNEDY in the night club of the Sands Hotel, during this period, but has no idea as to the identity of any possible female companion. He stated that when Senator KENNEDY was in Miami, Fla., an airline hostess named SUSAN STALLINGS, who is a native of Baltimore, Md. was sent to visit Sen. KENNEDY. He stated that he learned this from an airline hostess whom he did not want to involve and whom he declined to identify. He stated that he had no idea of the date Sen. KENNEDY was in Florida.

██████████████ stated that all of the above information has come from members of the hoodlum element he has met and their associates, and he does not desire to identify them, and in some instances does not know the identities of some of these individuals. He stated that there is no way he can check the accuracy of this information as he is afraid to ask questions of any of these individuals, but he believes that this information is correct.

██████████████ said that he was considerably disturbed when he learned this information, as he would hate to see a pawn of the hoodlum element such as SINATRA have access to the White House.

Although it is realized that the above information as furnished by PCI ██████████████ is to a great extent non-specific, it is being brought to the Bureau's attention in view of the prominence of Senator KENNEDY. ██████████████ advised that he will be proceeding to ██████████████ within the next few days where he will be a guest in the ██████████████ while negotiating with the ██████████████ movie industry for distribution rights of

█████████████ motion pictures in the United States. He stated his stay in ████████████ will be indefinite. Upon his return, █████████████ will be followed closely to assure that any additional information received by him is made available to this office.

On March 21, The New York Times broke a story that threatened to damage the Kennedy campaign: Sinatra had hired his old friend Albert Maltz to do a screenplay for The Execution of Private Slovik, *the story of the only U.S. soldier in either world war shot for desertion. Maltz had been imprisoned in 1950 and blacklisted for refusing to cooperate with the red-baiting House Un-American Activities Committee. Sinatra wanted to break the blacklist and restore Maltz's name, and initially, he stood by him.*

The FBI began looking into the matter right after the story broke. The resulting memos were seasoned with rumors about sex involving Kennedy.

March 29, 1960

By teletype dated 3/22/60 and radiogram dated 3/23/60, the Los Angeles Office furnished the following information concerning Frank Sinatra hiring Albert Maltz to do the script for the film "Execution of Private Slovik."

Richard J. Collins, film writer and one-time communist party member, advised the Los Angeles Office that Frank Sinatra's film producing company, reported to be Essex Productions, had contracted writer Albert Maltz. This deal was handled for Sinatra by Martin Gang, well known Hollywood attorney, while Maltz's end was negotiated by attorney Martin Popper, of New York, and talent agent George Willner, former Los Angeles Security Index subject, now residing in New York. Another former communist party member, Martin Berkeley, film writer and source of the Los Angeles Office, advised that various film companies in the past have been interested in doing a film on this subject but the Defense Department has wanted to forget the episode and has refused all cooperation to would-be producers. He said that Sinatra was expected to direct the film but not appear in it himself and that he would receive no cooperation from the Defense Department. Financial arrangements for production not known, however, Sinatra's partner is reported to be film and TV star Peter Lawford, brother-in-law of Senator Kennedy, which was probable reason contracting parties have been loath to announce the deal.

Lewis Meltzer, member of Screen Writers Council of the Writers Guild of America, furnished the following information, based upon a confidential conversation he had with Dalton Trumbo 3/22/60 (Trumbo has had numerous communist connections). Meltzer said that Trumbo is a close contact of Maltz and Maltz is upset with Trumbo for having filed an application for reinstatement in the Writer's Club.

Trumbo thinks the Sinatra-Maltz deal was a bad thing politically and told Maltz so. According to Trumbo, Senator John Kennedy has requested Sinatra, probably through Peter Lawford, to hold off on confirmation of the Sinatra-Maltz deal until after the recent New Hampshire primaries. However, following Kennedy's success in the New Hampshire primary the Senator withdrew his objection to releasing confirmation of the deal.

The Los Angeles Office, by letter dated 3/22/60, advised that a criminal informant indicated that the editors of Confidential Magazine have had a reporter in the Los Angeles area during the past few days for the purpose of checking into a rumor regarding an alleged indiscreet party recently held at Palm Springs in which participants were said to be Senator John Kennedy, his brother-in-law Peter Lawford, the actor, and Frank Sinatra. The informant said that the last time Senator Kennedy was in California for a visit he stayed in Sinatra's home in Palm Springs. He advised that Sinatra and Lawford are the owners of Puccini's Restaurant in Beverly Hills, California.

The informant also advised that Confidential Magazine was attempting to obtain private investigators to verify or disprove the rumors concerning the party. The Los Angeles Office has no verification or other information concerning this matter. The informant, however, is in a position to know of investigative activities conducted by Confidential Magazine.

* * *

An editorial appearing in the March 23, 1960 edition of the Los Angeles Herald and Express severely criticized Sinatra for hiring Albert Maltz and, among other things, pointed out "the impact of Mr. Sinatra's move may also cause dismay in the campaign camp of Senator John F. Kennedy, through no fault of his own. Mr. Sinatra has put himself forward as a strong Kennedy supporter and the Sinatra recording of 'High Hopes' is the Kennedy campaign song."

A UPI news release dated 3/26/60 stated that Frank Sinatra charged yesterday his critics were hitting below the belt by linking presidential hopeful Senator John Kennedy with Sinatra's hiring of Albert Maltz. Sinatra said, "I make movies. I do not ask the advice of Senator Kennedy on whom I should hire. Senator Kennedy does not ask me how he should vote in the Senate."

A UPI news release of 3/25/60 stated that Robert T. O'Leary, National Commander of the Catholic War Veterans, said his organization planned to boycott the movie "The Execution of Private Slovik," if accused communist leader Maltz wrote the screen play.

There has been widespread criticism of Sinatra by the news media and other sources for his hiring of Albert Maltz.

Attached are brief résumés of communist party connections of Maltz and Sinatra.

FRANK SINATRA

Frank Sinatra has been affiliated with or lent his name and prestige to the following organizations:

> Young Communist League
> American Youth for Democracy
> World Youth Council
> Action Committee to Free Spain Now
> Veterans of Abraham Lincoln Brigade

American Committee for Yugoslav Relief
American Committee for Spanish Freedom
American Crusade to End Lynching
American Society for Cultural Relations With Italy, Inc.
Committee for Democratic Far Eastern Policy
Free Italy Society
Independent Citizens Committee of the Arts, Sciences
    and Professions
International Workers Order
Joint Anti-Fascist Refugee Committee
Mobilization for Democracy
"New Masses"
Southern Conference for Human Welfare
Committee for the First Amendment

ALBERT MALTZ

Maltz is self-employed writer from residence which is Calle S.
Yarto 14, San Angel Inn, Mexico City, D.F. He has resided in Mexico
since 1951 and has been prominent member and leader of
American-Communist group in Mexico. Considered leader of group
in 1959. During summer of 1959, subject and wife toured several
satellite countries in Europe and Russia. He is member of Writers
Union in Moscow. He and wife were disillusioned in results of Soviet
domination of Russia and Soviet occupation of satellite countries
because of anti-Semitism and living conditions. He translated book
on the Rosenberg case by John Wesley into Spanish.

Affiliated with 34 cited organizations. Active since 1951, Board
of Directors, National Council of Arts, Sciences and Professions.
1946-1949-1951 listed as sponsor of Joint Anti-Fascist Refugee
Committee and Los Angeles Chapter of Civil Rights Congress in
1947. From 1951–1954 contributed to . . . Council of African
Affairs, American Peace Crusade, Jefferson School of Social
Science, Civil Rights Congress, American Committee for Protection
of Foreign Born, Veterans of Abraham Lincoln Brigade, Hollywood
Arts, Sciences and Professions Council, Independent Production

Corporation, Daily Worker and Daily People's World, contributed to Committee to Honor Memory of Israel Amter, contributed to Powell-Schuman Defense Fund. In 1950, he was fined $1,000 and sentenced to serve one year in Federal prison, Mill Point, West Virginia (began serving 6-29-50; released 4-2-51).

In February, 1960, Maltz advised an individual that moves by Stanley Kramer and Otto Preminger to bring "progressive" screen writers back into movie industry under their true names is developing into a full-scale conflict with the American Legion. Maltz said he had just received a telephone call from Frank Sinatra in Hollywood offering him the contract for writing a screen play for Sinatra and that it appeared the time had come for the "Hollywood 10" and fellow writers who sympathized with them to make an all-out stand to re-establish themselves in the movie industry. Maltz [said] he intended to return to Hollywood as soon as the current screen writers' [conflict] has been settled.

The bureau's curiosity aroused over Sinatra's links to Kennedy, one of Hoover's closest associates, Tolson, asked for a summary report on the FBI's Sinatra files. It was delivered to Alan Belmont (who later led the FBI's probe of President Kennedy's assassination).

TO: Mr. A. H. Belmont   DATE: March 30, 1960
FROM: Mr. G. H. Scatterday
SUBJECT: FRANCIS ALBERT SINATRA
         ALSO KNOWN AS FRANK SINATRA

The following memorandum is submitted pursuant to Mr. Tolson's request 3-29-60 for a summary of information contained in Bureau files concerning Frank Sinatra.

The attached memorandum, captioned as above, from Mr. M. A. Jones to Mr. Nichols dated 1-23-57, reveals information contained in Bureau files concerning Sinatra and is summarized as follows:

Sinatra was born 12-12-15 or 12-12-16 at Hoboken, New Jersey, and began his singing career in 1933. He has been married and divorced twice, the second marriage to actress Ava Gardner in 1951 ended in approximately two years.

In February, 1944, the FBI made limited inquiries concerning Sinatra's Selective Service status as a result of an anonymous complaint which alleged he had paid $40,000 to obtain a deferment. Inquiries revealed Sinatra's rejection was in conformance with Selective Service regulations. In 1955 Sinatra was investigated by the FBI relative to possible false statements in a passport application with regard to membership in subversive organizations. Investigation developed no evidence of Communist Party (CP) or front organization membership other than 1946 membership in the Independent Citizens Committee of the Arts, Sciences and Professions, which organization was cited by the California Committee on Un-American Activities as a communist front.

Information was received during the 1940's and 1950's which linked Sinatra's name as an associate of well-known hoodlums, including Joseph and Rocco Fischetti, members of the Capone gang; Willie Moretti, former underworld boss of Bergen County, New Jersey; and James Tarantino, an associate of Benjamin "Bugsy" Siegel. Identification Division records reveal Sinatra was arrested November, 1938, and charged with seduction; this charge was later changed to adultery and dismissed after a Grand Jury returned a no true bill.

In September, 1950, Sinatra offered his services to the FBI and the Director noted agreement with Mr. Tolson's comment that we "want nothing to do with him."

In addition to the foregoing contained in the above-mentioned memorandum, Bureau files reveal the following concerning Sinatra:

In July, 1959, it was reported Sinatra and singer Dean Martin flew to Miami, Florida, from the west coast to attend the wedding of the daughter of Chicago hoodlum, Samuel M. Giancana. In November, 1959, an informant advised Giancana had taken over a theatrical booking and managing agency, and that Sinatra (a close associate) was among the clientele of this agency.

A news release dated 9-23-59 revealed Sinatra was to be the

master of ceremonies on the occasion of Nikita Khrushchev's visit to a motion picture soundstage in Hollywood, California, to observe movie making.

On 3-22-60 an informant advised that "Confidential" magazine was investigating rumors concerning an indiscreet party held in Palm Springs, California, which was allegedly attended by Senator John Kennedy of Massachusetts, Kennedy's brother-in-law and business partner of Sinatra, Peter Lawford, and Sinatra. It was reported that on his last visit to California, Senator Kennedy stayed at Sinatra's home in Palm Springs.

On 3-22-60 a confidential source advised Sinatra's film production company had contracted to hire Albert Maltz, a security index subject and one of the "Hollywood Ten," who was convicted of contempt of Congress, to write the film script for "The Execution of Private Slovik." This story concerns the only American soldier in either World War who was executed for desertion. There was considerable newspaper publicity which criticized Sinatra's contract with Maltz, and pointed out this may cause dismay to the Presidential campaign camp of Senator Kennedy in view of Sinatra's announced intention to support and assist in Senator Kennedy's Presidential campaign. A newspaper account also reported that Sinatra had considered keeping the news of hiring Maltz a secret until after the Democratic National Convention in July, for fear it might jeopardize the political hopes of Senator Kennedy. A newspaper account reported that Senator Kennedy had "no comment" concerning Sinatra's having hired Albert Maltz.

On 3-23-60 it was reported that strict speculation by persons around Warner Brothers Studio revealed Sinatra did not have enough brains to know whether Albert Maltz is a good, bad or indifferent writer. It was further speculated that someone, possibly Lewis Milestone, who was in the past at least very close to the CP, may have influenced Sinatra to tie up with Maltz; that someone is or may be trying to promote Sinatra, Sammy Davis, Jr., the Negro star, and their crowd as "fair-haired boys" known to Senator Kennedy in case the Senator gets to the White House. It was further speculated that Sinatra may, through Peter Lawford and Lawford's wife, have been able to get Senator Kennedy to take a financial interest in Sinatra's film producing enterprise.

ACTION:
  None. For Mr. Tolson's information.

As the Slovik affair continued to create controversy, top FBI officials monitored the resulting bad press for Sinatra with seeming approval.

April 3, 1960

MR. MOHR:

COMMUNISTS IN HOLLYWOOD
  Jim O'Neil, Publisher of The American Legion Magazine, handed me the attached dummy proof concerning the hiring by Frank Sinatra of Albert Maltz, the communist in Hollywood, California. This is a very hard-hitting article regarding the entree of communists once again on the scene in Hollywood. The article will appear in the May 1, 1960, issue of The American Legion Magazine which will be disseminated to four million members throughout the United States.
  The Domestic Intelligence Division may desire to see the attached article.

RESPECTFULLY,

C. D. DE LOACH

Widespread public dismay at Sinatra's deal with Maltz spooked the Kennedy campaign. The family patriarch, Joseph Kennedy, reportedly told Sinatra, "It's either Maltz or us." So Sinatra fired the writer but paid him in full, $75,000.
  Meanwhile, Hoover continued to receive increasingly salacious reports

about Sinatra and Kennedy. This one came from the special agent in charge of Los Angeles, relaying information provided by a confidential information (CI) in that city, identified only as LA 4222-C.

4/1/60

AIR MAIL

TO: DIRECTOR, FBI
FROM: SAC, LOS ANGELES
RE: CRIMDEL—CRS

CONFIDENTIALLY

On 3/22/60 LA 4222-C provided information that he had picked up from a representative of "Confidential" magazine (Crimdel 3/22/60). The rumor being checked by the magazine concerned Senator JOHN KENNEDY, actor PETER LAWFORD and actor FRANK SINATRA, who were said to have been involved in some sort of indiscreet party.

Yesterday this CI, a notorious private investigator who has in the past performed investigations for "Confidential," added some details. He said he had declined an offer to do the investigating on this matter. Nevertheless, he was recently in Las Vegas and did pick up some amplification tending to verify the information "Confidential" magazine already has in affidavits, allegedly from two mulatto prostitutes in New York.

At Las Vegas LA 4222-C participated in a conversation with Senator KENNEDY's campaign manager, whose name the CI does not recall, ROCKY MARCIANO and BELDEN KATELMAN.

The campaign manager bewailed KENNEDY's association with SINATRA, stating something to the effect that the Senator is vulnerable to bad publicity only because of his associations with SINATRA. This worried man, according to CI, added that there are certain sex activities by KENNEDY that he hopes never are publicized. CI said he learned that these parties involving the Senator and SINATRA occurred in Palm Springs, Las Vegas and New York City.

BELDEN KATELMAN, prominent Las Vegas investor, made the point that KENNEDY had stayed at the Sands with SINATRA while in Las Vegas. KATELMAN said it is a known fact the Sands is owned by hoodlums and that while the Senator, SINATRA and LAWFORD were there, show girls from all over town were running in and out of the Senator's suite.

Sinatra and the Rat Pack, including Sammy Davis, Jr., Dean Martin, and Peter Lawford, sang "The Star-Spangled Banner" at that summer's Democratic National Convention in Los Angeles. On the day Kennedy secured the Democratic presidential nomination, DeLoach, Hoover's lieutenant, received an extraordinarily detailed memo on the senator—the good and bad, including the FBI's close relationship with the Kennedy family, the seamier side of JFK's friendship with Sinatra, and the mob's interest in his candidacy.

TO: Mr. DeLoach   DATE: 7-13-60
FROM: M. A. Jones
SUBJECT: SENATOR JOHN F. KENNEDY
                OF MASSACHUSETTS

SYNOPSIS:
    This memorandum prepared to briefly summarize high lights of pertinent available data concerning Kennedy in view of strong possibility he will be Democratic candidate for President.* Bureau and Director have enjoyed friendly relations with Senator Kennedy and his family for number of years. Kennedy's father, Joseph P. Kennedy, former Ambassador to Great Britain, is SAC contact of Boston. Director sent autographed copy of "The FBI Story" and "Masters of Deceit" to Joseph Kennedy, John Kennedy and Robert Kennedy.
    Kennedy family is known to SA David J. Murphy, Jr., of Washington Field Office and SA William H. Carpenter, Resident Agent at Hyannis, Massachusetts, as well as SAC's at Boston. SA Carpenter attended Senator Kennedy's wedding in 1953. Director

has seen Robert Kennedy several times in recent years—particularly in connection with McClellan Committee (labor-management) matters.

Director and Senator Kennedy have exchanged friendly correspondence concerning such matters as operation performed on Senator Kennedy in 1954 to correct crippling effects of World War II PT boat crash; awarding of Cardinal Gibbons Medal to Senator Kennedy in 1956; and re-election of Kennedy to Senate in 1958.

Robert Kennedy has advocated establishment of Federal Crime Commission, and Senator Kennedy has expressed opposition to loyalty oaths for students getting Federal scholarship loans. Senator Kennedy was cosponsor of bill designed to deal with hate bombings. Allegations have been received concerning immoral conduct on the part of Kennedy and hoodlum connections of Kennedy.

RECOMMENDATION:
   None. For information.
   *Subsequently nominated on first ballot.

DETAILS
   The purpose of this memorandum is to briefly summarize high lights of pertinent available information concerning Senator John F. Kennedy and his favorable attitude toward the Bureau in connection with the strong probability that he will be nominated as the Democrat candidate for the Presidency.

*   *   *

FRIENDLY RELATIONS WITH BUREAU:
   The Bureau and the Director have enjoyed friendly relations with Senator Kennedy and his family for a number of years. The Senator's father, Joseph Patrick Kennedy, is an SAC contact of the Boston Office. He has expressed deep admiration for the Director. Joseph Kennedy is an outstanding financier and industrialist. Known to the Director as "Dear Joe," he was U.S. Ambassador to Great Britain at the time World War II broke out. In June, 1939, the "Foreign Observer" quoted remarks from a London publication which stated

that the British were bewildered as to why Ambassador Kennedy was allowed to remain in his post considering his record as an appeaser and apologist for Chamberlain.

In 1957, the Director sent autographed copies of "The FBI Story" to Joseph Kennedy, John Kennedy and Robert Kennedy. In 1958, the Director sent autographed copies of "Masters of Deceit" to these three prominent members of the Kennedy family.

In January, 1953, SA David J. Murphy, Jr. (Washington Field Office, now in GS-13), called Mr. Holloman in the Director's Office and advised that he was a personal friend of Senator Kennedy; that the Senator had expressed to him (Murphy) a desire to tour the Bureau and meet the Director later in January. Mr. Holloman telephoned Senator Kennedy's Administrative Assistant whom Holloman had known for some time. Holloman mentioned the matter of Kennedy's visiting the Bureau, and Reardon said that as soon as things quieted down on the Hill, he and Kennedy would come over for a tour.

In September, 1953, SA William H. Carpenter (Resident Agent at Hyannis, Massachusetts, now in GS-13) attended the wedding of Senator Kennedy and the wedding reception. SA Carpenter is well-known to the Kennedy family. SA Carpenter stated that Senator Kennedy was very complimentary of the Director and the Bureau and stated he was anxious and willing at all times to support Mr. Hoover and the FBI. This statement was made to SA Carpenter in the presence of Senators Saltonstall, Green and Smathers, as well as the Reverend John Cavanaugh of Notre Dame and Joseph Kennedy.

In October, 1953, SAC James Kelly (then at Boston, currently at Baltimore) met Senator Kennedy at Joseph Kennedy's home. According to SAC Kelly, the Senator said he felt the FBI to be the only real Government agency worthy of its salt and expressed admiration for the Director's accomplishments. He said that upon returning to Washington in January, 1954, he would enjoy meeting the Director at the Bureau. The Director wrote Senator Kennedy about the remarks he made to SAC Kelly and told him to visit the Bureau any time it was convenient.

In the Fall of 1954, Senator Kennedy underwent a painful

operation to correct the crippling effects of the PT boat crash he had been involved in during World War II. In November, 1954, the Director wrote both Joseph Kennedy and Senator Kennedy to wish the Senator speedy and complete recovery.

In October, 1956, the Director wrote Senator Kennedy to congratulate him upon his being selected to receive the Cardinal Gibbons Medal for 1956. (The Director also has received this Medal, presented by the Catholic University Alumni Association.)

In November, 1958, the Director wrote John Kennedy to congratulate him upon his re-election to the Senate, and Senator Kennedy sent the Director a friendly reply stating "if I or my office can be of any help to you, do not hesitate to call upon me."

With regard to Senator Kennedy's staff members, it is noted that at the suggestion of Joseph Kennedy, the Director sent a copy of "Communist Illusion and Democratic Reality" to the Senator's Legislative Assistant, Theodore Sorensen, in November, 1959.

In July, 1959, Uniform Crime Reports material and other data containing crime statistics were sent Pierre Salinger, Assistant Chief Investigator for the McClellan (Labor-Management) Committee, following receipt of a call from Salinger advising that Senator Kennedy desired FBI data concerning crime—possibly for use in speeches.

Kenneth O'Donnell (who managed Kennedy's last Senatorial campaign, was Administrative Assistant of the McClellan Committee on labor-management racketeering, and is very close to Senator Kennedy and his brother Robert Kennedy) is well-known to Inspector Courtney Evans of the Investigative Division. In March, 1959, O'Donnell spoke to Inspector Evans regarding Senator Kennedy's suspicion that there might be a tap on one of his telephones. O'Donnell inquired whether it would be possible for the FBI to check Kennedy's phones; however, within a matter of minutes, he again called Inspector Evans to request that the Bureau forget the entire matter since he, O'Donnell, could make arrangements to handle the matter himself. Additionally, in March, 1959, O'Donnell discussed with Inspector Evans the publicity being given remarks made by Robert Kennedy concerning alleged offers of political support for Senator John Kennedy if Robert Kennedy would "go easy" on certain witnesses before the McClellan Committee. O'Donnell advised that Robert Kennedy stated the press had unduly enlarged on his remarks, and O'Donnell said he did not believe the Kennedys have the facts necessary to back up Robert Kennedy's reported statements.

Kenneth O'Donnell also advised Inspector Evans in March, 1959, that he had been informed that Cardinal Cushing was extremely displeased at the reaction of some Catholic Church publications to statements made by Senator Kennedy regarding the separation of church and state. O'Donnell said that Senator Kennedy's position that no public tax money should be used for parochial schools was the position of the Church and that Cardinal Cushing felt the critical remarks of the Church publications regarding Kennedy's statements were unwarranted.

John Kennedy is acquainted with former SA J. Philip O'Brien, whose resignation ███████████████ was accepted at Oklahoma City in May, 1960, following ███████████████ In this regard, O'Brien wrote the Director in June, 1960, to request reinstatement and/or acceptance of his resignation without ███████████████ In his letter to the Director, O'Brien stated that Senator Kennedy had written him (O'Brien) as recently as 11-2-59 to state, "Dear Phil . . . I am certainly glad to hear that you are doing so well in Oklahoma. . . ."

ROBERT KENNEDY: ADVOCATE OF FEDERAL CRIME COMMISSION:

Robert Kennedy, the Senator's 34-year-old brother, has seen the Director on a number of occasions in recent years. In September, 1959, he called upon the Director to advise that he was resigning as Chief Counsel of the McClellan Committee and to express appreciation for the excellent cooperation which the Bureau had extended him. He specifically mentioned the help of Inspector Courtney Evans. The Director addresses him as "Dear Bob."

Early this year, Robert Kennedy published a book, "The Enemy

Within," dealing with graft, corruption and criminal influences in the labor movement—particularly James Hoffa's Teamsters Union. In this book, Kennedy makes special mention of the advice and assistance given him by the Director.

Although he has displayed a very friendly attitude toward the Bureau, Robert Kennedy has been an outspoken advocate of the establishment of a Federal Crime Commission. He has stated, "In my opinion our first and most urgent need is for a national crime commission. This commission would serve as a central intelligence agency, a clearinghouse to which each of the seventy-odd Federal agencies and the more than ten thousand local law enforcement agencies throughout the country would constantly feed information on the leading gangsters. The commission would pool and correlate all its information on underworld figures and disseminate it to the proper authorities."

WEST VIRGINIA PRIMARY ELECTIONS:

In connection with the recent hotly contested primary elections in West Virginia, several charges of improper actions were made to the Bureau, including allegations that votes were bought, that a polling place in Logan County was moved to prevent qualified West Virginians from voting, and that voting officials in Logan County pulled voting machine levers for local citizens. With regard to Senator Kennedy's religion, improperly labeled anti-Catholic literature was distributed by a nonexistent organization called the "Protestant Information Center."

POLITICAL VIEWS:

In a syndicated column datelined Washington, D. C., 1-14-57, Fulton Lewis, Jr., described Kennedy as "conscientious and sincere" in his Senate duties and stated, "Kennedy tempers his political liberalism with enough realistic conservatism that the Walter Reuther–Americans for Democratic Action leftists mistrust his independence. That was the real reason they threw the No. 2 (Vice

Presidential) nomination to Kefauver in Chicago (at the Democratic National Convention) last August."

*   *   *

The 3-11-59 issue of "Human Events" made reference to the "wrist-slapping labor-reform bill" which Senator Kennedy had placed before the Senate. "Human Events" stated that Kennedy claimed the bill would "virtually put (James) Hoffa and his associates out of business"; whereas Utah Senator Wallace Bennett exposed the falseness of this assertion. Senator Bennett stated that far from putting Hoffa out of business, the Kennedy bill "would fall far short of correcting the evils brought out by the McClellan committee." . . .

With regard to subversive matters, it is interesting to note that in March, 1960, Governor Wesley Powell of New Hampshire (a staunch Nixon supporter) accused Senator Kennedy of "softness toward communism." Kennedy called upon the Vice President to repudiate Powell's accusation, and Nixon's press representative issued a statement in Washington saying "the Vice President has known and worked with Senator Kennedy since they served together on the House Labor Committee in 1947. While they have differences on some issues, they have always been in complete agreement in their unalterable opposition to communism at home and abroad."

*   *   *

MISCELLANEOUS:

As you are aware, allegations of immoral activities on Senator Kennedy's part have been reported to the FBI over the years. These allegations are not being treated in detail in this memorandum. They include, however, data reflecting that Kennedy carried on an illicit relationship with another man's wife during World War II; that (probably in January, 1960) Kennedy was "compromised" with a woman in Las Vegas; and that Kennedy and Frank Sinatra have in the recent past been involved in parties in Palm Springs, Las Vegas and New York City. Regarding the Kennedy-Sinatra information,

"Confidential" magazine is said to have affidavits from two mulatto prostitutes in New York.

Allegations also have been received concerning hoodlum connections of Senator Kennedy. Again, in the interest of brevity, no effort is being made to list these allegations in full detail—much of the information being unsubstantiated. In March, 1960, for example, it was reported that Frank Sinatra has purposely cultivated Kennedy's brother-in-law (actor Peter Lawford) and that Sinatra would assist in Kennedy's campaign so that Joe Fischetti and other notorious hoodlums could have an entre to the Senator.

Regarding Kennedy's book, "Profiles in Courage," George Sokolsky advised L. B. Nichols in May, 1957, of a rumor circulating in New York to the effect that Arthur Krock actually wrote the book. According to Sokolsky, a group of New York people were attempting to verify whether Krock did, in fact, write the book—and if Krock did, they were going to charge fraud in connection with the awarding of a Pulitzer Prize to Kennedy.

Though the previous memo mentions questions about the integrity of Kennedy's crucial breakthrough victory in the West Virginia primary, books by biographer Kitty Kelley and Sinatra's daughter Nancy tell a fuller story.

Kelley's biography reported that Sinatra's pals, Chicago boss Giancana and associate Paul "Skinny" D'Amato, exerted influence on local political machines in the state to deliver votes for Kennedy. Nancy Sinatra's book said Joseph Kennedy himself suggested to Sinatra that he enlist Giancana's help, though she contends her father made sure his friend knew that his assistance was "not a quid pro quo" with the future president. Seymour Hersh's The Dark Side of Camelot alleges that Giancana also helped deliver Chicago votes to secure Illinois in the general election.

Giancana's motives were transparent: In 1957, Hoover had begun a "Top Hoodlum Program" that targeted, among many others, Giancana and his Chicago operation. He desperately wanted to get the FBI off his back. His agreement to help was all the more remarkable in that Jack Kennedy had served on Senator John McClellan's rackets committee, which relentlessly investigated the mob for years. Robert Kennedy served as the panel's chief counsel—and publicly ridiculed Giancana when he invoked the Fifth Amendment to avoid testifying.

At some point, Hoover became aware of dealings between Joseph Kennedy and the mob, as evidenced by this entry in a June 8, 1964, summary of information in Sinatra's FBI files. The information came from a source whose name the FBI redacted. A visit by Giancana to the hotel mentioned here would later cause Sinatra considerable difficulty.

██ advised that he had heard from numerous sources that prior to the last presidential election, Joseph Kennedy (father of John F. Kennedy) had been visited by many gangsters (not identified) who had gambling interests. A deal was made which resulted in Peter Lawford, Frank Sinatra, Dean Martin and others obtaining a lucrative gambling establishment, the Cal-Neva Hotel, at Lake Tahoe, California. Joseph Kennedy was staying at the Cal-Neva at the time of the meeting.

Two weeks after the Democratic convention, DeLoach got more sex tidbits on Kennedy and Sinatra.

TO: Mr. DeLoach   DATE: 7-26-60
FROM: M. A. Jones
SUBJECT: POTENTIAL CRIMINAL INFORMANT (PCI)
                ████████████████ HOLLYWOOD, CALIF., CALL
                GIRL

The captioned individual is a high-priced Hollywood call girl and ████████████████ of Fred Otash, private detective in Los Angeles who has been convicted of horse race fixing. She advised Agents of our Los Angeles Office on July 11, 1960, that Otash contacted her on 7-10-60 requesting information relating to her participation in sex parties involving Senator John Kennedy, his brother-in-law, movie actor Peter Lawford, Frank Sinatra and Sammy Davis, Jr. ████████████████ said she told Otash she had no knowledge of such activities involving these men. He then asked her to name any girls who might have been present at parties with these men. She told the Agents that she was unaware of any indiscretions or girls involved with the four men specified by Otash.

On July 11, 1960, Los Angeles Agents had occasion to talk to Otash in his office. During the conversation he inadvertently—or his actions indicated inadvertence—[indicated] that some operator, unnamed and unidentified, was attempting to spy on Senator Kennedy's hotel room. He inferred to the Agents that "Confidential" magazine is "looking for dirt on Kennedy or Lawford" for use in a series of articles planned for publication before the November election.

In the evening of 7-11-60 ███████████████ told Agents that Otash had telephoned her wanting to know if she could arrange to be introduced to Senator Kennedy. He suggested that he would like to equip her with a recording device for taking down any "indiscreet statements" the Senator might make. She said she refused this suggestion and invitation.

RECOMMENDATION:
For information.

Later, the FBI overheard a bugged subject (identified only as Eddy M.) discussing Sinatra and Kennedy's sexual exploits while complaining that agents had questioned an associate's wife about her husband's caddish ways. (This 1962 transcript, edited here for clarity, was obtained from the National Archives, not the FBI files released in 1998.)

EDDY M: What is this, Russia? You know what they did? They went over to Gil Beckley's and said to his wife, "Do you know that Gil is living with a girl in NYC?"

Why don't they come in and say this to me? I'll say, "One minute, I'll call up the newspaper, see, and I'll say, 'Now, here's an FBI man who said I'd been sleeping with a girl. Since when is [having sexual intercourse] a federal offense? And if it is a federal offense, I want the president of the U.S. indicted, because I know he was whacking all those broads Sinatra brought him. And I can mention some names. And do you want me to mention some names? You know, this will really kill him. Is that a federal offense? And if it is, I want to get it straightened out.' "

What I'm going to say is, "Say, well, one minute, let's put this down on record. I want it down that [sexual intercourse] is a federal offense, and I want to see what the president has to say about that, because I know he's been [having sexual relations] with [a woman] in Palm Beach. And I know a couple of other girls that Frank Sinatra flew out there, flew from California to Palm Beach, and I can prove it. Now, let's—why don't we investigate it." [Laughter]

You know what will happen? They'll run, they'll hide, they'll get with their heads down under the rocks. All I'll say is, "Let me have your card, I want to talk to your boss. I don't want to answer this question. Just let me have your card." That's all a girl has to say: "A crime? Let me have your card," because they're Boy Scouts.

After Kennedy won the presidency in November 1960, he asked Sinatra to take control of the festivities surrounding the January 20, 1961, inauguration. America's very own Camelot had begun, and Sinatra was leading the orchestra.

A pair of FBI memos suggests that the inauguration wasn't the only thing that kept Sinatra busy that week. The first, between top FBI officials Alex Rosen and Alan Belmont, recounted an incident two days before the inauguration. (Note that the price of such services hadn't increased markedly since Sinatra's encounter with the too-drunk hundred-dollar prostitute in 1947, an incident recounted by Rosen in an earlier memo, in chapter 3.)

TO: MR. BELMONT   DATE: October 23, 1961
FROM: A. ROSEN
SUBJECT: WHITE SLAVE TRAFFIC ACT

PURPOSE

This memorandum is to advise you concerning an investigation by the Washington Field Office concerning possible violations of the White Slave Traffic Act and involving several prominent individuals

as customers, who may possibly be called upon to testify before the
Federal Grand Jury in the near future.

SUMMARY OF FACTS

This case involves ███████████████████████ The activities of
███████████████ have been primarily concerned with sex parties,
which involve commission of various natural and unnatural sex acts
simultaneously by three or more participants, both male and female.
Several female victims have furnished signed statements admitting
their participation in these orgies. Other victims have involved
████████████████ as individuals who arranged numerous prostitution
dates for them.

CONTEMPLATED PROSECUTION

The Assistant U. S. Attorney handling this case has advised that
he plans to present the facts to the Federal Grand Jury, possibly in
early November, 1961. He requested interviews of several customers
of the victims to obtain necessary corroborating testimony of
victims' statements and he has indicated a possibility that these
individuals may be subpoenaed before the Federal Grand Jury. The
Assistant U. S. Attorney pointed out that travel within the District
of Columbia constitutes a violation of the White Slave Traffic Act
and it is possible that the male customers have committed a
technical violation of the law. Conceivably they could be indicted by
the Federal Grand Jury, but this action is not contemplated.

PROMINENT PERSONS INVOLVED

████████████████ an employee in the office of ███████████████
and a victim in this case, has furnished a signed statement setting
forth her prostitution activities, which include sex parties with
subject ████████████████ and on separate occasions with
████████████████ An interview with ████████████████ is not
contemplated.

*   *   *

███████████████████████████████████████

One prostitute has admitted several prostitution dates with
███████████████ the dates having been arranged through subject
███████████████ In connection with a separate investigation
concerning James Riddle Hoffa, it has been learned that
███████████████ has contacted Hoffa on several occasions to obtain
loans granted by the Teamsters Pension Fund.

FRANK SINATRA

Well-known entertainer was a guest at the Statler Hotel on the
night of 1-18-61. ███████████████ one of the victims in this case,
has stated that she went to the Statler Hotel after receiving a
telephone call from ███████████████ and she filled a prostitution
date with Sinatra, receiving $110 for her services.

███████████████ will be interviewed at the request of the
Assistant U. S. Attorney, but he (Assistant U. S. Attorney) has
stated that interview with Frank Sinatra is not necessary.

The following customers have been interviewed and orally
substantiated allegations by victims to the effect that victims filled
prostitution dates with them after arrangements for the dates had
been made by the subject ███████████████

1. ███████████████
2. ███████████████
3. ███████████████
4. ███████████████
5. ███████████████

In connection with the above individuals, the prostitution dates
with them included only the victim and the customer.
███████████████ is the only customer who allegedly participated in
the sex orgies of three or more persons previously referred to.

ACTION

The prosecutive action in this case will be closely followed.

Three weeks after the inauguration, Hoover caught wind of another in-
cident involving Sinatra's visit to Washington that week. This time, he used
the incident to inform the president's brother and new attorney general,
Robert F. Kennedy, in a "personal" note that his brother the president was
hanging out with an "associate of well-known hoodlums" who also had ties
to "communist fronts." Hoover, always on the lookout for any advantage to
make himself hard to fire, wasn't one for subtlety.

TO: The Attorney General   DATE: February 10, 1961
FROM: Director, FBI   PERSONAL
SUBJECT: FRANK SINATRA

I thought you would like to know that recently a highly
confidential source in Washington, D.C., stated that Frank Sinatra is
regarded as having control of the entertainment industry in Las
Vegas, Nevada. The source indicated that when someone in Las
Vegas desires entertainment, arrangements must be made through
Sinatra who negotiates for this entertainment to his financial
benefit.

A confidential informant of our Washington Field Office has
advised that on the weekend of January 21, 1961, the Spartan
American Club, 1016-A 14th Street, Northwest, Washington, D.C.,
was visited by Frank Sinatra and George Raft. The Spartan
American Club is operated by Joseph Nesline, a notorious
Washington, D.C., gambling figure.

The informant advised that while at the club, both Sinatra and
Raft lost heavily at the crap table. Raft was heard to say that he had
never seen a larger crap game outside of Las Vegas or Reno, Nevada.

There is enclosed additional information concerning Frank
Sinatra which may be of interest to you.

Enclosure

February 10, 1961

FRANK SINATRA

Sinatra was born December 12, 1915, or December 12, 1916, at Hoboken, New Jersey, and began his singing career in 1935. He has been married and divorced twice, the second marriage to actress Ava Gardner in 1951 ended in approximately two years.

In February, 1944, on the basis of an anonymous complaint alleging he had paid $40,000 to obtain a deferment, the FBI made inquiries concerning Sinatra's Selective Service status. These inquiries revealed that Sinatra's rejection for military service was in conformance with Selective Service regulations.

In 1955, the Bureau conducted investigation relative to possible false statements reportedly made by Sinatra in a passport application with regard to membership in subversive organizations. This investigation developed no evidence of Communist Party or front organization membership other than 1946 membership in the Independent Citizens Committee of the Arts, Sciences and Professions, which organization was cited by the California Committee on Un-American Activities as a communist front.

Information available reflects that Sinatra has reportedly been associated with or lent his name to sixteen organizations which have been cited or described as communist fronts.

Information was received during the 1940's and 1950's which linked Sinatra's name as an associate of well-known hoodlums, including Joseph and Rocco Fischetti, members of the Capone Gang; Willie Moretti, former underworld boss of Bergen County, New Jersey; and James Tarantino, an associate of Benjamin "Bugsy" Siegel.

A confidential source advised in June, 1958, that during the first part of that year when Sinatra was appearing at the Sands Hotel in Las Vegas, Nevada, Sinatra was with Samuel M. Giancana, described as a notorious Chicago hoodlum, and accompanied him to the El Rancho Vegas, which is located in Las Vegas.

During a search of Giancana by Customs officers in Chicago,

Illinois, during June, 1958, the notation "Sinatra, Office 5-4977, Home Crestview 4-2368" was found among his effects. Crestview 4-2368 is the private number for Frank Sinatra in Los Angeles, California.

A confidential source advised in August, 1958, that Joseph Fischetti, Frank Sinatra and Dean Martin were driven from the Ambassador East Hotel to the residence of Anthony Accardo, referred to as a notorious Chicago hoodlum, in River Forest, Illinois. At the Accardo residence, Martin and Sinatra gave a "command performance" for numerous Chicago hoodlums.

Based on information from a confidential informant that notorious hoodlums Vito Genovese, Thomas Lucchese and Samuel Giancana were at Atlantic City, New Jersey, as guests of Frank Sinatra, investigation was conducted in that city. It was ascertained that the Sinatra party rented the entire first floor of the Claridge Hotel in Atlantic City from July 25, 1959, to August 2, 1959. The presence of Genovese and Lucchese was not ascertainable but a hotel employee identified the photograph of Samuel Giancana as being in the hotel on several occasions as a visitor in connection with the Sinatra party. Notorious Chicago hoodlum Joseph Fischetti was also identified as being with Sinatra at the Claridge Hotel.

In July, 1959, it was reported Sinatra and singer Dean Martin flew to Miami, Florida, from the west coast to attend the wedding of the daughter of Chicago hoodlum Samuel M. Giancana. In November, 1959, an informant advised Giancana had taken over a theatrical booking and managing agency and that Sinatra was among the clientele of this agency.

███████████████ advised during September, 1959, that in ███████████████ she went to Frank Sinatra's suite at the Hotel Fontainebleau, Miami Beach, Florida, in connection with efforts to sell him a painting. She said that among those present in the Sinatra suite was Joseph Fischetti and added that she assumed that it was common knowledge Fischetti and Frank Sinatra were close friends and that Sinatra had the "hoodlum complex."

███████████████ advised in January, 1960, that he had known

Mickey Cohen, Los Angeles, California, hoodlum figure, for several years and had met Frank Sinatra through Cohen.

In March, 1960, a confidential source reported that Sinatra's company had contracted to hire Albert Maltz, one of the "Hollywood Ten," who was convicted of Contempt of Congress, to write the film script for the movie "The Execution of Private Slovik."

Files of the Identification Division of the FBI reveal that Frank Albert Sinatra, born December 12, 1915, or December 12, 1916, Hoboken, New Jersey, was arrested by the Sheriff at Hackensack, New Jersey, on November 26, 1938, and charged with seduction. This charge was dismissed on January 24, 1939.

Enclosed is a photograph which includes Sinatra which was found among the effects of James John Warjac, one of the FBI's Ten Most Wanted Fugitives, at the time he was apprehended on July 22, 1960, at Los Angeles. The photograph shows Sinatra at a gambling table dealing "blackjack" in the Sands Hotel, Las Vegas, Nevada. He is standing between Rudy Duran, a young movie actor, and Shearn Moody, Jr., a wealthy Texan, who are seated.

SIX

SINATRA, THE KENNEDYS, AND THE MOB— THE ESTRANGEMENT

"He made a donation to the campaign . . . but was not getting his money's worth."

Not surprisingly, Robert Kennedy's principal initiative as attorney general was a crackdown on mobsters. Building on Hoover's "Top Hoodlum Program," the initiative would lead to even more aggressive tactics against Sam Giancana and his Chicago syndicate. That, of course, didn't sit well with the boss and his associates, who were overheard on hidden FBI microphones bitterly complaining that Sinatra and the Kennedys had failed to show sufficient gratitude for their campaign support in West Virginia and in Illinois.

The Justice Department's war on organized crime had one significant unintended consequence—Hoover's discovery of evidence suggesting that the president was consorting with a lady friend of two of the attorney general's principal targets.

She was the same woman the New Orleans FBI office had mentioned several weeks after Jack Kennedy had met her in 1960, as recounted early in chapter 5. Frank Sinatra had introduced Jack Kennedy to his former girlfriend, Judith Campbell (later Judith Exner), during a Rat Pack show at the Sands in Las Vegas on February 7, 1960. A while later, Sinatra also introduced Campbell to Giancana. She was also friendly with Johnny Roselli, Giancana's man in Hollywood and in Las Vegas.

All these players—the two alleged mobsters, the Kennedy brothers, Campbell, Sinatra, and Hoover—soon were entangled in increasingly bizarre plot lines. First, Campbell and Kennedy became lovers. Then, the CIA enlisted Giancana and Roselli to assassinate Fidel Castro. By 1962, Hoover had learned something was up between the president and Campbell and made sure the Kennedys knew what he knew.

Ever his brother's keeper, Robert Kennedy moved to limit the damage.

Hoover thought it best to keep his boss apprised of the relationship between the president's friend Sinatra and Giancana. Hoover sent this memo to RFK two days after a hidden FBI mike picked up some hoodlums discussing how Giancana and Sinatra "almost got into a fistfight" over who was going to buy the drinks one night.

TO: The Attorney General   DATE: November 24, 1961
FROM: Director, FBI
SUBJECT: SAMUEL M. GIANCANA
          ANTI-RACKETEERING

Information was confidentially received November 23, 1961, concerning the close association between Chicago hoodlum Samuel M. Giancana and entertainers Frank Sinatra and Tony Bennett on occasions when Sinatra and Bennett visit Chicago.

During such visits, according to our information, Giancana and his associates, John Mattassa, a former Chicago Police Department Detective, and Dominic "Butch" Blasi, accompany Sinatra and Bennett on their rounds of various night clubs reported to be hangouts and possible enterprises of Giancana. On some past visits, Sinatra and Giancana have held contests to determine who could spend the most money buying drinks and trinkets for the party.

Giancana is one of the individuals selected as a target for early prosecution. Reports containing the results of our inquiries into his activities have been furnished to the Criminal Division.

On December 6, 1961, a Giancana underling named Johnny—either Roselli or Johnny Formosa—was overhead in Chicago telling his boss about a talk he'd had recently with Sinatra about trying to get the attorney general to lay off Giancana. (The transcript, obtained from the National Archives, has been edited here for clarity.)

JOHNNY: I said, "Frankie, can I ask one question?" He says, "Johnny, I took Sam's [Giancana's] name and wrote it down and told Bobby Kennedy, 'This is my buddy. This is my buddy. This is what I want you to know, Bob.' " . . . Between you and I, Frank saw Joe

Kennedy three different times. He called him three times, Joe Kennedy, the father.

* * *

GIANCANA: He better make it, because after this administration goes out, he'll have a headache.

JOHNNY: He says, "Johnny, I have to protect myself."

GIANCANA: He'll protect himself.

JOHNNY: I say he's [Kennedy's] a one-termer. He [Sinatra] says, "I got to watch myself." He says he's got an idea that you're mad at him. I says that I wouldn't know. "I must ask you this question," I said.

GIANCANA: He must have a guilty conscience. I never said nothing. . . . If he [President Kennedy] starts campaigning, I'm not giving him one penny. . . . That [expletive] better not think of taking this [expletive] state.

* * *

GIANCANA: Well, I don't know who the [expletive] he's [Sinatra's] talking to, but . . . after all, if I'm taking somebody's money, I'm gonna make sure that this money is going to do something. Like, "Do you want it or don't you want it?" If the money is accepted, maybe one of these days, the guy will do me a favor.

JOHNNY: That's right. He says he wrote your name down.

GIANCANA: Well, one minute he tells me this and then he tells me that. And then the last time I talked to him was at the hotel in Florida, a month before he left, and he said, "Don't worry about it, if I can't talk to the old man [Joe Kennedy], I'm going to talk to *the* man [President Kennedy]." One minute he says he talked to Robert, and the next minute he says he hasn't talked to him. So he never did talk to him. It's a lot of [expletive]. Either he did or he didn't. Forget about it. Why lie to me? I haven't got that coming.

* * *

JOHNNY: If he can't deliver, I want him to tell me, "John, the load's too heavy."

*   *   *

GIANCANA: When he says he's gonna do a guy a little favor, I don't give a [expletive] how long it takes, he's got to give you a little favor.

JOHNNY: He says he put your name, buddy, on—

GIANCANA: Aw, [expletive]. Out of a jillion names, he's gonna remember that name, huh?

JOHNNY: What's happened, Frank says to me, "Johnny, he ain't being bothered."

GIANCANA (pausing, taking a deep breath and then shouting): I got more [expletive] on my [expletive] than any other [expletive] in the country! Believe me when I tell you!

JOHNNY: I know it, Sam.

GIANCANA (still shouting): I was on the road with this broad, there must have been . . . twenty guys! They were next door, upstairs, downstairs, surrounded, all the way around! Get in a car, somebody picks you up. I lose that tail—boom!—I get picked up someplace else! Four or five cars . . . back and forth, back and forth!

JOHNNY: This was in Europe, right?

GIANCANA: Right here in Russia: Chicago, New York, Phoenix!

A few days later, Hoover summarized Giancana's complaint in a memo to Attorney General Robert Kennedy.

TO: The Attorney General   DATE: December 11, 1961
FROM: Director, FBI   PERSONAL
SUBJECT: GAMBLING ACTIVITIES
                LAS VEGAS, NEVADA

Information has been received that persons connected with gambling activities in Las Vegas are becoming increasingly apprehensive concerning the intensity of investigations into gambling.

In this connection, information has been received indicating that Samuel M. Giancana, a hoodlum figure, has sought to enlist Frank Sinatra to act as an intermediary to intercede on Giancana's behalf with the Attorney General. In this regard, consideration was allegedly given to making such overtures through the father of the Attorney General. However, Sinatra is reported to have rejected this idea.

Information has been received that Giancana complained bitterly concerning the intensity of investigation being conducted of his activities, and that he made a donation to the campaign of President Kennedy but was not getting his money's worth. Giancana allegedly indicated he would not donate one penny toward any future campaign.

This is being furnished for your personal information.

On December 21, 1961, Johnny Roselli analyzed Sinatra's relationship with the Kennedys in another talk with Moe Giancana—and obliquely suggested getting tough. (This transcript also was obtained from the National Archives.)

ROSELLI: He's got big ideas, Frank does, about being ambassador or something. You know, [Kennedy spokesman] Pierre Salinger and them guys, they don't want him. They treat them [sic] like they treat a whore. You [expletive] them, you pay them and then they're through. You got the right idea, Moe—go the other way: [expletive] everybody. Every [expletive], we'll use them every [expletive] way we can. They only know one way. Now let them see the other side of you.

On January 4, 1962, Giancana was still grumbling about the situation. According to this edited transcript (also from the National Archives), he and an unknown associate discussed a law limiting appeals by criminal defendants.

GIANCANA: Got a new law where we can't go back and forth to the courts. Bobby Kennedy's bright idea.

ASSOCIATE: How about his friend, and your friend, Sinatra?

GIANCANA: Aw, that [expletive]. Johnny Roselli is out there. I told John to tell him to forget about the whole thing and tell him to go [expletive]. Lying [expletive]. If I ever listen to that [expletive] again—if he [Kennedy] had lost this state here, he would have lost the election. But I figured with this guy [Sinatra], maybe we'll be all right. I might have known this guy would [expletive] me.

ASSOCIATE: Well, at the time, it looks like you done the right thing, Sam. Nobody can say different, after it's done.

GIANCANA: Well, when a [expletive] lies to you . . .

ASSOCIATE: What was his motive?

GIANCANA: Who knows.

A couple of weeks later, on the evening of January 31, 1962, Giancana discusses the matter with another associate, John D'Arco, a Democratic Chicago alderman, comparing President Kennedy at one point to somebody else who crossed him. (This edited transcript also comes from the National Archives.)

GIANCANA: He's like Kennedy: He'll get what he wants out of ya', but you won't get anything out of him.

*   *   *

D'ARCO: That [expletive] Kennedy. Is Sinatra going to work on [him]?

GIANCANA: No.

D'ARCO: I heard that the president, when he is in California, is with Sinatra all the time.

GIANCANA: He can't get change for a quarter.

D'ARCO: Sinatra can't?

GIANCANA: That's right. Well, they got the whip, and they're in office, and that's it, and they got the money behind 'em. So they're gonna knock us guys out of the box and make us defenseless. They figure if you got money, you got power; if you don't have money, you don't have power.

D'ARCO: That's probably what it is. They're trying to break you, and they don't give a [expletive] what happens as long as they stop your income.

Bitterness about the Kennedy administration's crackdown on alleged mobsters ran deep in Chicago's Italian-American community. Later in this conversation, D'Arco discusses what Frank Annunzio, a Democratic ward committeeman and later a congressman, told an FBI agent questioning him about his relationship with Giancana. The agent was William Roemer, head of the FBI detail investigating Giancana.

D'ARCO: Frank [Annunzio] said, "And another thing, Roemer, . . . the irony of all this is that the Italian-Americans elected Kennedy, and this is the appreciation they get, by him harassing anybody and saying he's a criminal if he's Italian. . . . Why is it you ask about this man when this man was responsible for Kennedy being elected? Without this state, Kennedy was in a lot of trouble. They'd ask for a recount in a few other states and it would have shown that Kennedy was beat. If it wasn't for the Italian voter in this city, Kennedy would never have got in. They went for him 100 percent, and this is what they get for it."

During yet another talk, Giancana and his colleague Johnny Formosa were overheard discussing how to avenge the slight, according to this excerpt from Kelley's book:

FORMOSA: Let's show 'em. Let's show those asshole Hollywood fruitcakes that they can't get away with it as if nothing's happened. Let's hit Sinatra. Or I could whack out a couple of those other guys. [Peter] Lawford and that [Dean] Martin, and I could take the nigger [Sammy Davis, Jr.] and put his other eye out.

GIANCANA: No . . . I've got other plans for them.

*Eddy M., the bugging subject mentioned in chapter 5, also was over-
heard talking about revenge in 1962, according to this transcript from the
National Archives.*

EDDY M.: I'd like to hit that Kennedy in the kisser with a bomb.
If I could just hit Bob Kennedy in the kisser with a stink bomb, some
kind of bomb that will explode, I would gladly go to the penitentiary
for the rest of my life, believe me. Is that too much to ask?

*By early 1962, Hoover had enough information to know that something
was up between the president and Campbell. He quickly informed the attorney general and a top White House aide.*

TO: Mr. Belmont   DATE: 2/26/62
FROM: C. A. Evans
SUBJECT: JOHN ROSELLI
            ANTI-RACKETEERING

With respect to the information previously received that Judith E.
Campbell of Los Angeles was in telephonic contact with Evelyn
Lincoln, the President's Secretary, the following additional
information has been received from the Los Angeles Office.
    Campbell has associated with John Roselli, prominent West
Coast hoodlum, who is on the second list of forty hoodlums
designated to receive intensified investigation.
    Campbell states she formerly was employed by Jerry Lewis
Productions in a public relations capacity, but is presently a free
lance artist. Campbell is divorced from William Campbell, a
television producer.
    Campbell, when interviewed by Bureau Agents, admitted
meeting Sam Giancana, Chicago underworld figure, in Miami
Beach, Florida, but refused to furnish names of acquaintances who
introduced her to Giancana.
    A review of her telephone toll calls reveals four calls in
December, 1961, to the Palm Springs, California, residence of Frank
Sinatra.

ACTION

1. If approved, that the attached letters be forwarded to the Attorney General and to P. Kenneth O'Donnell, Special Assistant to the President.

2. The Los Angeles Office is being instructed to vigorously pursue the investigation of Campbell to determine the exact nature of her relationship with Roselli and Giancana.

TO: The Attorney General   DATE: February 27, 1962
FROM: Director, FBI
SUBJECT: JOHN ROSELLI
          ANTI-RACKETEERING

Information has been developed in connection with the investigation of John Roselli, one of the second group of forty hoodlums receiving concentrated attention, that he has been in contact with Judith E. Campbell.

A review of the telephone toll calls from Campbell's Los Angeles residence discloses that on November 7 and 15, 1961, calls were made to Evelyn Lincoln, the President's Secretary, at the White House.

The relationship between Campbell and Mrs. Lincoln or the purpose of these calls is not known.

Information has also been developed that Campbell has associated with Sam Giancana, a prominent Chicago underworld figure.

Campbell, a free-lance artist, is divorced from William Campbell, a television producer.

This information is being made available to Honorable P. Kenneth O'Donnell, Special Assistant to the President.

You will be advised of all significant developments in this matter.

Now it was clear that President Kennedy was consorting with two people with mob affiliations—Sinatra and Campbell. The potential for a disastrous scandal must have been obvious to Hoover and the Kennedys, especially given what the FBI had been hearing in recent months about Gi-

ancana and Roselli. The two men were involved with CIA operatives in a plot to assassinate the president's principal foreign policy nightmare, Cuba's Fidel Castro. The public wouldn't find out about the plot until years later, and it has never been known for sure whether it was a rogue operation or an authorized undertaking.

In 1975, a Senate committee headed by Frank Church, an Idaho Democrat, conducted a sweeping investigation of reports that the CIA had been involved in assassination attempts. Its report described the Castro plot in meticulous detail (though it didn't name Campbell, discretely describing her only as "a close friend of President Kennedy.") The excerpts that follow have been extensively condensed and edited to delete repetition and extraneous detail.

In August 1960, the CIA took steps to enlist members of the criminal underworld with gambling syndicate contacts to aid in assassinating Castro. Colonel Sheffield Edwards, Director of the Office of Security, recalled that Richard Bissell, CIA's Deputy Director for Plans and the man in charge of CIA's covert action directorate, asked him to locate someone who could assassinate Castro.

Edwards and the Chief of the Operational Support Division of the Office of Security [name withheld] decided to rely on Robert A. Maheu to recruit someone "tough enough" to handle the job. Maheu was an ex-FBI agent who had entered into a career as a private investigator in 1954.

Sometime in late August or early September 1960, the Support Chief approached Maheu about the proposed operation. As Maheu recalls the conversation, the Support Chief asked him to contact John Roselli, an underworld figure with possible gambling contacts in Las Vegas, to determine if he would participate in a plan to "dispose" of Castro. The Support Chief testified that Maheu was told to offer money, probably $150,000, for Castro's assassination. At first Maheu was reluctant to become involved in the operation because it might interfere with his relationship with his new client, Howard Hughes. He finally agreed to participate because he felt that he owed the Agency a commitment.

Roselli introduced Maheu to two individuals on whom Roselli intended to rely: "Sam Gold," who would serve as a "back-up man," and "Joe," whom "Gold" said would serve as a courier to Cuba and make arrangements there.

The Support Chief testified that he learned the true identities of his associates one morning when Maheu called and asked him to examine the "Parade" supplement to the *Miami Times*. An article on the Attorney General's ten-most-wanted criminals list revealed that "Sam Gold" was Momo Salvatore Giancana, a Chicago-based gangster, and "Joe" was Santos Trafficante, the Cosa Nostra chieftain in Cuba. The Support Chief reported his discovery to Edwards, but did not know whether Edwards reported this fact to his superiors. Maheu recalled that it was Giancana's job to locate someone in Castro's entourage who could accomplish the assassination.

Shortly before the 1960 election, the FBI learned that Giancana was involved in a plot against Castro—but not that the CIA was involved, according to a memo quoted in the Church committee report.

An October 18, 1960 memorandum from J. Edgar Hoover to Bissell, stated that "a source whose reliability has not been tested" reported that:

> During recent conversations with several friends, Giancana stated that Fidel Castro was to be done away with very shortly. When doubt was expressed regarding this statement, Giancana reportedly assured those present that Castro's assassination would occur in November. Moreover, he allegedly indicated that he had already met with the assassin-to-be on three occasions. Giancana claimed that everything has been perfected for the killing of Castro, and that the "assassin" had arranged with a girl, not further described, to drop a "pill" in some drink or food of Castro's.

The plot against Castro might not have been Giancana's only clandestine foray that fall. He suspected that his girlfriend was involved with an-

other man, who ended up being bugged with the help of the CIA, according to the Church committee report. (Though the report didn't identify them, it later became known that the girlfriend was the singer Phyllis McGuire and the target of the eavesdropping device was the comedian Dan Rowan, according to Curt Gentry's Hoover biography.)

After discovering the Las Vegas wiretap on October 31, 1960, the FBI commenced an investigation which quickly developed that Maheu and Giancana were involved in the case. In April 1961, Roselli's involvement was discovered.

Meanwhile, the Castro plot continued, as detailed by the Church committee.

There is some evidence that Giancana or Roselli originated the idea of depositing a poison pill in Castro's drink to give the "asset" a chance to escape. The Support Chief recalled Roselli's request for something "nice and clean, without getting into any kind of out and out ambushing," preferably a poison that would disappear without a trace. The Agency had first considered a "gangland-style killing" in which Castro would be gunned down. Giancana reportedly opposed the idea because it would be difficult to recruit someone for such a dangerous operation, and suggested instead the use of poison.

Edwards rejected the first batch of pills because they would not dissolve in water. A second batch, containing botulinum toxin, "did the job expected of them" when tested on monkeys. The Support Chief received the pills, probably in February 1961, with assurances that they were lethal, and then gave them to Roselli.

The record clearly establishes that the pills were given to a Cuban for delivery to the island some time prior to the Bay of Pigs invasion in mid-April 1961. Roselli reported to the Support Chief that the pills had been delivered to an official close to Castro who may have received kickbacks from the gambling interests. The official returned the pills after a few weeks, perhaps because he had lost his position in the Cuban Government, and thus access to Castro, before he received the pills. Yet another attempt was made in April 1961, with the aid of a leading figure in the Cuban exile movement. He was paid advance money to cover his expenses, probably in the amount of $10,000. The money and pills were delivered at a meeting between Maheu, Roselli, Trafficante, and the Cuban at the Fontainebleau Hotel in Miami. As Roselli recalled, Maheu:

> opened his briefcase and dumped a whole lot of money on his lap and also came up with the capsules and he explained how they were going to be used. As far as I remember, they couldn't be used in boiling soups and things like that, but they could be used in water or otherwise, but they couldn't last forever. It had to be done as quickly as possible.

The attempt met with failure. Edwards believed the scheme failed because Castro stopped visiting the restaurant where the "asset" was employed.

Continuing its wiretap investigation of Giancana, the FBI contacted Maheu, the former agent. Acting on previous instructions, Maheu told the FBI that the bug had been placed as part of a CIA operation and referred the bureau to Edwards, the CIA security director. Hoover apprised Attorney General Robert Kennedy of the situation in a memo on May 22, 1961. The whole mess didn't go over well with the FBI, according to the Church committee report.

Sam Papich, the FBI liaison with the CIA during this period, stated that the FBI was furious when it learned of the CIA's use of Maheu, Roselli and Giancana because it might inhibit possible prosecutions against them in the wiretap case and in others.

Entries in the FBI files, however, indicate that the FBI vigorously pursued its investigation of the wiretap case. Then, on August 16, 1961, the Assistant United States Attorney in Las Vegas reported his reluctance to proceed with the case because of deficiencies in the

evidence and his concern that CIA's alleged involvement might
become known. The Department of Justice files indicate no activity
between September 1961, when the FBI's investigation was
concluded, and January 1962, when the question of prosecution in
the case was brought up for reconsideration.

It was in the following month, February 1962, that the FBI had discov-
ered the evidence tying President Kennedy to Judith Campbell. The FBI
later heard from Fred Otash—the private eye who had tried to set up Jack
Kennedy in July 1960—that Campbell and the President were romantically
involved. So now, Hoover had enough information to put it all together:
Kennedy was sleeping with a friend of two alleged mobsters, Roselli and Gi-
ancana, who in turn were friends with the president's buddy Sinatra and
who were under investigation for illegal bugging. And Giancana—the same
man who had helped the Kennedy campaign and therefore was angry with
Sinatra for not getting Robert Kennedy and the FBI off his back—was se-
cretly working with Roselli and the CIA against Castro.

It was time to go see the president. The Church committee tried in vain
to find out what happened at that meeting.

On March 22, 1962, Hoover had a private luncheon with
President Kennedy. What actually transpired may never be known,
as both participants are dead and the FBI files contain no records
relating to it.

It's clear, however, that President Kennedy was finally coming to grips
with his own recklessness. Robert Kennedy, increasingly troubled by his
brother's public camaraderie with the mobster-friendly Sinatra, persuaded
the president to distance himself from the singer. Sinatra reportedly flew into
a rage when, after he spent considerable sums fixing up his Palm Springs es-
tate to accommodate presidential visits, Kennedy canceled plans to stay
there that March in favor of Bing Crosby's place. President Kennedy also
ended the affair with Campbell, who at some point became romantically in-
volved with Giancana, too.

For his part, Hoover decided to force the CIA's hand on the question of whether to prosecute the men under Giancana and Roselli who planted the illegal bug, as detailed by the Church committee.

The day immediately following his luncheon with the President, at which Roselli and Giancana were presumably discussed, Hoover sent a memorandum to Edwards stating:

> At the request of the Criminal Division of the Department of Justice, this matter was discussed with the CIA Director of Security on February 7, 1962, and we were advised that your agency would object to any prosecution which would necessitate the use of CIA personnel or CIA information. We were also informed that introduction of evidence concerning the CIA operation would be embarrassing to the Government.
>
> The Criminal Division has now requested that CIA specifically advise whether it would or would not object to the initiation of criminal prosecution for conspiracy to violate the "Wire Tapping Statute."

The CIA, of course, objected, and word was passed on to Robert Kennedy, the Church committee said.

In a memo dated April 24, 1962, Herbert J. Miller, Assistant Attorney General, Criminal Division, advised the Attorney General that the "national interest" would preclude any prosecutions based upon the tap. Following a briefing of the Attorney General by the CIA, a decision was made not to prosecute.

The briefing for Robert Kennedy occurred on May 22, 1962. In the Church committee report, one of the CIA officials recalled the attorney general's reaction on being told that the CIA had conspired with the mob to kill Castro.

If you have seen Mr. Kennedy's eyes get steely and his jaw set and his voice get low and precise, you get a definite feeling of unhappiness. . . . [He said,] "I trust that if you ever try to do business with organized crime again—with gangsters—you will let the Attorney General know."

Nevertheless, the Church committee discovered that the CIA plot against Castro continued. Another CIA official, William Harvey, had been put in charge of the project in late 1961.

Harvey, the Support Chief and Roselli met in New York on April 8–9, 1962. Four poison pills were given to the Support Chief on April 18, 1962. The pills were passed to Harvey, who arrived in Miami on April 21, and found Roselli already in touch with the same Cuban who had been involved in the pre–Bay of Pigs pill passage. He gave the pills to Roselli, explaining that "these would work anywhere and at any time with anything." Roselli testified that he told Harvey that the Cubans intended to use the pills to assassinate Che Guevara as well as Fidel and Raul Castro. According to Roselli's testimony, Harvey approved of the targets, stating "everything is all right, what they want to do."

The Cuban requested arms and equipment as a *quid pro quo* for carrying out the assassination operation. Harvey procured explosives, detonators, rifles, handguns, radios, and boat radar costing about $5,000.

Roselli kept Harvey informed of the operation's progress. Sometime in May 1962, he reported that the pills and guns had arrived in Cuba. On June 21, he told Harvey that the Cuban had dispatched a three-man team to Cuba.

Harvey met Roselli in Miami on September 7 and 11, 1962. The Cuban was reported to be preparing to send in another three-man team to penetrate Castro's bodyguard. The second team never left for Cuba, claiming that "conditions" in Cuba were not right. Harvey terminated the operation in mid-February 1963. At a meeting with Roselli in Los Angeles, it was agreed that Roselli would taper off his communications with the Cubans. Roselli testified that he simply broke off contact with the Cubans. However, he never informed them that the offer of $150,000 for Castro's assassination had been withdrawn.

Sinatra, meanwhile, didn't completely drop out of Camelot. Kennedy called his old friend while the star was hosting a mob wedding party in Atlantic City, according to a later summary of references in the Sinatra FBI files.

The following references . . . set out information pertaining to Frank Sinatra in connection with his appearance in Aug., 1962 at the 500 Club in Atlantic City with Dean Martin, reportedly as a special favor to Paul D'Amato, partner of Sinatra in the Cal-Neva Lodge at Lake Tahoe, Nev. D'Amato possibly had an interest in the 500 Club. Sinatra took over the first floor of the Claridge Hotel which guests invited to attend the wedding on Aug. 26 of the daughter of Angelo Bruno, head of the Italian mob in Philadelphia, could occupy. Information in connection with the hoodlum element was set out including contacts and associates of Sinatra. One contact was a personal telephone call which he received from President Kennedy on 8/23/62, the nature of which was not described.

Hoover wrote to his ostensible boss again that summer about the president's call to Sinatra.

TO: The Attorney General   DATE: August 27, 1962
FROM: Director, FBI   PERSONAL
SUBJECT: FRANK SINATRA

While conducting inquiry at the Claridge Hotel in Atlantic City, New Jersey, in connection with an investigation under our Criminal Intelligence Program, Agents of our Newark Office were confidentially advised by an official of this hotel that Frank Sinatra had received a personal telephone call from President John F. Kennedy on August 23, 1962. It is noted that Sinatra reserved a floor of this hotel during the latter part of the week of August 19–25,

1962, in connection with his appearance with Dean Martin at the 500 Club in Atlantic City.

His dreams of a favored seat at the court of Camelot dashed, Sinatra continued to associate with mobsters, though he may have been wearing out his welcome, as this snippet from a surreptitiously recorded September 13, 1962, conversation shows.

GIANCANA: That Frank, he wants more money, he wants this, he wants that, he want more girls, he wants . . . I don't need that or him. . . . I broke my [expletive] when I was talking to him in New York.

Meanwhile, RFK's Justice Department began to close in on Sinatra. An October 1962 FBI memo suggested that Sinatra had put his private plane, a car, and his home at Giancana's disposal for assignations with his steady girlfriend, the singer Phyllis McGuire of the McGuire Sisters.

FRANK SINATRA

The Los Angeles Division advised on October 2, 1962, that a physical surveillance reflected that a white Ford Falcon belonging to the Frank Sinatra Enterprises arrived at the Palm Springs Airport at 3:40 AM October 2, 1962, and contained one female and two males. FRANK SINATRA's airplane bearing Number N71DE arrived at the Palm Springs Airport at 4:50 AM on October 2, 1962. PHYLLIS MC GUIRE at that time joined the individuals in the Ford Falcon described above. One of the individuals in the Falcon appeared to be SAM GIANCANA.

███████████████ advised on September 22, 1962, that PHYLLIS MC GUIRE called telephone number 328-2105 in Palm Springs, California. At the time the call was placed, the informant advised that GIANCANA was present with MC GUIRE.

The Los Angeles Office advised on September 23, 1962, that telephone number 328-2105 is the unlisted number of FRANK SINATRA, Tamarisk Country Club, Cathedral City, California. The telephone number is billed to SINATRA's agent, SAM BURK, Suite 419, 9350 Wilshire Boulevard, Los Angeles, California.

██████████████ advised in August, 1962, that GIANCANA had made plans to be in Atlantic City, New Jersey commencing with the week end of August 25, 1962.

The Newark Office advised on August 22, 1962, that GENE CATENA, brother of GERALDO CATENA and JOSEPH PECORA were in Atlantic City, New Jersey for several days commencing with August 22, 1962.

The Newark Office advised on August 27, 1962, that FRANK SINATRA was due to appear at the 500 Club in Atlantic City to perform with DEAN MARTIN on the last night of MARTIN's singing engagement at that club.

Surveillances conducted by Agents at the Newark Office indicated that many individuals came to the Atlantic City area for two-fold purposes, that is to attend the wedding of ANGELO BRUNO's daughter on August 26, 1962, and a performance of FRANK SINATRA–DEAN MARTIN–SAMMY DAVIS, JR., at the 500 Club.

FRANK SINATRA arrived in Atlantic City on August 27, 1962, for the above scheduled appearance with DEAN MARTIN and took over the first sleeping floor of the Claridge Hotel, Atlantic City, which consists of approximately 40 rooms. SINATRA's representatives allowed no one on the hotel floor, including the hotel management, except by invitation.

██████████████ advised ██████████████ that SINATRA and MARTIN were appearing at the 500 Club as a personal favor to PAUL D'AMATO, also known as "SKINNY," for which they would receive no money but would have all of their expenses taken care of by D'AMATO.

SINATRA's personal airplane landed at the Atlantic City Airport on August 25, 1962, and departed from the Airport in an unmarked Atlantic City Police car.

██████████████████████ observed SAM GIANCANA in company with ██████████████████████ in a private

dining room on SINATRA's floor of the Claridge Hotel as of
██████████████████

PHYLLIS MC GUIRE

██████████████ advised on September 19, 1962, that PHYLLIS
MC GUIRE moved into her temporary residence of 2223 Edgewood,
Las Vegas, Nevada, as of approximately September 15, 1962. Her
residency there was for the period when the MC GUIRE sisters
appeared at the Desert Inn Hotel Night Club.

██████████████ advised on September 22, 1962, that
GIANCANA arrived at the above residence during September 21,
1962.

At this point, refer to that section of this report relating to
FRANK SINATRA whereby MC GUIRE was observed in the
company of an individual believed to be GIANCANA at Palm
Springs, California, on September 25, 1962.

MC GUIRE, according to ██████████████ was in contact with
GIANCANA at the SINATRA residence in Cathedral City,
California, as of October 1, 1962.

Las Vegas Division advised on September 25, 1962, that
GIANCANA had departed Las Vegas on September 25, 1962, via
chartered aircraft to Palm Springs, California. The plane was
identified as a Cessna 310 and the plane was chartered by
GIANCANA under the name of GEORGE GOLDBERG.
PHYLLIS MC GUIRE had chartered an aircraft to depart Las Vegas
at 1:45 AM, September 26, 1962, for Palm Springs. The aircraft and
pilot were to return to Las Vegas at 5:00 PM, September 26, 1962.

Records of the Palm Springs Airport as made available by
██████████████ to SA [Special Agent] ██████████████ on
September 25, 1962, revealed that a chartered plane, described as a
Cessna 310 aircraft, number 865, arrived at the Palm Springs,
California, airport at 8:45 AM, September 25, 1962. The plane
belongs to the Alamo Airways and arrived from Las Vegas.

At 3:16 AM, September 26, 1962, PHYLLIS MC GUIRE was

observed departing from a private plane at Palm Springs Airport and was met by three unknown males in a station wagon determined to be a 1962 Buick, bearing California License XDP318. This wagon is registered to the Essex Productions, 9229 Sunset Boulevard, Los Angeles, California, an enterprise of FRANK SINATRA. After Miss MC GUIRE entered this wagon, it proceeded to the vicinity of the Tamarisk Country Club, Cathedral City, California, and the vehicle was observed shortly thereafter parked in the carport of the residence of FRANK SINATRA.

On September 26, 1962, at 4:55 PM, PHYLLIS MC GUIRE and an unknown male Negro were observed proceeding to a Cessna 310 plane, Registration Number N6848T, belonging to Alamo Airways. This plane is the same aircraft in which MC GUIRE arrived earlier that day. After the above plane departed, the Buick Station which delivered Miss MC GUIRE, proceeded from the airport at Palm Springs to the FRANK SINATRA residence in Cathedral City, California.

It would appear from the observation of surveilling agents at the Palm Springs airport that GIANCANA was one of the individuals who met Miss MC GUIRE upon her arrival at the Palm Springs Airport at 3:16 AM, September 26, 1962.

███████████████ advised ███████████████ that GIANCANA as of that date was in Hot Springs, Arkansas, with PHYLLIS MC GUIRE and was scheduled to remain there until August 12, 1962.

It is noted that the MC GUIRE sisters singing team made an appearance at the Vapors Club, Hot Springs, Arkansas, on August 4, 1962, and on that date after the completion of the first show of the MC GUIRE sisters, GIANCANA was observed by Bureau Agents at Hot Springs, entering an automobile at the Velda Rose Motel with the MC GUIRE sisters at approximately 9:20 PM on August 4, 1962, and traveled to the Coy's Steakhouse, in Hot Springs, where this party had dinner. After dinner, GIANCANA drove the MC GUIRE sisters to the Vapors Club and then returned to Room 64, Velda Rose Motel, which at the time was occupied by PHYLLIS and CHRISTINE MC GUIRE. GIANCANA was not observed from

that time until the evening of August 6, 1962, when he departed
Room 64 of the Velda Rose Motel and took a short walk.

*By then, it had become clear what Giancana had meant many months
back when he told his underling, Johnny Formosa, that he had "other plans"
for Sinatra and the rest of the Rat Pack. He wanted their services for a gig at
the Villa Venice, a supper club outside Chicago. Continuing their investigation of Giancana, FBI agents picked up on the story and recounted it in various memos about his business enterprises.*

Villa Venice Supper Club,
Milwaukee Avenue,
Northwest Suburban Cook
County, Illinois

This well-known restaurant and lounge was owned and operated
by ALBERT "PAPA" BOUCHE, until October, 1956, at which time
BOUCHE was bought out by the MEO brothers, with backing of
"the Syndicate." Although the ostensible purchasers of the property
were the MEO brothers and their wives, ALFRED and TRIP
(TRIPOLINA) and JAMES and STELL, the real operator of the
Villa Venice is SAM GIANCANA, commonly referred to as
"MOONEY," while JIMMY MEO is the "front." When
GIANCANA appears on the scene, it becomes obvious to all he is
the "top dog" in the operation of the place, as all the others,
including JIMMY MEO, become subservient to him and jump at his
command. GIANCANA regards the Villa Venice as his toy and
insists on it being run strictly according to his dictates, and he
personally rebukes employees when their dress or conduct are not up
to his standards.

CG T-37 [a confidential informant] continued that although
GIANCANA was frequently at the Villa Venice prior to the . . .
hearings of the Senate Rackets Committee (McClellan Committee
or more properly, the Senate Select Committee on Improper
Activities in the Labor or Management Field), he went to Cuba

while the hearings were in progress and did not return until the hearings ended. GIANCANA and other "wheels in the Syndicate" held a private party at the Villa Venice to celebrate the conclusion of the hearings. At this gathering, in one of the many private rooms in the Villa, several guards were posted at strategic points on the grounds to challenge anyone not known to them. The Villa has gradually been becoming a headquarters for "the Syndicate," as indicated by closed meetings complete with "lookouts" and by frequenting of the Villa by friends of GIANCANA, who are paid considerable deference by the MEO brothers.

One of the principal attractions of the Villa for the "hoodlums" was the fact it was a "floating house of prostitution." The "floating" aspect of the Villa refers to the canals and gondolas which comprise part of the Villa's seven or eight acres of grounds. Prostitutes were brought to the Villa by hustlers and turned their tricks on the gondolas with the male customers. Most of these sexual activities did not follow conventional patterns.

*   *   *

The Maitre d' of the Villa, known to the informant only as "LOUIE," knows extremely little regarding the duties of a Maitre d', but the word has gone around that he is the son of one of the better known syndicate "hoodlums," who requested that GIANCANA give his son the job, and GIANCANA obliged.

*   *   *

It has been reported that the Villa Venice Supper Club has been an enterprise of GIANCANA since approximately 1960. From April 1960 through the spring of 1962, the Villa Venice was utilized primarily for private parties, weddings, etc., and was not considered as a money-making proposition. During the summer months and early fall the Villa Venice underwent a remodeling and reopened on November 9, 1962. The featured entertainer for the opening date was EDDIE FISHER. He was followed by SAMMY DAVIS, Jr., and then by FRANK SINATRA and DEAN MARTIN. During the week of the engagement of MARTIN and SINATRA, the act was joined by SAMMY DAVIS, Jr. Following the appearance of MARTIN and SINATRA, SAMMY DAVIS, Jr., remained at the Villa Venice through December 4, 1962. Following December 4, 1962, the Villa Venice was closed and plans are not known at this time as to their reopening.

███████████ advised ██████████ that SAM GIANCANA advised that the Villa Venice will definitely be a "going" proposition and was keeping in close contact with the operation. Advance reservations were made at the Villa Venice for the entire booking of SAMMY DAVIS, Jr., and FRANK SINATRA.

███████████ advised ██████████ that SAM GIANCANA is definitely the owner of the Villa Venice, and has spent many hours overseeing the remodeling operation of the Villa Venice during the past several weeks. GIANCANA is referred to at the Villa Venice as "Mr. FLOOD."

*   *   *

████████████ learned recently that the Villa Venice is financially in trouble, and for this reason, FRANK SINATRA and his associates are scheduled to entertain at this establishment. SINATRA, et al., are not going to receive the amount of money they reportedly were scheduled to receive in return for their services. . . .

*   *   *

███████████ advised ██████████ that SAM GIANCANA has been at the Villa Venice on at least five occasions since the opening of that establishment on November 9, 1962.

████████████ stated that on the opening night, GIANCANA was present and was in a very expansive mood, and was in the lobby of the Villa Venice greeting everyone who came in. Among other persons observed at the Villa Venice on opening night by ████████████ were FELIX ALDERISIO, ROCCO POTENZO, MARSHALL CAIFANO, ANTHONY DE MONTE, and LEONARD GIANOLA.

During these appearances at the Villa Venice, GIANCANA was normally accompanied by either BUTCH BLASI or an individual believed by ████████████ to be TONY SABONA (ph), who drives a 1963 dark blue Oldsmobile bearing 1962 Illinois license FG 8525. This is registered to CHRISTINE COSCIONI, 4840 North Neva, Chicago, Illinois, on an Oldsmobile.

A physical surveillance was conducted by SAs [Special Agents] ████████████ at the Villa Venice Club on November 27, 1962. FRANK SINATRA and DEAN MARTIN were observed entering the Villa Venice for the second show at approximately 12:30 a.m. on November 28, 1962, accompanied by JOSEPH FISCHETTI. JOSEPH FISCHETTI is a former Chicago member of the Chicago criminal organization, now residing in Miami, Florida, where he is part-owner of Puccini's Restaurant in Miami.

████████████ advised ████████████ that FRANK SINATRA and EDDIE FISHER accompanied by SAM GIANCANA, recently flew from Los Angeles, California, to Reno, Nevada, en route to Lake Tahoe, Nevada, in FRANK SINATRA's private plane.

* * *

████████████ advised in October, 1962, that GIANCANA and several other individuals made arrangements for other acts to appear at the Villa Venice and among the performers that they either have definite commitments for or are planning to schedule for the Villa Venice are DINAH SHORE, JIMMY DURANTE, and DANNY THOMAS.

* * *

Throughout the interview, ████████████ suggested that the person to contact regarding the Villa Venice would be FRANK SINATRA.

Indeed, this memo shows that Sinatra had interceded when it appeared that Eddie Fisher had an engagement that conflicted with the Villa Venice's originally proposed reopening date.

TO: Mr. Belmont   DATE: October 12, 1962
FROM: C. A. Evans
SUBJECT: FRANK SINATRA

Further indication of the control and influence of the Chicago hoodlum organization in the operation of Las Vegas gambling casinos is evident in connection with the forthcoming appearance of singer Eddie Fisher as the star attraction at the reopening of the plush Villa Venice Supper Club, Wheeling, Illinois, on October 31, 1962. Also appearing at this supper club following Fisher's engagement are Sammy Davis, Frank Sinatra and Dean Martin. Wheeling is a suburb of Chicago.

Fisher, who is now appearing in New York, was to follow his New York appearance with a month's engagement at the Desert Inn in Las Vegas. The Chicago hoodlum organization of Samuel Giancana, however, made it known that they wanted Fisher to appear at the Villa Venice on October 31, 1962. They told the Desert Inn that Fisher could split his Las Vegas engagement in order to make a week's appearance in Chicago. Later they decided they wanted Fisher for three weeks instead of one week.

The operators of the Desert Inn headed by Morris Barney Dalitz felt that such an arrangement would be bad for Desert Inn business. Fisher and his manager were of the opinion that such an arrangement would have an adverse effect on Fisher's career, going from a smash New York engagement to an unknown supper club in Wheeling, Illinois. Neither Morris Barney Dalitz nor Fisher nor his manager had the courage to express their reluctance for this arrangement.

Frank Sinatra reportedly said to Eddie Fisher, "Look, you're going over here for 18 days, never mind about the Desert Inn, I already handled that. I take care of that. They do what I tell them."

According to our source, the instructions and messages relating to these arrangements were sent by Samuel Giancana to Las Vegas with ▬▬▬▬▬ believed to look out for the interests of the Chicago group at this hotel.

ACTION

The information above is from our highly confidential source ▬▬▬▬▬ We are closely following the operation of the Villa Venice Club and the investigation of ▬▬▬▬▬ is being intensified.

The Rat Pack ended up doing sixteen shows in seven nights at "The New Villa Venice." At one of the shows, Dean Martin sang parody lyrics about his fee for the gig:

> I love Chicago, it's carefree and gay
> I'd even work here, without any pay
> I'll lay you odds it turns out that way
> That's why this gentleman is a tramp.

That apparently made it a doubly good deal for the club's backers.

A December 20, 1962, FBI memo quoted a press account detailing the operations of a gambling joint, the Flamingo Motel, near the Villa Venice. The Rat Pack headliners were meant to draw in the high rollers, who were then shuttled to crap games.

Flamingo Motel
Intersection of US 45 and Milwaukee
Avenue, Northwest Suburban
Cook County, Illinois

Refer to that section of this report relating to the Villa Venice. It should be noted that the Flamingo Motel is located approximately one and one half blocks North of the Villa Venice.

Report of SA [Special Agent] ▮▮▮▮▮▮▮▮▮▮ dated May 5, 1961, at Chicago, Page 130, contains information relating to the Flamingo Motel which reflects that this is an alleged GIANCANA enterprise.

The "Chicago Daily News" Red Streak Edition dated November 30, 1962, contained the following article relating to a gambling operation at the Flamingo Motel. This operation is referred to in the newspaper as the Quonset Hut. It is noted that this particular Quonset Hut is located immediately adjacent to and North of the Flamingo Motel. The article is as follows:

"A king-size quonset hut two blocks north of the Villa Venice has been the site of big money dice games since the River Road night club reopened, The Daily News learned Friday.

"Elaborately concealed and guarded, the dice games and other gaming-den diversions have been restricted to well-heeled suckers whose identities were well known to the gamblers.

"Rocco (Parrot Nose) Potenza, 48, of 8857 N. Kildare, Skokie, gaming lieutenant for Sam (Mooney) Giancana, has presided over the nightly sessions. He has been aided by Sam Rosa, West Side bookmaker and associate of Charles (Chuck) English.

"Beneath the silvery, metal exterior of the hut, a fantastic operation was devised. Patrons with the proper credentials enter through a door at the rear of the building. As they step into the heavily carpeted and air-conditioned hut, an attendant parks their cars in parking spaces at the adjacent Flamingo Motel at River Rd. and Milwaukee, in unincorporated territory south of Wheeling.

"Next stop for patrons of the hut is the hat check room and then, most important, the cashier's cage.

"Chips are mandatory, unlike previous suburban gaming action in which the big money game was played with cash only.

"At the two dice tables, the limit is $100 for a single bet, but Potenza has lifted it for big shooters. Blackjack tables and roulette wheels complete the equipment in the hut. A small bar and light refreshment counter are also provided.

"During the last 20 days since singer Eddie Fisher started off the new star policy at the Villa, a heavy toll has been levied at the hut on the patrons. Individual losses of as much as $25,000 have been reported.

"A shuttle service has been provided for some of the customers who want to leave their cars at the Villa. The hut is camouflaged with old trucks and pieces of road machinery.

"The front inner area, which is sealed off from the gaming room, is cluttered with a ladder and building materials.

"At least four top crime syndicate figures went unnoticed in the Villa Venice opening night crowd last Monday night for Frank Sinatra and 'rat pack' members Dean Martin and Sammy Davis Jr. Jimmy (The Monk) Allegretti, North Side vice boss and Marshall Caifano, mob enforcer, both had front tables.

"More secluded were Felix (Milwaukee Phil) Alderisio, juice loan racketeer, and Giancana, who sat further back. Giancana has paid several visits to the hut while some 40 or 50 patrons were there.

"Thursday night Potenza's black 1963 auto was parked directly in front of the Patio, a restaurant operated in conjunction with the Flamingo.

"Joe Iacullo, the motel overseer for Giancana, asked a Daily News reporter who was sitting in a car near the motel, what he wanted.

" 'I want to see Rocky,' the reporter said.

" 'Rocky who?' Iacullo asked. 'Is he registered in the motel? If he was here, what do you want to see him about?'

"The reporter pointed at the quonset hut.

" 'Don't put words in my mouth,' Iacullo said as he walked around the corner of the motel, 'I don't know any Rocky, but now I know who you are and you can stay as long as you want.'

"The reporter did, but Potenza didn't. Both he and his car disappeared moments later and the game was shut down. Iacullo walked over to the hut and turned on a big floodlight that bathed the front of the hut in light, apparently a signal that the game was over."

The FBI questioned some in the Rat Pack about all this. One answer attributed to Sinatra here would later be contradicted in Nancy Sinatra's biography of her father: "The shows were Dad's way of paying back Giancana for the help he provided to the Kennedy family," she wrote.

SINATRA and MARTIN denied all knowledge of the gambling, and SINATRA claimed he arranged all the appearances merely as a favor to Mr. LEO OLSEN, the owner of the club, for past favors, and that GIANCANA had nothing to do with it. Available information indicates otherwise.

At around the same time, Sinatra was looking to expand the Cal-Neva casino resort on the California-Nevada border, in which he had acquired a 36.6 percent interest in 1961. The FBI suspected that Giancana had a secret interest in the establishment. He had been overheard saying that he was "gonna get my money out of there" but still "end up with half the joint," while an associate fretted that the expansion would bring unwanted "attention."

Sure enough, the FBI learned that Sinatra was seeking a multimillion-dollar Teamsters pension-fund loan to finance the expansion. It suspected that the mob was using cheap loans from Jimmy Hoffa's Teamsters to expand its Nevada operations. The FBI inquiry was short-lived, as shown by these three memos:

Los Angeles, California
April 17, 1963

On January 16, 1963, FRANK SINATRA and MILTON A. RUDIN, Attorney at Law and Financial Advisor to SINATRA, were interviewed at the offices of Essex Productions, 9229 Sunset Boulevard, Suite 512, Los Angeles, California, concerning the Cal-Neva Lodge, Crystal Bay, Nevada.

During the course of this interview Mr. RUDIN, with the consent of Mr. SINATRA, advised that their current plans for the Cal-Neva Lodge included quite a substantial expansion of the hotel which would necessitate the bringing in of some $4,000,000.00 of added capital. RUDIN stated that he found out by checking into the loan situation that banks and insurance companies, in order to make loans, would ask for stock options, which they are not ready to agree to.

Mr. RUDIN advised that he has become familiar with some of the pension fund loans from reading the series of articles run by the "Los Angeles Times" on investigations of loans by the Teamsters to various Nevada casinos and that these are straight forward loans. He advised that he had gone to Chicago and had talked to various Teamster officials in the Chicago area concerning the possibility of securing a loan for Cal-Neva. He advised that the Cal-Neva, at the next meeting of the trustees for the pension fund in March, will, according to their present plans, apply for a loan in order to achieve their expansion program.

Both RUDIN and SINATRA advised they wished to go on record that there were no under-the-table payments of any kind involved, that this was a simple straight forward business transaction with sufficient collateral involved. Mr. RUDIN advised that the person he had contacted regarding the possibility of such a loan was HAROLD GIBBONS. SINATRA mentioned that DORIS DAY had secured a similar type loan from the Teamsters for a motel that she owns, and he had asked her if she had had to cut anybody in, and she advised him that it was not necessary, that it was a straight loan.

Chicago, Illinois
May 31, 1963

A review of the minutes of a meeting held on September 21, 1962, by the Trustees of the Central States, Southeast and Southwest Areas, Pension Fund of the International Brotherhood of Teamsters revealed the following pertinent information:

Mr. Milton A. Rudin appeared before the Trustees on behalf of Park Lake Enterprises, Incorporated, Cal-Neva Lodge, Nevada.

The borrower was seeking an immediate loan of $3,000,000 with an additional commitment for $2,000,000. This loan was to be used for the purpose of developing the resort.

Trustee James R. Hoffa summarized the application as follows:

The request for the loan was on Park Lake Enterprises, Cal-Neva Lodge, Nevada, for a $3,000,000 present loan with an additional commitment of $2,000,000. Hoffa asked Rudin to explain the application.

Mr. Rudin advised the Trustees that Mr. Frank Sinatra was the principal stockholder of the corporation. Cal-Neva had been operated for 30 years at Lake Tahoe. Sinatra had acquired majority control over the past two years and started an expansion program without permanent financing.

Rudin detailed the application and said they were asking for $5,000,000 with the understanding that the additional $2,000,000 which would be only 60% of the applicant's actual cash was additional investment in additional construction.

In response to a question asked by Trustee Albert Matheson, Rudin stated that Sinatra and others will have $540,000 plus some monies they have loaned in, namely, a quarter million dollars from various companies.

Rudin continued that it was their intention to put other Sinatra ventures into this which would supply income and additional capitalization rather than put in tax paid dollars. Rudin also stated that if the Fund put $5,000,000 into this project the property would then be worth from $8,000,000 to $10,000,000.

A motion was made by Trustee Frank Fitzsimmons that the loan be rejected on the basis presented and "that the man come in" and give a definite presentation for a future request on the actualities of what is going to be entailed in his request for money.

The motion which was seconded by Trustee John Spickerman was carried with dissent.

After the vote, Hoffa who was acting as chairman, advised Rudin as follows:

"The committee has rejected the presentation presented today and recommends that you present at the next meeting here, more concise program—namely, exactly how much money you are going to spend, how much money you are going to have in this from Sinatra and the other stockholders' interest in it, and what your projection is going to be for the next five years, so we will know exactly what this Fund is investing in. Plus, we want to have an outline as to what other enterprises will Sinatra put into this operation to show that there will be ability to pay back the money he borrows from us."

This document contains neither recommendations nor conclusions of the Federal Bureau of Investigation. It is the property of the Federal Bureau of Investigation and is loaned to your agency; it and its contents are not to be distributed outside your agency.

TO: SAC, Las Vegas   DATE: 7/2/63
FROM: Director, FBI   PERSONAL ATTENTION

This case should be placed in a closed status in view of the fact that the trustees of the Teamsters Union Pension Fund during the 9/21/62 meeting rejected the loan application in this matter.

All offices in the future should be alert to any indication this loan is being reactivated. Should this occur, the Bureau and other interested offices are to be furnished a letterhead memorandum suitable for dissemination. No open inquiries are to be made in connection with this loan in absence of specific advice from the Bureau.

Soon after Sinatra was interviewed about the Teamsters loan, the FBI's special agent in charge for Los Angeles asked Hoover for authorization to look into planting a bug (a "misur installation" in bureau jargon) in Sinatra's Palm Springs home—the same house where the singer had hosted Giancana and JFK.

DATE: April 24, 1963
TO: DIRECTOR, FBI
FROM: SAC, LOS ANGELES
ATTENTION: ASSISTANT DIRECTOR COURTNEY EVANS
RE: FRANK SINATRA
    "Francis Albert Sinatra" (True Name)
    ANTI-RACKETEERING

The Los Angeles Division during recent weeks has been in receipt of information that would tend to indicate the above-captioned individual apparently intends to spend more of his time in the Palm Springs area, than in Los Angeles. He has had installed a direct telephone line between his home in Palm Springs and his personal offices at 9339 Sunset Boulevard, Los Angeles.

A review of information that has accrued during the years, especially the past few years, has shown a constant association of SINATRA with some of the more infamous individuals of modern times, i.e., during the late 40's with LUCKY LUCIANO, and he was reputedly a money courier for the benefit of LUCIANO; during the 30's, various pieces of information tend to indicate an alliance with the late WILLIE MORETTI of New Jersey.

Currently and for the past several years, and reported by the Chicago, Las Vegas and Los Angeles Division of the Bureau, he has tied up with SAM "MOONEY" GIANCANA, with GIANCANA apparently issuing him orders as regards to appearances at the Villa Venice, the use of SINATRA's house at Palm Springs for assignations with PHYLLIS MC GUIRE, accompanying of SINATRA recently in Acapulco, and during the past season at Cal-Neva having JOHNNY FORMOSA present at Cal-Neva Lodge with apparently a great deal to say in its operation.

Chicago sources have advised of GIANCANA's disappointment in SINATRA's apparent inability to get the administration to tone down its efforts in the anti-racketeering field.

On at least two occasions during past years, SINATRA has been in Atlantic City, and taking over the floor of one of the major hotels has had a number of prominent hoodlums such as BONANNO of Phoenix, FISCHETTI of Miami, GIANCANA and others in attendance with all local hotel help barred from the floor.

SINATRA is an owner of considerable points in the Sands Hotel, Las Vegas, and at present is about a 100% owner of Cal-Neva Lodge at Lake Tahoe.

In interviews concerning this ownership, he has maintained he is the owner in fact as well as of record, that he represents no one other than himself and that GIANCANA is someone he recalls meeting at an airport and he has no connection other than as an entertainer keeping himself before the public. Confidential sources tend to furnish information to the contrary.

*   *   *

The long continued association of SINATRA as a possible front for investments for hoodlums of both national and international stature has led to the belief by this division that a confidential source if established in Palm Springs concerning SINATRA would undoubtedly develop information of extremely valuable intelligence nature, and furnish a picture of top level criminal investments and operations.

Authority is requested to conduct a preliminary survey to determine the feasibility of a misur installation at SINATRA's residence in Palm Springs, California.

No action will be taken in this matter without Bureau authority. Full security is assured.

SINATRA's home near Palm Springs has the mailing address of 70-558 Wonder Palms Road, Rancho Mirage, California.

But, surprisingly, Hoover rejected the request.

TO: SAC, Los Angeles   DATE: 4/29/63
FROM: Director, FBI
SUBJECT: FRANK SINATRA
          "Francis Albert Sinatra" (True Name)
          ANTI-RACKETEERING

Re your airtel 4/24/63.

Bureau authority not granted at this time to conduct a survey to
determine the feasibility of a misur installation in Frank Sinatra's
Palm Springs, California, residence. In the event you develop
information which would warrant such an installation, you may
resubmit your recommendations. You are reminded that all misurs
must be completely justified.

*The FBI, however, continued to keep a close eye on Giancana as part of
RFK's mob clampdown. In June of 1963, agents in the Chicago FBI office
started harassing Giancana with what they called "lockstep surveillance." It
drove him to distraction. Desperate, Giancana sued to get the FBI to back
off, but he also made an extraordinary overture involving Sinatra, as recounted in this Hoover memo to RFK.*

TO: The Attorney General   DATE: July 9, 1963
FROM: Director, FBI
SUBJECT: SAMUEL M. GIANCANA

We have learned through our surveillance of Giancana that he
has resumed holding meetings in the Armory Lounge in Forest Park,
Illinois. Giancana's lieutenants have been shuttling carloads of
individuals to and from this location where Giancana "holds court"
at a large table just inside the entrance.

Last week one of Giancana's top lieutenants, Charles "Chuck"
English, contacted our Agents and requested an interview. This
interview took place in the Armory Lounge at a time when
Giancana was also present in another part of the lounge. At one
point Anthony Tisci, attorney, son-in-law of Giancana and now his

representative in the First Ward, joined in the conversation. Tisci admitted that Giancana's reason for instituting court action was a "desperation measure" caused by his extreme agitation over FBI surveillance. Tisci stated further, "We are putting all our eggs in one basket."

Toward the end of the interview, English, who was slightly intoxicated, attempted to persuade Giancana to talk with the Agents. Giancana declined but as the Agents were driving away, English came out with a message from Giancana that, "If Bobby Kennedy wants to talk to me, I'll be glad to talk to him and he knows who to go through." In this respect English had previously mentioned Frank Sinatra as a person who could arrange such a meeting.

Nothing ever came of the overture. On July 16, 1963, Giancana's court action resulted in the FBI being ordered to back off. Until the FBI could get the order reversed, other law enforcers picked up his trail, "much to the consternation of Giancana, [who] shouted a steady tirade of verbal abuse" every time he noticed he was being followed, an FBI memo reported. That same month, Giancana made a fateful visit to the Cal-Neva. This excerpt from a later FBI memo described the result: Sinatra was forced to divest himself of interests in both the Cal-Neva and the Sands.

██████████████ furnished information in ████████████████ which reflected that SAM GIANCANA immediately upon cessation of FBI surveillance eluded a surveillance placed by the Cook County Sheriff's Department and proceeded on two separate occasions in July of 1963, to Lake Tahoe, California area where he met with PHYLLIS MC GUIRE, and reportedly stayed at the Cal-Neva Lodge, of which FRANK SINATRA is a part-owner.

*   *   *

██████████████████ advised that during GIANCANA's stay at the Cal-Neva Lodge, an incident occurred on one evening whereby GIANCANA became involved in a brawl with one VICTOR

COLLINS, who was at that time the road manager of the
MC GUIRE sisters.

As word of GIANCANA's appearance in Lake Tahoe spread, it
came to the attention of the Nevada Gaming Control Board, who
began an investigation based on the Board's regulations, to the effect
that persons whose names were contained in the "Nevada Black
Book" were not allowed access to the gambling facilities in Nevada.
According to the Nevada Gaming Control Board rules, if owners of
gambling establishments in that state failed to accede to these
regulations, they are liable to lose their gambling license.

During a subsequent investigation by the Gambling Control
Board, it was determined that GIANCANA had in fact been at the
Cal-Neva Lodge in the company of PHYLLIS MC GUIRE and upon
further investigation by the Gaming Control Board Investigators, it
was brought out that persons employed at the Cal-Neva Lodge
attempted to bribe investigators of this organization. According to
newspaper releases on the situation, EDWARD OLSON, Chairman
of the Gaming Control Board, advised that SINATRA had used
highly insulting language upon OLSON in connection with these
hearings.

The Gaming Control Board gave SINATRA and his attorney,
HARRY CLAIBORNE until October 7 in which to present
evidence in refutation of the charges made.

On October 7, 1963, CLAIBORNE made a press release to the
effect that SINATRA was divesting himself of all of his gambling
interests in Nevada. The release continued that SINATRA claimed
that he had several months previously instructed his attorney to
dispose of these interests inasmuch as he intended to take control of
the Warner Brothers Studio in Hollywood, California.

SINATRA failed to file any answer to the complaint filed by the
Gaming Control Board. In that no answer was filed by midnight of
October 7, the Nevada Gaming Commission automatically revoked
SINATRA's license at the Cal-Neva Lodge.

*Another FBI memo picks up the story and provides a glimpse at the reac-
tion of Giancana's hometown newspaper.*

Information was received in October, 1963, from the Las Vegas Division that SINATRA had agreed to sell his interest in the Sands Hotel in Las Vegas, Nevada to Sands, Inc. The arrangement was that SINATRA would resell his nine points at an agreed price of $43,500 per point. In this regard it is pointed out that information was received that SINATRA, when originally purchasing these points, had paid an estimated $5,000 per point. At this same time, it was learned that SINATRA was selling his interest in the Cal-Neva Lodge located at Lake Tahoe, Nevada. As noted previously, these sales were the direct result of an investigation conducted into SINATRA's association with SAM GIANCANA. In this regard the following editorial concerning GIANCANA's and SINATRA's relationship appeared in the "Chicago Tribune" of October 24, 1963:

"THAT OLD GANG OF MINE"

"The narrow-minded, sanctimonious, and bigoted state Gaming commission of Nevada has dealt a cruel and unjust blow to Frank Sinatra, the warbler, by stripping him of his licenses to operate so-called games of chance for the visiting rubes. Frankie Boy has been held a peril to the high ethics of Nevada gambling because he provided a royal welcome at one of his joints to Momo Giancana, a Chicago gangster, who has a high rating in the hoodlum Cosa Nostra bluebook.

"Giancana was a guest at Sinatra's Lake Tahoe lodge, and his mere presence was deemed, under the bluenose standards prevailing in Nevada, to be a contamination of all that is pure and virtuous in the gambling racket. So now the revered Leader of the Hollywood Rat Pack will have to divest himself of a 3½ million dollar interest in sucker traps at Tahoe and Las Vegas.

"Well, this is an hour when true friends will close ranks around Sinatra in his time of trouble, while phonies and fair weather fakers will suddenly remember they have dates elsewhere.

"Frankie has stood by Momo. Will Momo stand by Frankie? And will the Pack come running with the crying towel? When the roll is called out yonder, will Sammy Davis be there? Will Peter Lawford, the brother-in-law of President John F. Kennedy, rally round the Leader? How about Dean Martin, another member of The Clan? Anybody seen him? Will Frankie Boy's Hollywood tailor, Don Loper, who outfitted him for the J.F.K. inauguration, turn up to renew his fealty or will he retire to the cutting room with a mouthful of pins?

"Yea, these are the times when the sheep are separated from the goats, and the trueblue Rat Packers from the finks.

"We put it flatly: Will Frankie's principal patron stand up and be counted? We refer, of course, to J.F.K., who has been entertained by the disbarred gambler at Las Vegas and who permitted Frankie and Pack to take over provision of the entertainment at the Kennedy inauguration ball in Washington. There, in Mr. Loper's finery, Frankie cut such a resplendent figure that Joe E. Lewis wired, 'May I have the first dance?'

"The least we should expect of Mr. Kennedy is to rush word by ZIP code that, tho they may have padlocked Frankie's Nevada joints, the latchstring at the White House is out. Perhaps, by way of compensation, Frankie could be awarded the gaming concession at the state department, with a bank of one-armed bandits, dice tables, wheels, and fare boxes, the whole to be known, in memory of Nevada days, as 'The New Frontier,' which we find infinitely more tasteful than, say, 'The Last Chance Saloon.'

"Bobby Baker, the get-rich-quick operator, has little to occupy him since his resignation as secretary of the Democratic Senate majority because of a flyer in vending machines. He might be made an honorary member of the Rat Pack and allowed to team up with Frankie long enough to restore the Sinatra fortunes."

One of RFK's top mob prosecutors, Dougald D. MacMillan, arrived in Los Angeles in 1963 to mount the feds' most serious effort to nail Sinatra. He had a high-profile plan to interview well-known celebrities close to Sina-

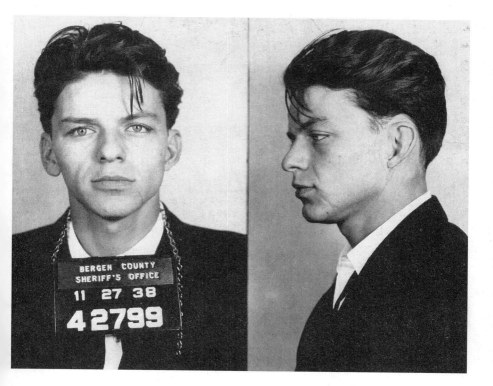

Mugshots showing Frank Sinatra on November 27, 1938—a couple of weeks shy of his twenty-third birthday—after his arrest in New Jersey for seduction under a false promise of marriage. The charge, recorded in the police report at left, was later changed to adultery and then dropped. In the side view, there appears to be a scar under his left ear, where an injury at birth later disqualified him from the World War II draft.

Sinatra signs papers in December 1943 at the Jersey City draft board with clerk Mae Jones. She told the FBI he didn't get special treatment, but she had the impression he knew he'd be rejected. *NEW YORK WORLD-TELEGRAM & SUN COLLECTION (LIBRARY OF CONGRESS)*

Sailors throw tomatoes at Sinatra's image on the marquee of New York City's Paramount Theatre in 1944. Historian William Manchester once called him "the most hated man of World War II" for becoming a millionaire heartthrob while others fought. BETTMANN/CORBIS

Dear Sir:

The other day I turned on a Frank Sinatra program and I noted the shrill whistling sound, created supposedly by a bunch of girls cheering. Last night as I heard Lucky Strike produce more of this same hysteria I thought: how easy it would be for certain-minded manufacturers to create another Hitler here in America through the influence of mass-hysteria! I believe that those who are using this shrill whistling sound are aware that it is similar to that which produced Hitler. That they intend to get a Hitler in by first planting in the minds of the people that men like Frank Sinatra are O.K. therefore this future Hitler will be O.K. As you are well aware the future of some of these manufacturers is rather shaky unless something is done like that.

sincerely,

This 1943 letter from a concerned citizen apparently is the first document the FBI placed in its Sinatra file.

Sinatra is as much to blame as are the moronic bobby-sopers.

H.

Hoover did not have a high opinion of the crooner. He scrawled this note on a 1946 FBI memo about how Sinatra's appearance in Detroit prompted many girls to skip school.

Sinatra, with Saul Chaplin on piano, entertains 10,000 soldiers in Italy in July 1945. The singer later would be denied permission to perform for troops in Korea amid suspicions that he was a Communist.

U.S. SIGNAL CORPS (NATIONAL ARCHIVES)

Sinatra and fellow performers Fay McKenzie, Phil Silvers, and Betty Yeaton in Naples, Italy, just before they returned from their 1945 USO tour.

U.S. AIR FORCE (NATIONAL ARCHIVES)

Columnist Lee Mortimer behind Sinatra in a Beverly Hills courtroom in April 1947. The star was facing charges for punching Mortimer. Sinatra's disdain for the press wasn't completely unjustified. A month later, Mortimer asked the FBI for derogatory information on the singer. The case was settled out of court in June.
BETTMANN/CORBIS

Sinatra Pays $9,000, Writer Drops Charge

By the Associated Press

BEVERLY HILLS, Calif., June 4. — Columnist Lee Mortimer has dropped his assault charge against Frank Sinatra — announcing that the crooner had agreed to pay him $9,000—but the boys didn't make up.

Former first lady Eleanor Roosevelt and Sinatra admire a statuette of her late husband in 1947. A congressman once derided Sinatra as "Mrs. Roosevelt in pants" for his liberal views.
FRANKLIN D. ROOSEVELT LIBRARY

Sinatra Is Playing With the Strangest People These Days

By ROBERT C. RUARK Scripps-Howard Staff Writer

HAVANA, Feb. 20—It is probably my wistful old worldliness cropping up again, but I am frankly puzzled as to why Frank Sinatra, the fetish of millions, chooses to spend his vacation in the company of convicted vice operators and assorted hoodlums from Miami's plush gutters.

In February 1947, the FBI's focus shifted from Sinatra's supposed Communist ties to his organized-crime contacts after the appearance of this column by Robert Ruark of the Scripps-Howard syndicate. Ruark, who happened to be in Havana, learned that Sinatra had traveled there with two Chicago mobsters and was seen at a casino, at a racetrack, and at parties with Lucky Luciano, the father of the modern Mafia.

FBI Director J. Edgar Hoover (left) and his top aide and closest friend, Clyde Tolson, in 1950. Tolson was the recipient or author of many FBI Sinatra memos. © *WASHINGTON POST*; REPRINTED BY PERMISSION OF THE D.C. PUBLIC LIBRARY

When the bureau heard from a third party that Sinatra was willing to help the FBI expose subversives, Clyde Tolson scrawled his recommendation on the bottom of this September 1950 memo about the overture. Hoover added: "I agree."

Hoover (left) and Richard Nixon at Griffith Stadium in Washington, D.C., probably in the 1950s. The man at right appears to be Tolson. Years later, despite FBI warnings that Sinatra associated with mobsters, President Nixon befriended the singer. © *WASHINGTON POST*; REPRINTED BY PERMISSION OF THE D.C. PUBLIC LIBRARY

Sinatra backstage in 1956 with columnist Walter Winchell. The singer had thanked Winchell years earlier for standing by him amid controversy, yet FBI documents indicate the scribe confidentially gave the bureau unsubstantiated tips that Sinatra was a draft-dodger and a Communist. PHOTOGRAPHER CHARLOTTE BROOKS; *LOOK* MAGAZINE COLLECTION (LIBRARY OF CONGRESS)

Chicago mob boss (and Sinatra pal) Sam Giancana invokes the Fifth Amendment before Senator John McClellan's rackets committee in 1959, prompting ridicule from the panel's chief counsel, Robert F. Kennedy. Sinatra was a friend of both Giancana and Senator John F. Kennedy, a member of the committee. Giancana later provided political muscle to JFK's presidential campaign while secretly plotting with the CIA to kill Fidel Castro. Sinatra's relationships with Giancana and the Kennedys became strained after RFK became attorney general and cracked down on the mob. BETTMANN/CORBIS

The Rat Pack—Sinatra, Dean Martin, Sammy Davis, Jr., and Peter Lawford—filming *Ocean's 11* in Las Vegas in January 1960. During a Rat Pack show at the Sands casino the next month, Sinatra introduced Senator Kennedy to a former girlfriend, Judith Campbell, who later became JFK's mistress.   PHOTOGRAPHER EARL THEISEN; *LOOK* MAGAZINE COLLECTION (LIBRARY OF CONGRESS)

Judith Campbell Exner attends a press conference with her husband, Dan Exner (left), in December 1975, shortly after her early 1960s affair with JFK was exposed. She also had an affair with Giancana. BETTMANN/CORBIS

Sinatra and Senator Kennedy at a fund-raiser in Los Angeles
in July 1960.   BETTMANN/CORBIS

Washington attorney Marvin Braverman greets Sinatra and Peter Lawford
(JFK's brother-in-law) at National Airport in January 1961, as the singer
prepares to oversee JFK's inaugural gala. The FBI later reported that Sinatra
visited a gambling house on inauguration weekend and "lost heavily."

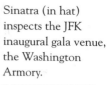

Sinatra (in hat) inspects the JFK inaugural gala venue, the Washington Armory.

© WASHINGTON POST; REPRINTED BY PERMISSION OF THE D.C. PUBLIC LIBRARY

President Kennedy meets with Hoover and Attorney General Robert Kennedy in February 1961, weeks after the director informed RFK that Sinatra was an "associate of well-known hoodlums."

JOHN FITZGERALD KENNEDY LIBRARY

The McGuire Sisters (Christine, Dorothy, and Phyllis) with hairdresser Frederic Jones and Phyllis's boyfriend, Giancana, in London, 1961. The couple later visited Sinatra's Cal-Neva Lodge in Lake Tahoe, causing a brouhaha that forced him to divest his casino interests in 1963.   CORBIS

How Hood Got Sinatra In a Jam

Giancana Flew To Nevada After FBI Watch Ended

BY JACK WILLNER

The day after U.S. District Judge Richard B. Austin ordered the FBI to limit its surveillance of hoodlum Sam Giancana, the mobster hopped a plane for a Nevada rendezvous with singer Frank Sinatra.

President Kennedy and Hoover in the Oval Office in May 1963, a year or so after FBI reports on Sinatra and Judith Campbell prompted JFK to distance himself from both.   JOHN FITZGERALD KENNEDY LIBRARY

Frank Sinatra and Mia Farrow in 1965 outside the Shubert
Theatre in New York. Two years later, a secondhand source told
the FBI that Farrow (by then Sinatra's wife) had lost $20,000
gambling in Las Vegas and that the enraged singer lost $50,000
trying to win it back.   *NEW YORK WORLD-TELEGRAM & SUN*
COLLECTION (LIBRARY OF CONGRESS)

Frank Sinatra, Jr., in Thailand to entertain
U.S. troops fighting the Vietnam War in
1966, three years after he'd been
kidnapped.   U.S. AIR FORCE
(NATIONAL ARCHIVES)

Nancy Sinatra chats with a wounded
American at a base in Vietnam in 1967.
She later wrote two affectionate biographies
of her father, which the editors of this book
consulted to help put the FBI documents in
context.   U.S. AIR FORCE
(NATIONAL ARCHIVES)

California Governor Ronald Reagan, Vice President Spiro
Agnew, and Sinatra hit the links in Los Angeles in August
1972, shortly after the singer was forced to testify before the
House Select Committee on Crime.
WHITE HOUSE (NATIONAL ARCHIVES)

Sinatra and Nixon in August 1972.
WHITE HOUSE (NATIONAL ARCHIVES)

Sinatra at the White House with President Giulio Andreotti of Italy, President Nixon, and the leaders' wives in April 1973. Nixon had asked Sinatra to come out of retirement to sing at a state dinner for the Italian leader, apparently disregarding FBI memos sent to the White House on Sinatra's continued association with mobsters.

President Reagan and his wife, Nancy, attend a party in December 1985
with an all-star cast, including Sinatra (standing to the left of Reagan)
and fellow Rat-Packer Dean Martin (to the right of Reagan).
COURTESY THE RONALD REAGAN LIBRARY

tra, but it struck other law enforcement types as ill-considered. Hoover was told of their doubts in a memo.

TO: DIRECTOR, FBI   DATE: 8/28/63
FROM: SAC, LOS ANGELES
SUBJECT: FRANK SINATRA
              AR [Anti-Racketeering]

On 8/27/63, Departmental Attorney DOUGALD MACMILLAN, Organized Crime Section, arrived in Los Angeles and immediately contacted THOMAS R. SHERIDAN, Chief, Criminal Division, U. S. Attorney's Office at Los Angeles. Mr. SHERIDAN said MACMILLAN was here to discuss data which the Department has available on FRANK SINATRA and a number of his associates. SHERIDAN requested Bureau Agents to be present.

On 8/28/63 Mr. MACMILLAN advised that he, over a long period of time, has been building up a file from excerpts taken from reports of the FBI and Internal Revenue Service (IRS) and other agencies concerning SINATRA. He advised that it appears there is some connection existing between the Fontainebleau Hotel, JOSEPH FISCHETTI and SINATRA and The Villa Venice, SAM GIANCANA and SINATRA and the purpose of his inquiry in this area was to solicit suggestions and organize a starting point in the possible interviewing of persons close to SINATRA. Such persons include DEAN MARTIN, SAMMY DAVIS, JR., DINAH SHORE and EDDIE FISHER and also the interviewing of RED SKELTON in connection with moneys that SKELTON allegedly lost while flying in a commercial aircraft last year ▮▮▮▮▮▮▮▮ Las Vegas.

Mr. MACMILLAN said he did not have authority to conduct any interviews directly with SINATRA or with persons directly connected with SINATRA in any of SINATRA's enterprises, such as SINATRA's attorney, accountants, or immediate staff. He did say he had authority to interview the others mentioned in the preceding paragraph.

Mr. SHERIDAN advised MACMILLAN that the proper starting

point for this type of investigation would be to secure all documentary evidence such as the contracts existing between SINATRA and others who appeared at the Fontainebleau Hotel, allegedly at the request of JOE FISCHETTI. The purpose of securing the documents would be that the person interviewing any of those named above would be in a position to intelligently discuss specific instances without being referred to booking agents, managers or attorneys.

Mr. MACMILLAN also observed that he was sure that in compiling his file he had missed many references concerning SINATRA and was considering the possibility of making inquiry of the Bureau of Washington, D.C., for a complete run down on SINATRA. No commitments were made by Bureau representatives present.

For a portion of the time, representatives of IRS were present and Mr. MACMILLAN repeated essentially the same material that appears above. ROBERT LUND, Chief of the Intelligence Division of IRS, told MACMILLAN that as far as he knew, IRS was not conducting any investigation of SINATRA other than the usual audit of returns of persons in high revenue brackets.

It would appear that Mr. MACMILLAN, at the present time, does not have any organized plan of approach nor is he quite certain as to the goal he is attempting to achieve with the information which he has accumulated.

Days later, somebody scrawled on a related FBI memo, "MacMillan is a boy on a man's errand." On September 4, 1963, Hoover undercut MacMillan with a memo to the special agent in charge of Los Angeles, and MacMillan went home to formulate a "more productive" plan.

TO: SAC, Los Angeles
FROM: Director, FBI
SUBJECT: FRANK SINATRA
          AR [Anti-Racketeering]

Los Angeles should take no action whatever which could be interpreted as investigation of Frank Sinatra. Any requests for investigation should be brought immediately to the Bureau's attention and no action taken in the absence of specific authorization from the Bureau.

Keep the Bureau closely advised of any information coming to your attention relating to any inquiry being conducted concerning Sinatra.

TO: Director, FBI   DATE: 9/10/63
FROM: SAC, Los Angeles
RE: FRANK SINATRA
     ANTI-RACKETEERING

Re Los Angeles airtel dated 8/28/63 and Bureau airtel dated 9/4/63.

For the information of the Bureau, it was ascertained on a confidential basis from THOMAS R. SHERIDAN, Chief, Criminal Division, United States Attorney's Office, Los Angeles, California, that DOUGALD MAC MILLAN, Departmental Attorney, who was in the Los Angeles area regarding certain aspects of FRANK SINATRA, has now returned to the Department of Justice following the Labor Day Weekend.

According to SHERIDAN, MAC MILLAN, who originally had come to Los Angeles with an idea of interviewing certain prominent personalities, did not conduct any interviews and has returned to the Washington area to further study the material he has on hand in order to formulate some plan of action that might be more productive than the one that he originally proposed, that is interviewing persons such as DEAN MARTIN, SAMMY DAVIS,

Jr., DINAH SHORE, and EDDIE FISHER regarding the association of FRANK SINATRA with persons such as SAMUEL M. GIANCANA and JOSEPH FISCHETTI.

The Bureau will be kept advised of any information coming to the attention of this division regarding Mr. MAC MILLAN.

After MacMillan backed off, a further review by FBI agents of the old Sinatra files he had compiled turned up the possibly false statement that Sinatra had made in his interview with the IRS in 1959 (see chapter 4). In the memos excerpted below, the authorities considered whether to prosecute and detailed the evidence, the most significant of which was the recollections of a dancer and another witness who apparently had seen Giancana at the party in question.

TO: Mr. Belmont   DATE: October 9, 1963
FROM: C. A. Evans
SUBJECT: FRANK SINATRA
                ANTI-RACKETEERING

Based on information which we have supplied the Department concerning Sinatra's connection with the underworld, the Organized Crime and Racketeering Section of the Department assigned Departmental Attorney Dougald D. MacMillan to review all available information on Sinatra to determine whether prosecution could be initiated against Sinatra.

MacMillan has been in contact with Thomas R. Sheridan, Chief of the Criminal Division, United States Attorney's Office, Los Angeles, and also a special assistant to the Attorney General. MacMillan left his file on Sinatra with Sheridan in which he had apparently compiled all available data on Sinatra from FBI, Internal Revenue Service (IRS), and Federal Bureau of Narcotics reports. Sheridan, on an extremely confidential basis, made this file available to our Los Angeles Office for reviewing, indicating that he did not desire that the Department or MacMillan become aware of this.

In reviewing this file, Los Angeles noted a possible Fraud Against the Government violation in connection with apparently false statements made by Sinatra in an affidavit given to IRS, Los Angeles, in 1959. In this statement Sinatra denied the presence of Sam Giancana at a party in the Claridge Hotel, Atlantic City, New Jersey, in July, 1959. However, in our investigation of Sam Giancana we interviewed a professional dancer who advised that she was present at this party ███████████████████ She also identified several other hoodlums in attendance including Rocco and Joseph Fischetti.

RECOMMENDATION OF SAC, LOS ANGELES

SAC, Los Angeles recommends that this possible violation be brought to the attention of Mr. Sheridan and his opinion as to prosecution secured. SAC, Los Angeles points out if investigation is warranted a grand jury could possibly be convened at Los Angeles and Giancana, Joseph Fischetti and other personalities present at the 1959 meeting could be brought before the grand jury.

ACTION

Los Angeles is being authorized to bring this possible violation to the attention of the United States Attorney's Office at Los Angeles but to point out that any request for investigation should be channeled through the Department.

* * *

To substantiate the information of the violation are the following excerpts from FBI reports:

Pages 89–90 of September 12, 1960, FBI report entitled "Samuel M. Giancana" prepared by SA [Special Agent] ███████████████ reflected that ███████████████ advised on September 16, 1959 that he had recently been to the Claridge Hotel in Atlantic City, New Jersey, in order to see Frank Sinatra and was told SINATRA had reserved the entire first floor of the hotel. The informant stated when they got off the elevator on the first floor they were approached by two "tough looking men" and asked for identification and purpose of their visit. The informant stated one individual in SINATRA's suite at this hotel was identified to him as JOSEPH FISCHETTI, described as the "well known hoodlum from Miami."

Page 6 of July 13, 1962, FBI report entitled "Samuel M. Giancana" prepared by SA [Special Agent] ███████████ Chicago Office, reported that ██████████████████████████████
██

She stated that at the age of approximately eighteen she became employed as a professional dancer, appearing in chorus lines at various hotels, night clubs and casinos around the country. ████████████████████ she became acquainted with FRANK SINATRA during approximately 1958. During this period she traveled throughout the country and worked for some time at the Tropicana and Riviera Hotels in Las Vegas.

In July, 1959, she attended a party given by FRANK SINATRA in Atlantic City, New Jersey, at the Claridge Hotel. SINATRA at that time was appearing at the 500 Club as the featured entertainer. The party referred to lasted approximately two weeks and normally started at about 8:00 PM and lasted until about 4:00 or 5:00 AM the following morning. ████████████████████ She mentioned other persons in attendance at this affair, in addition to the ones mentioned above, as actress NATALIE WOOD, actor ROBERT WAGNER, then the husband of NATALIE WOOD, ROCCO FISCHETTI, his brother, JOSEPH FISCHETTI, JOHN FOREMAN (true name JOHN FORMOSA) and PAUL "SKINNY" D'AMATO.

* * *

Also in connection with this matter, the Newark Division in October, 1959, by airtel dated 10/28/59, TOP HOODLUM PROGRAM, Chicago Division, AR., advised that █████████████ at the Claridge Hotel, had been assigned to the SINATRA party from 7/25–8/2/59 and had identified the photograph of SAM GIANCANA as closely resembling an individual visiting the SINATRA party on two or three occasions.

But in the end, Sinatra was let off the hook, according to this November 4, 1963, memo.

TO: Director, FBI
FROM: SAC, Los Angeles
RE: FRANCIS ALBERT SINATRA, aka.
    ANTI-RACKETEERING

Re Los Angeles airtel to Bureau dated 10/7/63 and Bureau airtel to Los Angeles dated 10/10/63.

The material relating to the possible violation of Title 18, Section 1001 was brought to the attention of Special Assistant to the Attorney General, THOMAS R. SHERIDAN at Los Angeles on 10/29/63 and Mr. SHERIDAN advised that in his opinion this was an apparent, though a minor violation of Title 18, Section 1001, and of itself, in his opinion, was not sufficient to warrant a prosecutive effort. He added that this, of course, could be added to other charges of a more substantial nature if and when such charges were ever developed in the future.

He advised that this matter is now known to DOUGALD MAC MILLAN of the Department and he concurs in this opinion.

Two and half weeks later, on November 22, 1963, the president was assassinated. Sinatra was told the news while filming a scene for Robin and the Seven Hoods *in a Burbank cemetery, according to Nancy Sinatra's biography. After a brief talk with a White House staffer, he told the crew, "Let's shoot this thing, 'cause I don't want to come back here anymore." Roselli, meanwhile, went to Judith Campbell's hotel room in Los Angeles to console her in the aftermath of the murder of her former lover.*

Ever since Jack Kennedy's murder, there have been suspicions that the mob was behind the crime. Though no one has ever come close to substantiating such conjecture, some of the coincidences are extraordinary, as demonstrated by these excerpts from the FBI's files on what the Warren Commission had to say about Sinatra. (Reprise Records was Sinatra's record company, which employed Mike Shore.)

Volume 14 of The Report Of The President's Commission On The Assassination of President Kennedy, contains the following information concerning Frank Sinatra:

On 4/14/64, Robert Carl Patterson, a musician and singer of Dallas, Texas, testified in the office of the US Attorney, Dallas, that in approximately November (year not stated) Jack Ruby was interested in promoting a "rock 'n roll" record for Patterson. Ruby told Patterson that he had connections with Reprise, with which Sinatra had something to do, and that the record could be promoted by Reprise.

On 5/28/64, Mrs. Eva Grant, sister of Ruby, also testified before the US Attorney in Dallas, concerning the selection of attorneys to defend Ruby. She stated that her brother Earl Ruby made a trip (date not stated) to the West Coast to see Mike Shore (not identified), who knew Sinatra there, and "they" figured they would know somebody and that was how Melvin Belli came into the picture as a defense lawyer for Ruby.

This reference indicated that Ruby killed Lee Harvey Oswald, who allegedly killed President Kennedy.

There certainly is ample evidence in the files that the mob did bear a grudge against the Kennedy family.

██████████████ advised he had heard that LCN [La Cosa Nostra] members had allegedly planned to attack the characters of U.S. Senators Edward and Robert Kennedy, as well as their brother-in-law, Peter Lawford. This was to be accomplished through associates of Frank Sinatra, who were to get the victims in compromising situations with women.

In 1975, Giancana and Roselli both met violent deaths themselves, in the midst of the Senate investigation of the CIA plot to kill Castro. Giancana got a .22-caliber bullet in the back of the head while cooking up a midnight snack of sausages in June, just before he was to testify. In July, just after he testified, Roselli wound up asphyxiated in a 55-gallon drum floating off the coast of Key Biscayne, Florida.

SEVEN

SINATRA TURNS RIGHT

"Don't go overboard in praise."

Politically, Frank Sinatra changed with his times, but what didn't change was his desire to be close to people in power. Early on, he was a prominent supporter of left-leaning causes. He sipped tea in the White House with FDR and named his son after the president—Franklin—rather than Francis, his own given name.

In the 1950s and early '60s, when Sinatra and Hugh Hefner were the defining American male ideals of sophisticated virility, the swinging singer had cultivated a kinship with the suave Jack Kennedy. Later Sinatra campaigned for Hubert Humphrey, shunning the slain president's brother Robert, whose anti-mob crusade had targeted Giancana and other Sinatra associates. But once the Republican Richard M. Nixon won the White House, Sinatra drew close to Vice President Spiro Agnew and supported the Republican ticket's reelection.

Sinatra's rightward shift reflected the political climate of the times and the increasingly conservative views of some other Hollywood Democrats who switched to the GOP, notably Ronald Reagan. Not surprisingly, Sinatra stumped for Reagan's reelection as California's governor in 1970. In 1981, the transformation was completed when Sinatra produced the gala for Reagan's presidential inauguration.

But the mellowed entertainer had little opportunity to come to terms with the ultraconservative Hoover, who died in 1972. In any case, the FBI was still watching—and warning each successive politician who befriended Sinatra that he was trouble.

After President Kennedy's death, the Johnson White House requested the lowdown on a number of celebrities, including Sinatra. Hoover's reply was sent to President Lyndon B. Johnson's assistant, Bill Moyers (who would later become a noted broadcast journalist). The reason for the request isn't clear, for Sinatra wasn't all that close to Johnson and didn't become friendly with Vice President Hubert Humphrey until later.

THE WHITE HOUSE
WASHINGTON

November 16, 1964

Memo to Mildred Stegall
From Barbara Keehn

At Mrs. Carpenter's request—I would like to have FBI reports on the following entertainers—as quickly as possible.

Carol Channing (Mrs. Charles Lowe)—NYC
Frank Sinatra—9229 Sunset Boulevard, L.A., Calif.
Lena Horne—NYC
Debbie Reynolds—Beverly Hills, Calif.
Carol Burnett—NYC
Dame Margot Fonteyn
Rudolf Nureyev
Peter Gennaro—NYC
Danny Kaye—1103 San Ysidro, Beverly Hills, Calif.
Mike Nichols
Elaine May

November 20, 1964
BY SPECIAL MESSENGER

Honorable Bill D. Moyers
Special Assistant to the President
The White House
Washington, D.C.

Dear Mr. Moyers:

Reference is made to the memorandum dated November 16, 1964, from Mrs. Barbara Keehn to Mrs. Mildred Stegall requesting name checks concerning Carol Channing and ten other individuals who were described as entertainers.

The FBI has not investigated the following individuals and our files contain no derogatory information identifiable with them.

Carol Channing   Peter Gennaro
Debbie Reynolds   Mike Nichols
Carol Burnett   Elaine May

There are enclosed two memoranda setting forth information concerning Frank Sinatra and Dame Margot Fonteyn.

With reference to Lena Horne, our files reveal that a summary of information available concerning Lena Horne was furnished the Honorable P. Kenneth O'Donnell by letter dated January 5, 1962. In addition to the information contained in that summary, our files reveal that the "Los Angeles Times" for November 1, 1963, contained an article which indicated that the radio stations in Los Angeles, California, banned the playing of a recording sung by Lena Horne entitled "Now," describing it as containing a "biting, angry integration message." The article further described the record as voicing a "strong racial freedom message" and the lyrics called for action now strengthening, according to the newspaper, the racial unrest in the United States.

We have not investigated Rudolf Nureyev; however, our files reveal that he has been publicly identified as a Soviet ballet artist who defected from the Leningrad Ballet in Paris, France, in June,

1961. Representatives of this Bureau have interviewed Mr. Nureyev and he has furnished limited information to the FBI. He was contacted by a Russian intelligence service shortly after his defection, but he stated he refused to cooperate with them. Since his defection he has danced with the British Royal Ballet in the United States and elsewhere.

Our files reveal that summaries of information in our files concerning Danny Kaye have been furnished the White House on January 12, 1962, May 10, 1962, and October 19, 1964. We have no additional information identifiable with Danny Kaye.

Sincerely yours,

J. Edgar Hoover

Hoover enclosed a summary report on Sinatra. It included the usual stuff about the draft and Communists, as well as some more recent information about his alleged association with mobsters.

November 20, 1964

FRANK SINATRA

*   *   *

We have received information over an extended period of time from sources, who have furnished reliable information in the past and who have knowledge of general criminal activities in the United States, that Sinatra has been a close friend and associate of Samuel Giancana, a former chauffeur and bodyguard for Anthony Accardo, the acknowledged leader of the syndicate (La Cosa Nostra) in Chicago, Illinois, prior to 1956. Giancana, described as a cold, brutal killer, assumed leadership of the syndicate in Chicago in approximately 1956. Giancana has been a guest at various places owned or operated by Sinatra and at Sinatra's home in Palm Springs, California. It has been reported that due to Sinatra's close association with Giancana and other syndicate hoodlums he lost his license to operate gambling establishments in the State of Nevada.

As a result of this loss, Sinatra was reported to have sold his interest in the Sands Hotel, Las Vegas, Nevada, for $43,500 per point for a total of $391,000 and his entire interest in the Cal Neva Lodge at Lake Tahoe, Nevada. . . .

In March, 1963, an informant who has furnished reliable information in the past advised that Sinatra and Dean Martin, well-known singer, were long-time friends of John Anthony Matassa. Matassa is a former member of the Chicago Police Department, who resigned many years ago after taking the Fifth Amendment before the McClellan Committee and as of 1963 was a business agent for a Chicago, Illinois, local of the Teamsters Union and reportedly a close associate of Samuel Giancana and other syndicate hoodlums.

In early 1964 another informant, who has furnished reliable information in the past regarding general criminal activities in the United States, indicated among other things that Paul "Skinny" D'Amato, operator of the 500 Club, Atlantic City, New Jersey, and a business partner with Sinatra in Nevada, was a hoodlum and a member of the La Cosa Nostra syndicate. The informant stated that although Sinatra was not a member of the syndicate, he was big enough and close enough to the organization to obtain any favors he desired.

In January 1967, Sinatra testified behind closed doors before a federal grand jury in Las Vegas looking into casinos allegedly controlled by the mob. That May the Italian-American Anti-Defamation League tapped Sinatra to head a nationwide effort to discourage the stereotyping of Italians as mobsters. The choice of an entertainer publicly known to associate with accused gangsters seemed odd to some. Still, the new group helped persuade the producers of The Untouchables *television series to change some of its hoodlum characters' surnames.*

And it managed to land Vice President Humphrey as a speaker. A Justice Department official requested and received the usual briefing materials on Sinatra, which included some new information. (The next year, Sinatra returned the favor: He endorsed Humphrey for president in the Democratic primary over Robert Kennedy, who had quit the Justice Department in 1964 to become a senator from New York.)

TO: Mr. Gale   DATE: May 18, 1967
FROM: W. V. Cleveland
SUBJECT: PROPOSED SPEECH BY VICE PRESIDENT
        HUMPHREY BEFORE AMERICAN ITALIAN ANTI-
        DEFAMATION LEAGUE, INC., NEW YORK CITY,
        MAY 20, 1967

On the night of 5-17-67, Mr. John T. Duffner, Executive Assistant, Office of the Deputy Attorney General, telephonically requested name checks of the following: Frank Sinatra, Ross J. DiLorenzo and the American Italian Anti-Defamation League, Inc. Duffner stated he was requesting this information in connection with a proposed speech by the Vice President before the American Italian Anti-Defamation League, Inc., on May 20, 1967.

Frank Sinatra is well known for his hoodlum associations and, according to recent press reports, has been named National Chairman of the above-mentioned league. The Department has been previously furnished complete details on the background of Sinatra and his association with hoodlums. Ross J. DiLorenzo is the president of this league. With reference to this organization, recent newspaper publicity has criticized it for the appointment of Sinatra to a high position in this organization. In an article dated May 12, 1967, in the "New York Times," former New York Police Officer Ralph Salerno took this organization to task for appointing Sinatra as National Chairman and indicated strongly that the Italian American community should face the facts that some 10,000 Italian wrongdoers were disgracing the 20 million law abiding Italian American citizens and that this organization should devote its activities to assisting law enforcement in cleaning up that element of Italian American communities which is in violation of law and order.

Among the directors of the American Italian Anti-Defamation

League, Inc., are listed Anthony Scotto and Dr. Mario Tagliagambe, concerning whom we have received allegations from confidential informants that they are reported members of La Cosa Nostra.

With specific reference to Ross J. DiLorenzo, he is the individual who, in a letter to the Bureau in March of this year, endeavored to imply that a Bureau television show defamed Italian Americans. In our reply, we set the record straight and pointed out to DiLorenzo that no such defamation occurred and, in fact, the principal character of the show in question was named Roland which is not an Italian name.

May 18, 1967

FRANK SINATRA

*   *   *

During the summer of 1964 an informant who has furnished reliable information in the past indicated that he had learned from one of the top hoodlums in the syndicate that on one occasion Sinatra owed the syndicate "a lot of money." He also stated that although it was publicly reported that Sinatra divested himself of all financial interests in gambling establishments in Nevada, he had actually not "cut loose" from his night clubs but that the names were changed concerning reported ownership.

*   *   *

The May 4, 1967, issue of "The New York Times" newspaper, New York City, contained an article captioned "Sinatra to Head Antibias Group." This article indicates in part Sinatra had been named National Chairman of the American Italian Anti-Defamation League. A copy of this article is enclosed.

The May 12, 1967, issue of "The New York Times" contained an article captioned "Sinatra Assailed as Ethnic Leader." This article indicates in part that Ralph Salerno, a former member of the New York City Police Department's Central Investigation Bureau, criticized the selection of Sinatra as National Chairman of the

American Italian Anti-Defamation League stating Sinatra's friendship and association with identified members of the Mafia "hardly matches the image the league is seeking to project as representative of the 20 million Americans of Italian birth or ancestry." A copy of this article is enclosed. Details concerning Sinatra previously furnished Department.

Three months later, White House aide Mildred Stegall again asked for and received an update on the Sinatra file from the FBI, as shown in this excerpt.

August 21, 1967
BY LIAISON

Mrs. Mildred Stegall
The White House
Washington, D.C.
Dear Mrs. Stegall:

Reference is made to your request for a review of the information in FBI files subsequent to the previous name check which was made on November 20, 1964, regarding Frank Sinatra.

Our files reveal that Frank Sinatra continues to associate both socially and on a business basis with alleged members of La Cosa Nostra and other members of the hoodlum element in this country. Notable among such associates are Sam Giancana, Chicago, Illinois, who reportedly has been out of the country for the past year, and Joseph Fischetti, Miami, Florida.

Meanwhile, Sinatra kept showing up in reports about the FBI's routine surveillance of mob figures and hangouts.

TO: Director, FBI
FROM: SAC, Miami
SUBJECT: ELSUR [Electronic Surveillance]
FRANK SINATRA
4/18/68

In connection with the Anti-Racketeering investigation of JOSEPH FISCHETTI, aka, Miami installed an eavesdropping device in Puccini's Restaurant, 991 N.E. 79th St., Miami, Florida.

On 3/26/62, FRANK SINATRA and FISCHETTI came to Puccini's Restaurant for dinner and parts of the conversation were overheard concerning his, SINATRA's, returning to Los Angeles and the airport being "fogged in," and they discussed the possibility of chartering a plane to New Orleans. It was general conversation and nothing was disseminated nor learned of value.

Later that year, Sinatra canceled campaign appearances on behalf of Humphrey, after The Wall Street Journal *detailed his continuing mob associations. By 1969, Sinatra's politics had begun to lean right. Shortly after Nixon's inauguration, the FBI (presumably Hoover himself) wrote to Nixon's top aide, John D. Ehrlichman of Watergate fame, to fill him in on Sinatra's background.*

April 25, 1969

Honorable John D. Ehrlichman
Legal Counsel to the President
The White House
Washington, D.C.
Dear Mr. Ehrlichman:

This letter is being written to you to outline briefly association for many years by Frank Sinatra with many leaders of La Cosa Nostra. As you know, that organization is the dominant force in the country's organized crime underworld.

Sinatra, who was born December 12, 1915 (or 1916), in

Hoboken, New Jersey, was associated early in his singing career with the late notorious Willie Moretti, a long-time La Cosa Nostra leader in northern New Jersey who became the victim of a gangland type slaying in 1951. Also quite early in his career, Sinatra was quite friendly with Paul Emelio D'Amato, a La Cosa Nostra member who, for many years, was the proprietor of The 500 Club, a night spot in Atlantic City, New Jersey.

Sinatra's association with D'Amato, who has served a penitentiary sentence as a panderer, continued over the years with Sinatra appearing at The 500 Club during many summer seasons. It has been reported that during some of those appearances, Sinatra rented one or two entire sleeping floors in the Claridge Hotel in Atlantic City for party purposes, the party actually being a cover for clandestine meetings of La Cosa Nostra leaders.

D'Amato and Sinatra were associated in the operation of the Cal Neva Lodge at Lake Tahoe, Nevada, during 1963. Salvatore "Sam" Giancana, long-time "boss" of the Chicago "family" of La Cosa Nostra, was frequently Sinatra's guest at the Cal Neva Lodge during that period. These connections on the part of Sinatra provided a basis for the revocation of his gambling license in the State of Nevada and the disposal of his interest in the Cal Neva Lodge as well as the Sands Hotel in Las Vegas, Nevada.

Sinatra was present in 1947 in Havana, Cuba, with top leaders of La Cosa Nostra who had gone there to meet with Salvatore Lucania, more commonly known as Lucky Luciano, former "boss of bosses" of La Cosa Nostra in the United States. Luciano had entered Cuba surreptitiously from his native country, Italy, to which he had been deported under his parole from a New York State penitentiary where he had been serving a sentence on conviction for compulsory prostitution.

Sinatra has long been very friendly with the Fischettis, particularly Joseph and Rocco. The Fischettis were connected with the Chicago "family" of La Cosa Nostra once headed by their cousin, the late Al Capone. Their deceased brother, Charles Fischetti, was once "boss" of the Chicago La Cosa Nostra.

In addition to the foregoing, ██████████████ that Joseph
Colombo, a New York La Cosa Nostra leader, met with Sinatra
██████████████ of Raymond Patriarca, New England La Cosa
Nostra leader, ████████████████████████████████████
that Colombo was asked by Patriarca to meet with Sinatra because of
a close friendship between the two. In prior years, Sinatra, together
with his friend and fellow entertainer, Dean Martin, became a
director of the Berkshire Downs Race Track in western
Massachusetts. ████████████████████████████████████

It is thought that this known and alleged connection of Sinatra's
with La Cosa Nostra leadership might be of interest to you.

*Scotland Yard also requested information on the singer—through an
American legal attaché ("Legat") in London—to prepare for an audience
with England's Queen Elizabeth. The background summary prepared for
Scotland Yard included a bare-bones memo on the usual Sinatra background material, as well as the latest news—Sinatra being forced to testify
before a New Jersey crime commission. (Though the FBI didn't know it at
the time, Sinatra confirmed under oath that Skinny D'Amato and Sam Giancana were indeed his friends but denied knowing that they and various
other infamous figures with whom he'd allegedly associated were organized
crime members.)*

URGENT 3-10-70
TO DIRECTOR
FROM LEGAT LONDON NO. 33
FRANK SINATRA, FOREIGN POLICE COOPERATION
ON MARCH NINE LAST JOHN WALDRON, COMMISSIONER,
METROPOLITAN POLICE, NEW SCOTLAND YARD, ADVISED
SINATRA AND COUNT BASIE ORCHESTRA ARE APPEARING AT
ROYAL FESTIVAL HALL, LONDON, ON MAY SEVEN AND EIGHT
NEXT IN A CHARITY PERFORMANCE FOR BENEFIT OF SOCIETY
FOR PREVENTION OF CRUELTY TO CHILDREN. SOCIETY HOLDS
ANNUAL PERFORMANCE, IS ONE OF ROYAL FAMILY'S FAVORITE

CHARITIES, THEY ARE USUALLY INVITED AND USUALLY ATTEND.

THE COMMISSIONER IS EXTREMELY CONCERNED OVER RECENT PUBLICITY AFFORDED SINATRA OVER TESTIFYING RE MAFIA CONNECTIONS IN NEW JERSEY. COMMISSIONER MUST MAKE RECOMMENDATION FOR OR AGAINST APPEARANCE OF QUEEN AND OTHER MEMBERS OF ROYAL FAMILY. IF QUEEN ATTENDS SINATRA WILL BE PRESENTED TO HER AND HE FEARS UNFAVORABLE PRESS MAY RESULT.

COMMISSIONER WOULD BE MOST APPRECIATIVE FOR SUMMARY OF PERTINENT AVAILABLE INFO RE SINATRA TO INCLUDE IDENT RECORD, WHY HE HAD TO DISPOSE OF LAS VEGAS INTERESTS, RECENT NEW JERSEY MATTER, ETC. HE ASSURES ANY INFO WILL BE TREATED AS CONFIDENTIAL AND BUREAU POSITIVELY NOT IDENTIFIED AS SOURCE. HE NEEDS INFO AS SOON AS POSSIBLE AS ROYAL FAMILY HAS RECEIVED INVITATION.

IN VIEW TREMENDOUS AMOUNT OF BUREAU WORK HANDLED BY NEW SCOTLAND YARD AND COMMISSIONER'S OUTSTANDING COOPERATION IN ALL MATTERS, RECOMMEND SUMMARY OF INFO REQUESTED BE POUCHED SOON AS POSSIBLE IN FORM SUITABLE FOR DISSEMINATION TO HIM.

TO: Mr. DeLoach   DATE: 3/12/70
FROM: A. Rosen
SUBJECT: FRANK SINATRA

PURPOSE:

Attached memorandum and ident record regarding Sinatra outline pertinent data in Bureau files regarding him and were prepared for forwarding to Commissioner Waldron, New Scotland Yard, at his specific request.

BACKGROUND:

3/10/70 cablegram from Legat, London, forwarded a specific request from Commissioner John Waldron, New Scotland Yard, for pertinent data in Bureau files regarding Sinatra, who has been invited to perform at a charity performance in London on May 7, 1970. This performance will benefit one of the favorite charities of the British royal family, who usually attend this function. New Scotland Yard believes that Sinatra will be presented to the queen and desires to guard against any unfavorable publicity which may result as a result of Sinatra's past affiliations with criminal and hoodlum elements in this country.

Attached letterhead memorandum outlines Sinatra's affiliation over the years with such well-known hoodlums and members of the La Cosa Nostra as the late Willie Moretti, Paul Emelio D'Amato, and Salvatore "Sam" Giancana. Attached memorandum also includes the results of a security-type investigation conducted regarding Sinatra in 1955, which disclosed that his name had been associated with or lent to approximately 16 organizations in the early and middle 1940's which were either communist fronts or communist infiltrated. This investigation did not uncover any actual Communist Party or front membership on Sinatra's part.

Commissioner Waldron has been most cooperative with the Bureau in the past and he has assured Legat, London, that any information received will be treated on a strictly confidential basis and the Bureau will not be identified as the source.

RECOMMENDATION:

That the attached letter to Legat, London, enclosing the above-mentioned letterhead memorandum and identification record be approved and that Legat, London, be authorized to furnish the data regarding Sinatra to Commissioner Waldron of New Scotland Yard on a strictly confidential basis in response to his request.

March 12, 1970

FRANK SINATRA

*   *   *

In June, 1969, Sinatra was subpoenaed to appear before the New Jersey State Commission of Investigation which was probing organized crime and corruption in New Jersey. Sinatra refused to honor this subpoena and as a result, a warrant citing him for civil contempt was issued. Sinatra was purged of this contempt after testifying before the Commission on February 17, 1970, and the contempt citation was dismissed at that time. The nature of Sinatra's testimony before the Commission has not been made known.

The FBI's apparent warning and the continuing controversy surrounding Sinatra notwithstanding, the Nixon administration courted his support. He had initially bonded with Vice President Spiro Agnew, whom he met in mid-1969 at a political event, and later socialized with him regularly. Soon the White House was inviting Sinatra to attend official functions and to play golf with the president.

This memo between two Nixon aides (from the National Archives' Nixon Project files, not the FBI's) indicates that the White House was concerned about the propriety of inviting Sinatra to the White House, but not because of his unsavory mob acquaintances.

November 30, 1970

MEMORANDUM FOR MRS. CONNIE STUART
FROM: DWIGHT L. CHAPIN

As you will recall, Frank Sinatra endorsed Ronald Reagan when he ran for the Gubernatorial election this year. The President and Mrs. Nixon invited Sinatra to attend the Diaz Ordaz dinner in San Diego. Sinatra did not attend the dinner but he did fly in for the reception, although he opened the same night in Las Vegas. Last weekend Sinatra played golf with the Vice President in Palm Springs.

I talked with Paul Keyes today and he offered the suggestion that perhaps Sinatra might be available to do an Evening at the White House. There are obviously strong arguments pro and con in giving Sinatra the White House forum. I am sure that many of our friends in the entertainment field would think it wrong to have a former anti-

Nixon person entertain at the White House. I am fairly well convinced that the publicity value alone—not to mention the development of a relationship between Sinatra and the President would far outweigh the negatives.

I offer this only as a possibility that you may wish to explore with the First Lady and with Paul Keyes directly.

At times the FBI's information was very obviously flawed, as in this September 15, 1971, memo from the FBI's special agent in charge for New York.

TO: DIRECTOR, FBI
FROM: SAC, NEW YORK
SUBJECT: FRANK SINATRA
               MISCELLANEOUS—
               INFORMATION CONCERNING

███████████████ advised that FRANK SINATRA has been diagnosed as having terminal cancer, and estimates of life expectancy vary to as little as two months. According to the source, SINATRA has been examined at Columbia Presbyterian Hospital, New York City, and his presence in New York was kept secret, with the exception of an appearance at the recent funeral of BENNETT CERF, at which time SINATRA appeared to be in extremely poor health.

This exchange of memos from a year later (also from the National Archives) indicates that the White House consciously overlooked Sinatra's controversial background a few months after his announced retirement from entertaining. Still, Chief of Staff H. R. Haldeman didn't want to go too far, so Nixon sent him a perfunctory letter.

THE WHITE HOUSE
WASHINGTON

November 1, 1971

MEMORANDUM FOR ELISKA HASEK
FROM: DICK MOORE

Warren Dorn, Chairman of the Los Angeles County Board of
Supervisors (a Republican), phoned me this morning to request a
presidential letter or telegram for Frank Sinatra, who is being
honored with the Los Angeles County Distinguished Service Award
this Thursday, November 4. The award will be made at a reception at
the Music Center which will be attended by the Supervisors, Mrs.
Norman Chandler, and other civic officials and community leaders.

Dorn said that Governor Reagan is also sending a message.
Sinatra actively supported Reagan in his 1970 campaign and I keep
hearing that there is some likelihood that he may support President
Nixon in 1972.

*　　*　　*

While Sinatra has been controversial, he seems to have settled
down since his retirement and I would think that a presidential
message would be appropriate and well received. However, I am
sending a copy of this memo to Bob Haldeman in case he knows any
reason why the President would think differently.

cc: H. R. Haldeman
　　Ray Price

THE WHITE HOUSE
WASHINGTON

NOTE PER INFO FROM DICK MOORE:
 On receiving his copy of the attached memo, Mr. Haldeman called Dick Moore to let him know that he thought the President would want to send a wire to Sinatra—but that it should be brief and very general (don't go overboard in praise).

 Attached file on Sinatra shows President invited him to attend dinner last year in San Diego for Diaz Ordaz (after Sinatra's endorsement & support for Gov. Reagan's reelection) and also talked to him by phone in March of this year, but no indication of subject of conversation.

Claudia 11/2/71

Mr. Frank Sinatra
c/o Honorable Warren M. Dorn
Chairman, Los Angeles County Board of Supervisors
500 West Temple Street
Los Angeles, California 90012

 My wholehearted congratulations to you as you receive the Los Angeles County Distinguished Service Award. It is highly fitting that your deep humanitarian concern and your generous contributions to the community be recognized, and it is a pleasure to join with those who honor you on this occasion in conveying my best wishes for every success in the future.

RICHARD NIXON

Days later, the star offered a plane ride to Attorney General John Mitchell's wife, Martha. The offer prompted this tellingly captioned memo to Assistant FBI Director Tolson.

TO: MR. TOLSON   DATE: 11/9/71
FROM: J. P. MOHR
SUBJECT: PROTECTION OF THE ATTORNEY GENERAL

In my memo of 11/5/71 details were set out concerning the travel
of the Attorney General, his wife and his daughter, Marty. There
have been no changes in the travel schedule; however, there has
been one change in the mode of transportation.

SA [Special Agent] ▓▓▓▓▓▓▓▓▓▓ who has been assigned to
be with Mrs. Mitchell for the duration of her travels, telephoned
from San Francisco at approximately 2:30 p.m. today. He referred to
the previous arrangement where Mrs. Mitchell would be traveling
from San Francisco to Los Angeles via Jet Star aircraft owned by Mr.
Robert Flour of the Flour Corporation. Departure time is still the
same but instead of utilizing the airplane owned by Flour, the party
will travel on a Gulfstream II jet airplane owned by Frank Sinatra. It
will be flown by a pilot employed by Sinatra named Captain Johnny
Spotts. The Attorney General apparently is not aware of this change
as he is en route to Los Angeles and is not due to arrive there until
5:00 p.m. today, 11/9/71. It is apparent that Frank Sinatra is
becoming quite active in politics on behalf of the campaign to
reelect President Nixon.

RECOMMENDATION:
None. For information.

*Alexander P. Butterfield, the bit player in Watergate who revealed the
existence of the Nixon tapes, requested information on Sinatra in early
1972, a few months before the Republican party invited Sinatra and his
daughter Tina to Washington for a series of VIP meetings, including a visit
to the White House. The FBI gave him the standard rundown, as well as
some more up-to-date information, as excerpted below.*

February 18, 1972

Honorable Alexander P. Butterfield
Deputy Assistant to the President
The White House
Washington, D.C.

Dear Mr. Butterfield:

Reference is made to your name check request concerning James Ross MacDonald, Malcolm Charles Moos, and Frank Sinatra.

Attached are separate memoranda concerning these individuals.

This letter of transmittal may be declassified when the enclosures bearing a classification are removed.

February 18, 1972

FRANK SINATRA

By communication dated April 25, 1969, the White House was advised of captioned individual's association for a number of years with many leaders of organized crime. Since April, 1969, information coming to our attention indicates that Mr. Sinatra continues to be in contact with and is visited by individuals who are associated with the organized crime element.

*   *   *

In June, 1969, a confidential source who has furnished reliable information in the past advised that a group of individuals, including several members of the organized crime element in the Kansas City, Missouri, area, took a junket trip to Las Vegas, Nevada, sponsored by Caesars Palace Hotel. According to this source, Joe "Turk" Harris personally contacted Frank Sinatra, who was appearing at Caesars Palace, and had Mr. Sinatra and his daughter, Nancy, meet with these individuals.

Chester Zechowski, who is also known as Chester Gray, advised that Gray was in Las Vegas at Caesars Palace during the prior weekend and allegedly had some type of business contact with actor Frank Sinatra. Gray and three other individuals were arrested on

May 29, 1969, at which time a large quantity of stolen securities was recovered by FBI Agents of our New York Office. On November 1, 1971, Gray was sentenced in U.S. District Court, New York City, to serve a term of three years in prison.

A confidential source who was in a position to know advised in March, 1970, that Sam Giancana, nationally known organized crime figure, had a falling out with Frank Sinatra and was reportedly watching Sinatra's activities for possible retaliation. According to this source, Giancana felt that Mr. Sinatra's main ambition at that time was to be the number one man in the Italian hierarchy in the United States.

██████████████ a confidential source who has furnished reliable information in the past advised that Joseph Anthony Colombo, head of the Italian-American Civil Rights League (IACRL), and a leader of the organized crime element in the New York City area, had discussed the planned Italian-American rally to be held on June 29, 1970, at Columbus Circle, New York. According to this source, Frank Sinatra was to be one of three individuals from the show business world who would be at this rally. ████████████████

██

██

██

██

In December, 1970, a confidential source who has furnished reliable information in the past advised that Frank Sinatra was the godfather to one of David Robert Iacovetti's children. Iacovetti was described as a member of the organized crime element in the Miami, Florida, area.

* * *

Sinatra is one a number of individuals who are currently subjects in an Interstate Transportation in Aid of Racketeering—Extortion investigation initiated by the FBI in February, 1971. That investigation was based on information received from a confidential source who has furnished reliable information in the past that an attempt was made to extort $100,000 from one Ronald Alpert by the use of physical force and by threatening Alpert's life. According to this source, Alpert was seeking buyers for Computer Field Expressway stock and allegedly came up with an investor who bought $100,000 worth of this stock, reportedly put up by three individuals, who were described as active in organized crime circles, and Frank Sinatra. Subsequently, the value of this stock dropped and the $100,000 investment was lost.

A copy of an FBI Identification Record, Number 3 794 610, was sent the White House by communication dated August 21, 1967. The files of the Identification Division reveal no additional arrest record.

SECRET/NO FOREIGN DISSEMINATION

Unaware that the FBI had just informed the White House that her father associated with mobsters and himself was the subject of a racketeering investigation, Tina Sinatra requested a tour of FBI headquarters, but not a meeting with Hoover, who died a week later, at age seventy-seven. (Nothing ever came of the racketeering investigation, and several months later, Sinatra endorsed Nixon's reelection, at one point singing at a Young Voters for Nixon rally in Chicago.)

TO: Mr. Bishop   DATE: 4/25/72
FROM: G. E. Malmfeldt
SUBJECT: MISS TINA SINATRA
                 (DAUGHTER OF FRANK SINATRA)
                 SPECIAL TOUR OF THE BUREAU
                 WEDNESDAY, APRIL 26, 1972, 2:30 P.M.

We received a telephone call from the Vice President's office this morning. We were advised that Mrs. Agnew has a luncheon appointment with Frank Sinatra's daughter, Miss Tina Sinatra, tomorrow and that the young lady had expressed an interest in touring the FBI some time later that afternoon. We were informed that Tina Sinatra would be accompanied by her agent whose name is Jim Mahoney and by a young lady from the Vice President's office, Miss Connie Lykkee.

The Vice President's office was advised that we would be pleased to make special tour arrangements for Miss Sinatra and her companions and an appointment has been set up for them at the above indicated time. It was suggested that they present themselves in the Director's Reception Room where their arrival would be expected. There was no request to meet the Director.

RECOMMENDATION:

If you approve, we will have an Agent Supervisor from the Crime Records Division conduct Miss Sinatra and her party on a very special tour of the Bureau.

After Nixon returned from a summit in Moscow, Sinatra scrawled him a brief note, telling him "Bravo" for a job "well done." The president responded with seemingly heartfelt appreciation—though it's interesting to note that Nixon's letter to Sinatra was identical to one he sent to the Federal Reserve chairman, Arthur Burns, in response to his letter about the Moscow trip. (Both documents are in the National Archives.)

June 8, 1972

Dear Frank:

After any long journey, the best part is always coming home, and your warm words of greeting made this occasion especially happy.

In a very real sense, every American played a vital role in the success of the Moscow visit, for what was accomplished there reflected our people's abiding desire for enduring peace. With the agreements we have an unparalleled opportunity to build such a structure of lasting peace, and from your letter I know I can count on your support in this great undertaking. Needless to say, I am deeply grateful for your expression of confidence and encouragement.

With my best wishes,

Sincerely,
Richard Nixon

A month later, Sinatra was hauled before the House Select Committee on Crime as it investigated mob influence in professional sports. The Democrat-controlled panel had wanted to serve him with a subpoena while attending a gala with Agnew, but he ended up appearing voluntarily, according to Nancy Sinatra's biography of her father. He was questioned about his 1962 investment in a racetrack reportedly owned in part by alleged mob bosses Raymond Patriarca and Tommy Lucchese. Sinatra denied knowing Patriarca and said he'd met Lucchese a few times. Asked if he knew the man was a racketeer, he said, "That's his problem, not mine."

In April 1973, Nixon asked Sinatra to come out of retirement briefly to sing at a state dinner for President Giulio Andreotti of Italy. Several documents from the National Archives shed light on the White House's evolving view of the star. The Sinatra backgrounder prepared by Nixon's staff was considerably less juicy than those prepared by the FBI. (The former president later told Nancy Sinatra he'd dismissed as "nonsense" criticism that he shouldn't invite someone of Sinatra's "background" to the White House. Andreotti himself, it should be noted, subsequently faced allegations of consorting with the mobsters. Prosecutors in Italy charged him with protecting the Sicilian Mafia while in office; he was acquitted in October 1999.)

FACT SHEET: ENTERTAINMENT FOR ANDREOTTI DINNER

1. It might be good to mention how President Thomas Jefferson (who had earlier visited Italy) ordered that Italian musicians be recruited to be members of the Marine Corps Band in 1803. The band went on to become known as the Band of the President and 8 of its 19 directors have been of Italian birth or descent.

2. Francis Albert Sinatra was born on December 12, 1917 (some sources say 1915) in Hoboken, New Jersey. He first became interested in music when an uncle gave him a ukulele. He joined the school band and helped organize the glee club, worked as a

copy boy for a newspaper, and won first prize on the <u>Major Bowes Amateur Hour</u> which launched his career. He toured with Harry James, then Tommy Dorsey, and later the Lucky Strike Hit Parade. (He claims to have learned his distinctive phrasing and breathing technique from the way Dorsey played his trombone.) His motion picture career received major impetus when he won an Oscar for best supporting actor of 1953 in "From Here to Eternity." (His career had slumped and he was paid $8,000 for doing the role of Angelo Maggio.) He is often called "the Voice," or "the Chairman of the Board."

3. Both of Sinatra's parents were born in Italy. His mother, Dolly, came from Genoa, Italy at age two months. She was a politician of sorts, the "boss" of Hoboken's third ward. Told there was no opening for her husband, Martin, in the Fire Department, she responded by saying, "<u>Make</u> an opening," and they did.

4. Sinatra has been called "a one man Anti-Defamation League" for Italians in America. He donated his services to a 1945 movie, "The House I Live In," which won a special Academy Award for expressing the importance of tolerance in a democracy. He has been an active philanthropist—witness his world tour for children's charities a little over a decade ago. One major beneficiary was Boys' Town of Italy. He won the Gene Hersholt humanitarian award from the Academy of Motion Picture Arts and Sciences in 1971. Among other awards, he received the State of Israel's Medallion of Valor last November and was co-recipient with Vice President Agnew of the Thomas A. Dooley Foundation's Splendid American Award three weeks ago.

5. Serious musicologists such as Henry Pleasants rate Sinatra as one of the major singers of the century. Opera singers often collect his records. Technically he uses body placed tones (rather than head placed tones) in the upper register (which is supposed to be wrong). His range is two octaves—much greater than most pop singers. He is also said to be among the first to have understood

the potential for intimacy which the microphone gives the singer. And he is said to have "virtually invented" the proper pronunciation for English singing. "In brief," wrote Gene Lees in the Saturday Review, "Sinatra raised the singing of the tiny popular song to the level of an art form. Indeed, he, more than any other singer, discovered what a treasure of true art American popular music really is and showed it to the world."

Yet Sinatra says he has never taken a real music lesson and doesn't read a note of music. He learns the music by having someone play it a couple of times and learns the lyrics by writing them out in longhand.

6. Some Sinatra titles might have made good campaign theme songs last year. One could mention "All or Nothing At All," "High Hopes," or "I Did It My Way." There were some we did not want to hear, of course: "Put Your Dreams Away," or "Learnin' the Blues," or worst of all, "Softly As I Leave You." But in the end one Sinatra hit summed things up perfectly: "It Was A Very Good Year."

Nixon's staff also prepared some remarks for the president to deliver before and after Sinatra's performance. The crack about Sinatra's tax returns is noteworthy in that former White House attorney John Dean testified at that summer's Watergate hearings that Nixon had tried to obtain favors from the IRS for a number of entertainers, including Sinatra.

SUGGESTED INTRODUCTION OF FRANK SINATRA

Were I asked to describe the man I am about to introduce, I would have to say that Frank Sinatra is to music what the Washington Monument is to our landscape. He is the top.

As you know, Mr. Sinatra retired as a performer two years ago, and the fact that he will sing for you tonight surely makes this a night to remember. And I hope there is no conclusion to be drawn from the fact that Frank is coming out of retirement less than a full day after the tax returns had to be filed.

He is known to us by many names. There is Frank Sinatra, the man who has sung his way through our lives. That would make him Mister Music. There is Frank Sinatra, the man of untold charitable contributions in this country and all over the world, including his long and continued support of Boys Town of Italy. That would make him Mister Humanitarian. Then there is Frank Sinatra, the high school student who dreamed of becoming a newspaper reporter. And, on graduation, he became copy boy on the Jersey Observer. But he never became a newspaper reporter, because his dreams of becoming a singer won out. And that, of course, would make him Mister Good Sense.

I am happy to present him to you now. Mister Frank Sinatra.

SUGGESTED REMARKS FOR THE PRESIDENT FOLLOWING FRANK SINATRA

I think you'll all agree with me this has been a memorable evening in the White House. Now you're all invited to remain and dance and, above all, enjoy yourselves.

Unfortunately, I still have some work to do before retiring, so I'll be leaving you to do that. And also, I always try to watch the late news on television to see how the networks would have run the country today.

Finally, this internal White House memo provides background for a presidential thank-you letter—and expresses pleasant surprise at Sinatra's comportment. Nixon sent an effusive letter, and Sinatra did indeed come out of retirement shortly thereafter.

THE WHITE HOUSE
WASHINGTON

May 9, 1973

FOR: MARY FENTON
FROM: STEPHEN BULL
RE: Thank-You Letter to Frank Sinatra

Frank Sinatra appeared at the April 17th dinner for Prime
Minister Andreotti. Contrary to the practice of other performers,
Frank Sinatra held a rehearsal with Nelson Riddle on the 16th and
ran through all of his material. The purpose of this, basically, was to
permit an open dress rehearsal for the White House staff on the day
of the 17th. During the course of the dinner it was reported in the
newspapers that Frank Sinatra spoke with his dinner guests about the
impending birth of his first grandchild—his daughter Nancy was
pregnant. Upon returning to his residence after the performance he
received a telephone call from Nancy's doctor indicating that she
had had a miscarriage. This announcement put a damper on the
evening for him.

When Frank Sinatra was first invited to the White House in late
February, he began working strenuously to develop his voice so that
he could give a creditable performance. His work included physical
exercises, breathing practice, etc. He worked very hard in order to
put on a proper performance for the President in the White House.

As a result of his appearance at the White House, Frank Sinatra
made the decision to come out of retirement.

Generally, Frank Sinatra, the "Chairman of the Board" who is
reputed to be ornery and egotistical, was quite the opposite. He was
cordial and polite to all people with whom he worked. He had high
praise for members of the Marine Orchestra, the sound people, and
virtually everyone else whose job it was to put on this performance.

May 10, 1973

Dear Frank:

Once in a great while, a performer manages to hold everyone in the audience spellbound. You did just that during your appearance at the April 17 dinner for Prime Minister Andreotti. The selections which were included in your program were those which many of us have associated with you over the years, and that evening you made them sound even better than ever! Incidentally, your graciousness in rehearsing before the members of the White House staff really made their day—and some of the young ladies present were nearly walking on air when they returned to their desks.

Mrs. Nixon and I are most grateful to you for helping to make the evening of April 17 an unforgettable one, and she joins me in sending you our special thanks and warmest good wishes.

Sincerely,

Richard Nixon

Mr. Frank Sinatra
70-588 Frank Sinatra Drive
Cathedral City, California 92234

cc: Stephen Bull

The fifty-one-week tenure of former Justice Department official L. Patrick Gray III as acting FBI director ended in the spring of 1973 when it became clear that the Senate wouldn't confirm the man who oversaw the less-than-thorough initial probe of the Watergate burglary. Nixon appointed William Ruckelshaus as the agency's acting director—who almost immediately requested a dossier on the president's crooner friend. It included more up-to-date intelligence on the singer, including information suggesting that Sinatra may have had more influence with the Nixon administration than with the Kennedys.

TO: Mr. Cleveland   DATE: May 24, 1973
FROM: J. Keith
SUBJECT: FRANK SINATRA
                INFORMATION CONCERNING

This is in response to the Acting Director's inquiry. Following is a current brief concerning the above captioned individual.

*   *   *

A source who has furnished reliable information in the past advised on January 3, 1973, that Frank Sinatra is a close friend of Angelo DeCarlo of long standing.

Sources who have furnished reliable information in the past have described DeCarlo as a respected member of organized crime in the United States who holds a position of "caporegima" in the Genovese family of La Cosa Nostra.

On December 21, 1972, DeCarlo was released from the United States penitentiary, Lewisburg, Pennsylvania, after a commutation of his sentence by Presidential order.

A source who has furnished reliable information in the past advised ███████████ that DeCarlo's release came as no real surprise to certain associates of DeCarlo as they had been informed by someone very close to DeCarlo that he was expected to be released before Christmas.

This source further stated that these same associates are attributing DeCarlo's release to the intervention of singer Frank Sinatra, whose close personal relationship with Vice President Spiro Agnew allegedly served as the necessary "contact." The source stated that Sinatra's efforts had allegedly been in the works for "at least a couple of months."

Information concerning Sinatra's friendship with DeCarlo and DeCarlo's release from Federal custody was furnished to the Department by Newark's letterhead memorandum dated January 11, 1973.

On May 18, 1973, Mr. Jonathon L. Goldstein, United States Attorneys office, Newark, New Jersey, advised that he was contacted

on May 17, 1973, by ██████████████████████████.
██

claimed to have information indicating that initial contact to secure
the release of Angelo DeCarlo from Federal custody was made in
April, 1972, by DeCarlo to a singer with a rock group performing at
the Atlanta Federal Penitentiary. This singer (Frankie Valli of the
Four Seasons Quartet) was allegedly requested to contact Frank
Sinatra and have him intercede with Vice President Agnew for
DeCarlo's release. This request was ostensibly related to Mrs. Sinatra
who in turn supposedly forwarded to Frank Sinatra.

████████████████ continued that Frank Sinatra allegedly turned
over $100,000 cash to Maurice Stans as an unrecorded contribution.
Subsequently, due to the fact that Vice President Agnew had been
"stripped of his authority by White House aides," one Peter
Maletesta (possibly identical to Peter John Malatesta who was
employed as a staff assistant to the Vice President as recently as
January, 1971) allegedly contacted former Presidential Counsel John
Dean and got him to make the necessary arrangements to forward
the request to the Justice Department. Sinatra then allegedly "made
a $50,000 contribution to the President's campaign fund sometime
during December, 1972. DeCarlo's release followed."

A summary of Sinatra's background and association with
organized crime figures, prior to that information developed
concerning his friendship with DeCarlo has been made available to
The White House by letters dated August 21, 1967, April 25, 1969,
and February 18, 1972.

While Bufiles do not disclose this information, it is recalled from
recent newspaper articles that Sinatra was originally scheduled to
entertain at President Nixon's most recent Inaugural Ball and he
failed for some reason to make an appearance. About the same time
he reportedly had a strong verbal exchange with society columnist
Maxine Cheshire in which he reputedly used obscene language in
"chewing her out." Most recently Sinatra did appear at The White
House and entertained the President of Italy who was visiting this
country.

RECOMMENDATION:
None. For your information.

As Watergate closed in on the president, Sinatra stood by his friend. During his January 30, 1974, State of the Union message, Nixon defiantly declared to Congress and the nation, "One year of Watergate is enough!" Minutes after it ended, Sinatra sent Nixon a congratulatory telegram from Las Vegas, where he was playing Caesars Palace, which prompted another letter from the president. (This document is from the National Archives.)

February 12, 1974

Dear Frank:

Very shortly after delivering my State of the Union address to the Congress, I received your telegram, and this is just to let you know how much I appreciated your comments. As I stated that evening, this is a time of great challenge and great opportunities for America. I believe the measures outlined in my message can set the agenda for truly significant progress for this Nation and the world in 1974, and it is heartening to know I may continue to count on your support.

Again, my thanks and warm best wishes.

Sincerely,

Richard Nixon

Mr. Frank Sinatra
1041 North Formosa Avenue
Hollywood, California 90046

P.S. Incidentally, I have received reports about your very kind remarks during one of your Las Vegas appearances. I understand you expressed your love for, and your belief in, our country, and your continuing confidence in me. For this public expression of your support, and of your pride in our great Nation, I am deeply grateful.

Sinatra's friendship with Agnew lasted long after the vice president and Nixon resigned in disgrace. Agnew was one of only 130 guests invited to the singer's wedding to Barbara Marx on July 11, 1976. Agnew at the time had become pointed in his criticism of Israel, and Sinatra drew some of the resulting flack in the form of letters from outraged citizens, including several fans. A particularly threatening one prompted Milton A. (Mickey) Rudin, Sinatra's longtime attorney, to call the FBI. Federal agents interviewed him about it on August 9, 1976.

MILTON A. RUDIN, also known as, "The Judge," attorney, 9601 Wilshire Boulevard, Beverly Hills, California, business manager for FRANK SINATRA, was contacted concerning RUDIN's previous telephonic contact with the Federal Bureau of Investigation (FBI), Los Angeles, California, concerning a threatening letter received by SINATRA.

RUDIN furnished an envelope which was postmarked <u>(?)</u> shing, New York, on July 29. The envelope was typewritten, addressed to Mr. FRANK SINATRA, Palm Springs, California. RUDIN also furnished the letter received in the aforementioned envelope which states in part, that unless SINATRA arranges a well publicized press conference no later than August 15, 1976, in which he denounces his friendship with SPIRO AGNEW, that a chemically treated prickle will perforate one of his, SINATRA's eyes transmitted by an African Bushmen's blowing tube. RUDIN stated that the envelope and letter were received by SINATRA at Palm Springs, California, on Thursday, August 5, 1976. Upon receipt RUDIN stated SINATRA wrote on the front of the envelope, "Sarge—Important for The Judge." RUDIN further stated that the address label affixed to the front of the envelope beneath the typewritten address is a label that the Palm Springs Post Office put on the envelope when it was received at the Palm Springs Post Office. RUDIN stated that SINATRA advised him that he would not hold a press conference as advised on August 15, 1976. A copy of the envelope and letter are attached.

RUDIN stated that the only persons to handle the aforementioned letter and envelope were:

FRANK SINATRA (singer—entertainer)
Born December 12, 1916

IRVING "SARGE" WEISS
Messenger

MARY CAROL LOGAN
Secretary

HELEN MONTROSE
Secretary

MILTON A. RUDIN

RUDIN then furnished one Anti-Defamation League (ADL)
Digest, July/August, 1976 issue, and one ADL memorandum dated
May 26, 1976. RUDIN stated ADL memorandum and digest
furnished gives background concerning SPIRO AGNEW, in that
they feel AGNEW's statements to the American Press and on the
Today Show are "irresponsible, anti-Semitic, and are shocking and
unplausible." RUDIN stated that based on AGNEW's recent
statements, a number of people have written SINATRA concerning
his association with AGNEW and have recommended that his
association be severed. RUDIN furnished six letters that had been
received by SINATRA recently concerning SINATRA's association
with AGNEW. Copies of the six letters are attached.

RUDIN telephonically contacted SINATRA on August 9, 1976,
at SINATRA's residence in Pinyon Crest, California, and it was
determined that SINATRA had no suspects in this matter. RUDIN
stated that he had no suspects in this matter although one letter
furnished above to the FBI was postmarked at Flushing, New York,
July 31, 1976, from ████████████ Queens, New York. RUDIN
then furnished SINATRA's itinerary, which reflects that SINATRA
will be in Vancouver on August 20 and 21, 1976, and that from
August 21 through 27, 1976, SINATRA will be at the Waldorf
Astoria while performing during that period at Saratoga, New York,
and Holmdel, New Jersey. SINATRA is currently in Palm Springs,
California, and will remain there until August 19, 1976.

The letter:

To Frank Sinatra!
You will arrange a well publicized press-conference not later than <u>August 15, 1976.</u> You will denounce your good friend Spiro Agnew because he sold himself to the Arabs in order to be their spokesman and official anti-Israeli and anti-Semitic propagandist in the USA.

If you do not comply [with] this demand your life is <u>N O T</u> in danger. Death is not a punishment, it is a sudden end of life without suffering. Your famous Blue Eyes are in jeopardy.

Study the method of African Bushmen's blowing tubes. The prickle can be targeted very exactly from a distance of 100 feet or further. The tube could be a cigarette holder, could be a part of a photo camera, a binocular, a trompet or a dozen of other objects. It is absolutely undetectable.

No poison will be used but a chemically treated prickle perforates one of your eyes and a sympathetic ophtalmia follows. Consult your doctor, he will convince you.

Think about it which is better: keep the friendship of Agnew or spend the rest of your life in complete darkness.

The FBI undertook an extensive four-month investigation to determine the identity of the writer for a possible extortion prosecution. Agents checked the letter for fingerprints and took fingerprints from Sinatra employees known to have handled the letter. They did a detailed analysis of the letter's typing. They took precise measurements, including the thickness of the paper down to the ten-thousandth of an inch. They compared it to two other letters sent to Sinatra around the same time, an unsigned one warning him of imminent danger and a signed one from a woman criticizing his friendship with Agnew. They compared the letter to missives in the FBI's vast Anonymous Letter File. They came up dry.

Copy to: USA [U.S. Attorney], Los Angeles
　　　　　(Attention: AUSA [Assistant U.S. Attorney] EARL E.
　　　　　BOYD)
Report of: ██████████████　　　　Office: Los Angeles, California
Date: 12/1/76
Title: UNKNOWN SUBJECT;
　　　　FRANK SINATRA—VICTIM
Character: EXTORTION

Synopsis: On 8/9/76, Attorney and Business Manager of FRANK SINATRA, Beverly Hills, California, furnished a threatening letter which was addressed to SINATRA in Palm Springs, California. Envelope was postmarked at ___shing, New York, on 7/29/76. Attorney also furnished other communications received by SINATRA in the recent post concerning his association with SPIRO AGNEW and one of those was an envelope and letter postmarked 7/31/76, at Flushing, New York, from ███████████████, Queens, New York. AUSA, Los Angeles, contacted and advised he would consider prosecution of sender of letter contained in envelope postmarked 7/29/76, for violation of the Extortion Statute. Elimination fingerprints taken at SINATRA's office of employees that handled the threatening letter. FBI Lab reports set forth, which identified character of typewriting. FBI Identification Division reported no latent fingerprints developed on threatening communication. By a letter dated 8/30/76, from SINATRA's business office, FBI Los Angeles, was forwarded a communication which had been forwarded to SINATRA's business office by Secretary and Corporate Counsel, Caesars World, Inc., Las Vegas, Nevada. The letter had as enclosures an envelope postmarked at Chicago, Illinois, 8/20/76, addressed to Caesars Palace, Strip on the, Las Vegas, Nevada, and enclosed letter was addressed to FRANK SINATRA. The letter advised SINATRA to be careful of his food and medicine, etc. as individuals were planning to get rid of him. FBI, New York, determined threatening communication mailed in Flushing and a review of New York indices determined ████████████ could be

identical to

telephonically advised she was in Europe with her husband during the period June–September, 1976. On 12/1/76, AUSA, Los Angeles, declined prosecution as all investigation has been conducted in an attempt to identify sender of threatening communication received by SINATRA.

EIGHT

THE FBI AND SINATRA THE MAN

"I don't think the leopard will change his spots."

In Sinatra's case, the price of fame was not simply a surrender of privacy. In late 1963, the singer's son, Frank Sinatra, Jr., then nineteen, was kidnapped and briefly held, unsuccessfully, for ransom. The incident brought the bureau and the senior Sinatra closer together—but only so close, and it appeared to harden the star.

If the FBI files did not show that Sinatra was a draft-dodger, Communist, or criminal, in the end they certainly showed that he was a man in a very bright spotlight.

Frank Sinatra, Jr., was kidnapped on December 8, 1963, two weeks after the assassination of John F. Kennedy.

Attempting to launch his own singing career, the young Sinatra had been scheduled to perform in Lake Tahoe, Nevada. But as he and a bandmate ate dinner in his hotel room just after 9 P.M., somebody knocked on the door, announcing a delivery for Frankie Sinatra. When Sinatra opened the door, he faced a .38 revolver. Two men, both twenty-three, tied up the friend and spirited the teenager away to Los Angeles, where they held him for ransom with the help of a forty-two-year-old accomplice.

Hoover and Attorney General Robert F. Kennedy, still mourning his brother's recent assassination, made the case a top priority. A team of FBI agents quickly cracked the amateurish scheme. The perpetrators were arrested in Los Angeles three days after Sinatra Sr. and an FBI agent delivered $239,985 for the safe return of his son, not counting $15 spent by the FBI for a valise big enough to carry all that cash.

During the kidnapper's trial, defense attorneys infuriated the Sinatra family by suggesting that the whole thing was a hoax cooked up to gain publicity for the son's fledgling singing career. The depth of the elder Sinatra's anger was on display in this exchange of letters, prompted by a June 27, 1964, letter from a prison chaplain who counseled the two younger kidnappers after they were convicted.

UNITED STATES DEPARTMENT OF JUSTICE
BUREAU OF PRISONS
MEDICAL CENTER FOR FEDERAL PRISONERS
SPRINGFIELD, MISSOURI

Dear Mr. & Mrs. Sinatra,

As Catholic Chaplain of the United States Medical Center here in Springfield, I have become very well acquainted personally with Mr. Barry Keenan and Mr. Joe Amsler. I have spoken with both of these men on numerous occasions about the true Catholic approach to the crime of kidnapping your son. It is quite evident that both Barry and Joe are very much convinced both emotionally and intellectually that considering the event of the kidnapping from the eyes of God, that it was truly a non-Christian act. As soon as Barry and Joe arrived at this institution, I suggested to them that they enroll in the Catholic Religion Classes which I was holding at this institution, and both of them complied with my wishes. The attitude that these two men expressed in these classes was quite amazing to me as well as other students in the class.

While I am not speaking officially in the name of this institution, it is quite evident from my very close contact with Barry and Joe that basically they are good men. At the present time one of their greatest concerns is the hardship that was brought upon both of you. Again, speaking as Catholic Chaplain of this institution, I am very much convinced that they will both try to make amends to you for this hardship. No doubt you did experience a great deal of suffering and emotional anxiety during the kidnapping as well as perhaps some embarrassment during the trial. This is very understandable and for having caused you this suffering and embarrassment, Barry and Joe have often expressed their sorrow and regret.

While I have never had the opportunity to meet either of you personally, it is commenting on the obvious to say that from various sources, various modes of communication, I have heard a great deal about you, and with this letter I too would wish to express to you my regret and sorrow for what the recent event has caused you.

We as Christians, we who have been taken into this body of Christ and have hence become other Christs, must also try to express in our attitudes, in our relationships with other people, the attitude of Christ himself. Christ, this son of God, was also kidnapped and you and I know very well that the motives, the reasons why Christ was kidnapped far exceed the evil that may have been involved in the motives, in the reasons, why your son was kidnapped. We should at all times, I think, see ourselves as we really are, other Christs, and as St. Paul tells us over and over again that we should live this life of a Christian, that we should put on Christ. Even though Christ was scourged, was spit upon, was crucified, yet some of his last words were, "Father, forgive them for they know not what they do."

I am certain that both Barry and Joe, and again I speak from my rather close relationship with them as their Catholic Chaplain, have learned a great deal from this tragic event and if they are treated correctly the event of the kidnapping and all that was entailed in it have caused, and will continue to cause a new resurgence of religious fervor both in Barry Keenan and Joe Amsler. We know that Christ works among us in rather mysterious ways. Things that bring people closer to him and to his Father sometimes mystify us poor ignorant human beings. I know that the event of the kidnapping has brought Barry and Joe much more closely to God and have brought about within them a deeper realization of what in this world is really of value.

I was convinced, Mr. and Mrs. Sinatra, that as their director in the area of religion that I am bound to write this letter to you for your own good and for the good of Barry and Joe, for whom I have a very great deal of respect and love. Both of them have been very regular in their attendance at all of our religious services, and both have expressed a great deal of interest in the area of religion. Since Barry has come to this institution he has been trained to be Commentator at Mass, a position which he fulfills very well.

Mr. and Mrs. Sinatra, I hope very sincerely that this letter finds you well and happy, and I ask that you say many prayers for us here at this institution. Many of the men here are not bad men, but they are persons who have made mistakes in life. Many of the sins, translating it into theological terminology, that men commit in the world far exceed the gravity of acts that have prompted the incarceration of so many of our brothers. We ask God to forgive us our sins but we ask him to forgive our sins as we forgive the sins of our brothers.

Very sincerely yours in Christ,

Father Roger Schmit, O.S.B.
The Catholic Chaplain

But Sinatra rebuffed the priest with a six-page letter in which his anger over the kidnapper's hoax defense was clearly palpable. The letter is truncated here.

Frank Sinatra

July 27, 1964

Dear Father Schmit:

Since you have had no prior relationship to the Sinatra family, we assume that it was not the purpose of your letter to give us religious guidance. Accordingly, there could only be two possible purposes for your letter: (1) a request that we forgive Keenan and Amsler, and/or (2) that we take some action to express our forgiveness in order to alleviate the punishment the court has imposed upon them.

At the outset, I feel I must tell you that in my opinion it is presumptuous for you to ask us to forgive them.

* * *

Up to this time I have remained silent on the subject of the manner in which the trial was conducted and the harm done to my son by the claim of "hoax," but your letter, written in the name of God, has caused me to break that silence.

Very truly yours,

FRANK SINATRA

Then Sinatra forwarded to Hoover the exchange of letters with the priest. In a surprisingly cordial "Dear Edgar" letter, Sinatra thanked Hoover for his son's safe return, and said he thought Hoover would find the exchange with the chaplain "interesting, particularly insofar as it reflects my own attitude with respect to what has happened." Hoover's reply below is equally cordial—if you disregard the internal note added to the copy in the FBI files. In his letter to the singer, Hoover suggests that he shares Sinatra's harsh attitude toward mercy.

August 4, 1964

Mr. Frank Sinatra
9229 Sunset Boulevard
Los Angeles 69, California
Dear Frank:

I have received your letter of July 30th enclosing a copy of the letter Mrs. Sinatra and you received from Father Roger Schmit and your reply.

I can certainly understand your concern in this matter and appreciate your interest in sending me this correspondence. I also want to thank you for your very kind comments regarding our participation in the investigation relating to your son's kidnaping.

As for my feelings in matters such as these, I think you would be interested in my introduction to the April, 1964, issue of the FBI Law Enforcement Bulletin wherein it was stated, "In 1924, a New York City judge stated, 'The demand of the hour in America is for jurors with conscience, judges with courage and prisons which are neither country clubs or health resorts. It is not the criminals, actual or potential, that need a neuropathic hospital,' the judge added, 'it is the people who slobber over them in an effort to find excuses for their crime.'"

Sincerely,

J. Edgar Hoover

NOTE: Bufiles reflect Father Roger Schmit, a 29-year-old Catholic priest, was a Departmental applicant in 1963 at which time no derogatory information was developed concerning him. The Director is well aware of the background of Sinatra. Address per previous correspondence.

Years later, Nancy Sinatra wrote to Hoover concerning a book she was writing about her father. She wanted to include the director's recollections about her father. Hoover was less than verbose in his response. (She later included much of his reply in two affectionate biographies of her father.)

November 26, 1969

Miss Nancy Sinatra
9000 Sunset Boulevard
Los Angeles, California 90069
Dear Miss Sinatra:

I have received your letter of November 20th and appreciate your interest in communicating with me in connection with the book you are writing about your father.

In response to your request, I remember, in particular, a telephone conversation I had with your father in connection with the kidnapping of Frank, Jr. This took place on December 11, 1963, and I told your father how pleased I was that Frank, Jr., had been safely returned. I recall pointing out to him that although he would now be besieged by inquiries from the news media, we still had numerous productive leads to pursue and would be able to do so only if the case received a minimum of publicity. Your father, of course, cooperated in every possible way. Within a short time, our investigation was completed and early on the morning of December 14th, I had the pleasure of telephoning your father again to inform him that the kidnappers were in custody.

Please feel free to use the foregoing in the manner you indicated, and I do hope that your book will enjoy every possible success.

Sincerely yours,

J. Edgar Hoover

NOTE: Bufiles contain no derogatory information regarding Nancy Sinatra.

Frank Sinatra, Sr., developed a close relationship with agents on the kid-
napping case, especially the special agent in charge for Las Vegas, Dean
Elson. In this memo, Courtney Evans, the FBI's liaison to the Justice De-
partment, tells a colleague, Alan Belmont, that Elson wants to capitalize on
his budding friendship with the celebrity, who at the time was about to start
filming None But the Brave *in Hawaii.*

TO: Mr. Belmont   DATE: April 17, 1964
FROM: C. A. Evans
SUBJECT: FRANK SINATRA

In view of the long association which Frank Sinatra, the well-
known entertainer, has had with prominent hoodlums and
racketeers, I discussed this situation personally with SAC Elson of
Las Vegas on Saturday, April 11, after the conclusion of the
Organized Crime and Criminal Intelligence Conference held at Los
Angeles.

SAC Elson has a close personal relationship with Frank Sinatra,
his attorney and close business associates as a result of Elson's
handling these individuals during the kidnapping case in which
Sinatra's son was the victim. As evidence of the high regard in which
Elson is held by Sinatra, it is noted Elson and his wife have been
invited by Sinatra to attend social affairs being given by Sinatra at
his home in Palm Springs. Sinatra even offered to send his private
airplane to Las Vegas and transport the Elsons to California. SAC
Elson said he graciously declined these social invitations and that he
had written the Director about them sometime ago. I told Elson that
in the absence of contrary instructions from the Bureau it seemed
most proper not to accept social invitations extended because of
Elson's handling his FBI duties.

We did discuss, however, Sinatra's background, including his long
and close association with several major hoodlums and racketeers. It
seems obvious that Sinatra could supply extremely valuable
information about these individuals and their activities. SAC Elson

believes his relationship with Sinatra is so close that he might be able to induce Sinatra to cooperate with us.

There is attached a summary of information showing Sinatra's long association with major hoodlums.

ACTION TO BE TAKEN:

Frank Sinatra is currently reported to be in the Far East where he is on location making a motion picture. On his return to the United States it is believed we should have SAC Elson contact Sinatra and explore the possibilities of developing him as an informant. This could best be accomplished by having Elson go to Southern California on two or three weekends when Sinatra would not be tied up with his business affairs. We would, of course, have Sinatra believe Elson was in California on other business which would provide an appropriate cover for Elson's meeting with Sinatra and exploring the possibilities of his cooperating with us.

Elson is convinced that his relationship with Sinatra at this time is such that he could do this discreetly without any possibility of embarrassment to the Bureau. If we are to do this we should begin promptly on Sinatra's return to the United States as Elson's relationship with Sinatra will deteriorate if no contact is made and much time elapses.

If you approve SAC Elson will be advised telephonically when he next calls the Bureau to proceed along these lines.

The summary attached to Belmont's memo:

Frank Sinatra through the years has been associated with some of the most infamous individuals of modern times. During the 1930s when he was growing up in New Jersey, he was reportedly befriended by Willie Moretti, former underworld boss of Bergen County, New Jersey, and cousin of the notorious Joe Adonis. In later years Sinatra sang at the wedding of Willie Moretti's daughter.

In the 40s Sinatra's name was linked with such well-known hoodlums as Joseph and Rocco Fischetti, members of the Capone gang, Charles "Lucky" Luciano, and James Tarantino, associate of Benjamin "Bugsy" Seigel and editor and publisher of the magazine "Hollywood Night Life."

Newspapers on February 20, 1947, reported that Frank Sinatra had been in Havana, Cuba, for four days the previous week and that "his companion in public and private was Luciano, Luciano's bodyguard and a rich collection of gamblers and high-binders." The article indicated that Luciano and Sinatra were seen together at the racetracks, the gambling casinos and at special parties.

A September 11, 1947, column of Westbrook Pegler reported that when Frank Sinatra flew to Havana, Cuba, on February 11, 1947, he was accompanied by Joe and Rocco Fischetti.

In recent years considerable information has been reported concerning Sinatra ties with Sam Giancana. Reports of the use of Sinatra's Palm Springs home by Giancana and Phyllis McGuire and Giancana's disappointment in Sinatra's inability to get the administration to tone down its efforts in the Anti-Racketeering field constitutes the most significant information developed. On at least two occasions in past years Sinatra has been in Atlantic City taking over an entire floor of one of the major hotels for a private party which lasted several weeks and included hoodlum guests such as Giancana, the Fischettis and Joe Bonanno of Phoenix.

Until he was recently ordered to sell his interests in Las Vegas, Sinatra owned a percentage of the Sands Hotel in Las Vegas and was 100% owner of the Cal-Neva Lodge at Lake Tahoe. Informants have speculated that Sinatra was merely a front for hoodlum money invested in these gambling casinos. During the last year of operation, the Cal-Neva Lodge was managed by Paul "Skinny" D'Amato, long-time friend of Sinatra who also has a hoodlum background and has for years operated the 500 Club in Atlantic City.

When interviewed concerning his Las Vegas interests Sinatra maintained he represented only himself and that Sam Giancana was only someone he recalled meeting at an airport. Confidential sources in Las Vegas and Chicago, however, indicate a much closer association between Sinatra and Giancana. In the Fall of 1962,

Sinatra, Dean Martin, Sammy Davis, Jr., and Eddie Fisher made what appeared to be a command performance at the Villa Venice Supper Club near Chicago, apparently arranged by Sinatra for Giancana. When interviewed concerning it, Sinatra claimed he had arranged for these entertainers merely as a favor to Leo Olsen, owner of the Club and that Giancana had nothing to do with it.

It was Sinatra's continued association with Giancana that led to the revocation of his Nevada gambling license in September of 1963. This was brought about principally by the discovery of Giancana's presence at the Cal-Neva Lodge even though he was listed in the Nevada Black Book as a "undesirable" in Nevada.

ADDENDUM

I don't think the leopard will change his spots, but I recommend SAC Elson try his hand at this.

A. H. Belmont

Handwritten notation by Clyde Tolson: I do not agree. C.
Handwritten notation by Hoover: I share Tolson's views. H.
Handwritten notation by Evans: Elson advised to take no action in this matter. E. 4/23/64

Sinatra was apparently unaware of Hoover's low regard for him, as this item in the files about a party for Jack Warner of Warner Bros. Records shows.

By an undated letter addressed "Dear Friend" Frank Sinatra invited FBI Director, Mr. Hoover, to a testimonial dinner to be held on 4/25/65, in Beverly Hills, in honor of Jack Warner. The dinner was being sponsored by the Friars Club, Charity Foundation, Beverly Hills, Calif., of which Sinatra was Abbot Emeritus.

Years later, Elson continued to report to headquarters on Sinatra's activities, as shown by this memo from Tom E. Bishop to Cartha "Deke" De-

Loach, both top Hoover lieutenants. Sinatra was then in the midst of a two-week stand in Las Vegas at the Sands casino, where he had been a part owner until evidence of mob associations forced him to relinquish his casino interests in Nevada in 1964.

TO: Mr. DeLoach   DATE: September 11, 1967
FROM: T. E. Bishop
SUBJECT: FRANK SINATRA
              INFORMATION CONCERNING

SAC Elson from Las Vegas called this afternoon and spoke with Leinbaugh in my office. Elson said he had sent the Director a letter Friday regarding some of Sinatra's recent activities and wanted to bring the Bureau up to date.

Elson said that about 6 or 7 a.m. this morning Sinatra went into the casino at the Sands apparently to apologize to the pit dealers regarding his actions several nights ago. According to Elson some words were exchanged and when a security guard came walking over to Sinatra, Sinatra picked up a chair and hit the guard over the head, apparently injuring him seriously. Immediately thereafter Carl Cohen, casino manager, hit Sinatra in the mouth and in the words of our informant, "Really decked him." According to our source, Sinatra had at least two front teeth knocked out.

Elson commented that Cohen will be in real trouble now and he said that he will keep the Bureau closely advised of developments.

RECOMMENDATION:
The above is for the Director's information.

A later summary of Sinatra information in FBI files recounted the same episode in detail—and alleged a Machiavellian motive for the star's behavior: He wanted to end his contract with the Sands, which had just been bought by Howard Hughes, so he could instead perform at Caesars Palace, identified as a La Cosa Nostra (LCN) establishment. This reasoning seems unlikely, given that, according to Kitty Kelley's biography, Sinatra was al-

ready negotiating with Caesars at the time and had signed a $3 million per-formance contract on September 11, 1967—the same day as the fracas.

Informant stated that Sinatra, upon learning that his wife, Mia, had lost $20,000 gambling at the Sands Hotel, became furious and purchased $50,000 worth of chips in an attempt to win back his wife's losses. Within a 45 minute interval he had lost the $50,000. Upon learning of Sinatra's losses, Howard Hughes (not identified) ordered Sinatra's credit stopped. Sinatra, intoxicated, tore his room to shambles. He then obtained a golf cart and drove it all around the front of the Sands Hotel. Carl Cohen (not identified) attempted to calm Sinatra; however, Sinatra threw some chips in Cohen's face at which time Cohen punched Sinatra in the mouth causing the loss of teeth. Informant advised that it was indicated that this activity was planned in order to have Sinatra's contract at the Sands broken so that he could later be placed in Caesars Palace, since this establishment had Family* interests. Informant did not believe this was planned, however, to the extent that Sinatra would lose two teeth.

This reference indicated that [John] Roselli was active in LCN matters.

*LCN Family interests

After Frank Sinatra's mother, Natalie "Dolly" Sinatra, died at age eighty-two in the crash of a chartered plane on January 6, 1977, the FBI's current director sent condolences to Frank Sinatra, Jr.

January 10, 1977

Mr. Frank Sinatra, Jr.
Sinatra Way
Cathedral City, California 92234
Dear Mr. Sinatra:

Your friends in the FBI were deeply saddened at the news of your grandmother's death and extend heartfelt sympathy to you and the other members of your family. Although words are of little solace at times such as this, we hope you will be comforted by your many warm memories of her and the knowledge that others are thinking of you and share your sorrow.

Sincerely yours,

Clarence M. Kelley
Director

NOTE: Bufiles indicate prior cordial correspondence with Mr. Sinatra who has been friendly to the FBI and very cooperative with our Los Angeles Office. He met Mr. Kelley on 12-16-75 at the FBI Appreciation Day function held in San Francisco.

Sinatra occasionally was subjected to threatening letters or calls, usually from apparently deranged yet harmless people. An anonymous caller, for example, warned of a hand-grenade attack in Miami Beach. A tipster claimed two escaped mental patients from Massachusetts were bent on assassinating the singer. An anonymous letter said Henry Kissinger wanted to poison Sinatra for knowing too much about a planned coup.

In the earlier years, the FBI's inquiries were perfunctory. But later, as authorities at all levels began to take threats against celebrities more seriously, the investigations became ever more intensive, as shown by some of the final documents in the FBI's Sinatra files. Thus, by the twilight of Frank Sinatra's career, the FBI had come full circle, from relentlessly pursuing the star to relentlessly pursuing his tormentors.

*One of the last cases involved a threatening letter and phone calls just be-
fore a four-night Sinatra engagement in Atlantic City in May 1980. The
FBI spared no expense in trying to find the culprit. This memo detailed the
inquiry's origin.*

NARRATIVE OF OFFENSE:

This investigation was instituted upon request of information
from ███████████████ Intelligence Unit, Atlantic City Police
Department (ACPD), who reported that an unsigned letter,
containing a threat to kill entertainer FRANK SINATRA, had been
received on May 14, 1980, at the Reservations Office of the World
International Hotel (WI), Atlantic City, New Jersey. The
handwritten letter and envelope, postmarked Reading,
Pennsylvania, were obtained and examined. ████████████████
Clerk, WI, who received the subject correspondence, also advised
that she received suspicious calls on WI's out-of-state 800 telephone
line. Preliminary investigation was instituted to attempt to identify
unknown subject and to establish a violation of Title 18, United
States Code, Section 875–876. The threat letter appeared to be a
response to WI's promotional advertising for a package deal for the
scheduled SINATRA shows at the nearby Resorts International
Casino/Hotel, during the weekends of May 23–26, 1980, and May
31–June 1, 1980. Liaison was maintained with ACPD, Bell
Telephone Security Office, WI, Resorts and the SINATRA security
staff.

The primary piece of evidence was the letter itself.

EVIDENCE:

1. Envelope, postmarked at Reading, Pennsylvania, addressed to
World International Hotel, no return address listed; and its contents,
an unsigned one page, handwritten letter containing the following
wording:

"We are going to shoot
all Sinatra's guts out
we wanted to shoot him
for a long time he
never could sing and
he has been a old
crook all his life this
will be a good time
to get him.
    Watch and see
he is not worth 2¢
$189 ha ha."

The letter by the unknown subject (UNSUB, in FBI jargon) prompted a three-month investigation. Among the techniques employed was a "psycholinguistics" analysis, for which the FBI hired a consultant. He found an extraordinary amount of hidden meaning in the fifty-two-word note.

To: SSRA, Atlantic City
Attention: ███████████ Atlantic City
From: M. S. Miron, Psycholinguistics
Re: UNSUB; Frank Sinatra—Victim
     Hobb's Act

Photofacsimile of a one page communication addressed to World International, postmarked May 12, 1980 was transmitted from the Atlantic City office for analysis.

DEMOGRAPHIC PROFILE OF UNSUB

Based upon an analysis of the content and style of this communication, it is my opinion that UNSUB is a Caucasian male of foreign birth, who has resided in this country for at least 15 years and is between 45 and 55 years of age. I am not able to determine the nationality of the author from the evidence in hand, however given the clear signs of psychological identification this UNSUB feels for the victim and the distinctive orthography, it is not improbable that UNSUB is of Italian origin.

Given the content emphasis of money, it is most likely that UNSUB is unemployed or in a low-income, blue collar occupation.

PSYCHOLOGICAL PROFILE OF UNSUB

In my judgment, UNSUB's threat does not reflect content characteristics which would imply either the means or the determination for action. The threat is, I believe, instead based on UNSUB's resentments over not being able to indulge himself with a trip he wishes to take. The communication has the form of a "sour grapes" rationalization of the privation UNSUB feels.

Use of such defense and the gastro-intestinal form of the threat, imply that UNSUB is a dependent personality with inadequate and immature coping strategies. Such speculation further implies that UNSUB may tend toward alcoholism and other such letter writing activities. It is not unlikely that UNSUB has written similar anonymous letters to public officials and/or commercial institutions.

The form of the threat is consistent with an interpretation of lack of subterfuge; i.e., use of re-mailers or disguised handwriting. I, therefore, conclude that UNSUB is a resident of the post-marked area.

The unusual telephone calls to the advertised number for the referenced junket are entirely consistent with the behavior to be expected from this UNSUB.

UNSUB probably is an habitual lottery player and gambler, but, in my judgment would not be expected to have a criminal record.

Support for the conclusion that this UNSUB poses no danger to the victim is provided by the following data observations. Note that UNSUB chooses to cast his manifest resentment in the responsibility diffusing form of the plural pronoun. Instead of implying the organizational support UNSUB undoubtedly intended, it is instead inconsistent with the personal determination characteristic of more dangerous threats. Note further that UNSUB chooses to make salient his "wanting" to take action in a form which

is distinctly fantasy-like rather than action-oriented. UNSUB ends
with a reference to the passivity of "watch and see" which again is
antithetical to action and, I believe, is characteristic of the
passiveness of UNSUB himself.

The agent in charge of the probe summarized his or her efforts.

The following investigation was conducted by Special Agent
███████████████ at Atlantic City, New Jersey:

On May 22, 1980, ██████████████ Security Officer, New Jersey
Bell Telephone Company, ████████████████ was contacted
concerning the receipt of calls at the World International (WI)
Hotel on number 800-257-7912, which was identified as the toll-free
number utilized by WI in their out-of-state advertising for the
SINATRA weekend special. He referred this request for assistance to
his counterpart at Bell of Pennsylvania.

On May 22, 1980, ██████████████ Security Officer, Bell of
Pennsylvania, Philadelphia Office, number ███████████ was
contacted regarding this matter. He advised that arrangements would
be made to trap calls from the Reading area to the 800 number used
by WI. He also advised that he would attempt to retrieve any records
of such calls on May 17 and May 20, 1980.

On May 22, 1980, ████████████ and █████████████
Intelligence Unit, Atlantic City Police Department (ACPD) were
contacted for the purpose of reviewing their investigation in this
matter and coordinating future steps. ████████████ furnished
the original threat letter and its envelope (reported on separate FD-
302) and advised that he received it on May 16, 1980, from ACPD
employee ████████████ who received it from WI's Reservations
████████████ who received it from ████████████ confirmed
that the receipt of the threat had been reported to the intended
victim through ACPD ████████████ . ████████████
SINATRA appearances in Atlantic City. A coordinating conference
was subsequently scheduled for the following morning.

On May 23, 1980, Special Agent ████████████ attended a
meeting held at the office of ████████████ of Intertel, Resorts

International's Security Office, Seaside Motel Office, Atlantic City. Among the others in attendance were ████████████ (ACPD), ████████████ (ACPD), and ████████████ (New Jersey State Police—Division of Gaming Enforcement) (NJSP-DGE).

████████████ confirmed that he has reported the receipt of the threat, and has maintained contact regarding this matter with JILLY RIZZO, SINATRA's bodyguard and chief aid. RIZZO advised ████████████ that on occasion threatening-type letters are received by SINATRA. However, he could not recall any similar to the current one postmarked Reading, Pennsylvania, nor could he furnish any information of lead value. Security arrangements for SINATRA's performances May 23–26 and May 31–June 1 were coordinated between Resort's staff, SINATRA's personal guards, ACPD, and NJSP-DGE.

On May 23, 1980, ████████████ WI Hotel, was contacted and instructed regarding the proper handling of any future suspicious calls or correspondence. She agreed to advise all appropriate personnel. ████████████ was also contacted regarding the threat letter and suspicious calls (reported on separate FD-302). She agreed to search WI's reservations list for any individuals from Reading and to remain alert for same.

On May 23, 1980, Bureau Supervisor ████████████ contacted Special Agent ████████████ and suggested conferring with MURRAY MIRON, the Bureau's consultant in psycholinguistics, at number (315) 423-3661.

On May 27, 1980, MURRAY MIRON, of the Syracuse Research Corporation, was contacted and furnished a facsimile of the threat letter and envelope. He furnished an analysis and profile of unknown subject, which was subsequently confirmed in his report dated May 28, 1980.

On May 27, 1980, ████████████ was contacted and he advised that SINATRA's appearances over the weekend proceeded without incident.

On May 28, 1980, ████████████ advised that similar security precautions were planned for the second of SINATRA's weekend specials at Resorts.

On May 29, 1980, ██████████████ Bell of Pennsylvania, was recontacted and he advised that his efforts to locate and retrieve any record of May 17 and/or May 20, 1980, calls met with negative results. Also, to date no record has been printed out of any Reading-area calls to the 800 number. He agreed to continue this watch through June 1, 1980.

On May 31, 1980, Resorts International announced the cancellation of SINATRA's appearances that weekend, due to the performer's case of laryngitis.

On June 2, 1980, ██████████████ Bell of Pennsylvania, advised that there continued to be no record of any Reading-area calls to the 800 number.

SCIENTIFIC AND TECHNICAL REPORTS:

1. Psycholinguistical Analysis of M. S. MIRON, dated May 28, 1980.

2. Report of Federal Bureau of Investigation (FBI) Laboratory, Document Section, dated July 9, 1980.

3. Report of FBI Identification Division, Latent Fingerprint Section, dated July 25, 1980.

Alas, it was all for naught.

PROSECUTIVE STATUS:

On August 14, 1980, the facts of this matter were presented to Assistant United States Attorney (AUSA) THOMAS MC KAY, III, Camden, New Jersey, who concurred that all logical investigation had been pursued in an effort to identify the originator of the threat. AUSA MC KAY also noted that there were no indications of any followup to this threat nor have any similar threats been received. Based on these reasons he declined any prosecutive consideration in this matter.

Acknowledgments

Several people helped the editors in gathering material for this book that was not included in the batch of documents released by the Federal Bureau of Investigation in 1998. The editors express their gratitude.

Beth Crowley, a dogged news assistant in the Washington bureau of *The Wall Street Journal*, tracked down key electronic surveillance transcripts at the National Archives.

Sam Rushay and Pat Anderson, archivists for the National Archives' Nixon Project, helped locate noteworthy documents from that collection. Linda Kloss of the FBI's Freedom of Information Act Office knows where all the best documents are buried and found some of the most important Kennedy-related memos involving Sinatra that weren't included in the FBI's 1998 release. Jim Lesar of the Assassination Archives and Records Center supplied some documents related to Judith Campbell.

Numerous books proved quite helpful in putting these documents in context and were consulted liberally by the editors. These included *His Way: The Unauthorized Biography of Frank Sinatra* by Kitty Kelley; *Frank Sinatra: An American Legend* and *Frank Sinatra: My Father*, both by Nancy Sinatra; *All the Way: A Biography of Frank Sinatra* by Michael Freedland; *Sons and Brothers: The Days of Jack and Bobby Kennedy* by Richard D. Mahoney; *The Dark Side of Camelot* by Seymour Hersh; *J. Edgar Hoover: The Man and the Secrets* by Curt Gentry; *Hoover's FBI: The Inside Story of Hoover's Trusted Lieutenant* by Cartha D. "Deke" DeLoach; *Roemer: Man Against the Mob* by William F. Roemer, Jr.; and *The Mafia Encyclopedia* (second edition) by Carl Sifakis.

255

The editors also would like to thank our agent, Flip Brophy of Sterling Lord Literistic, Inc., for believing in this project from the start.

In addition, Tom Kuntz wishes to thank our brother Danny Kuntz and his wife, Rita, for their hospitality during this book's final stages.

Index

About the Editors

TOM KUNTZ is an editor for *The New York Times* Week in Review section, where he writes and edits "Word for Word," a column of verbatim excerpts on a variety of topics. Before joining the *Times* in 1988, he worked for *Newsday*, *The Hartford Courant*, and *The Miami Herald*.

His brother PHIL KUNTZ has been a staff reporter in *The Wall Street Journal*'s Washington bureau since 1994. Previously, he worked for *Congressional Quarterly* and *The Miami Herald*.